ATROPOS PRESS
new york • dresden

© 2013 by Cecilia Dougherty

ATROPOS PRESS
New York • Dresden

151 First Avenue # 14, New York, N.Y. 10003

ISBN 978-0-9885170-3-5

Acknowledgments

I would like to thank Prof. Wolfgang Schirmacher for excellent and very specific guidance regarding how to approach this unwieldy project, how to find the context for these ideas, and also for the enthusiastic encouragement to open up my topics and be as radical and as singular as they required. With this advice, I became truly open to the work of the authors, filmmakers and theorists, as well as to the ideas and histories, that I was about to jump headlong into. Those initial confusing steps then lead to moments of joyous realization that this book would be whatever I could make of it.

Many thanks to my professors at the European Graduate School, whose passion and fearlessness will always remain an inspiration. Avital Ronell, Alain Badiou, Sandy Stone, Friedrich Kittler, Geert Lovink, Bruce Sterling, and Giorgio Agamben created in their seminars situations of collective tension mixed with a palpable excitement for new ideas, and radically re-situated relationships of thought to element to practice.

I would like to thank Laurie Weeks for our many conversations about her novel *Zipper Mouth,* which inspired one of these chapters, and for discussing with me some of the most basic ideas I was investigating. Thanks also to filmmakers Charles Atlas and Barbara Hammer for creating inspiring and iconoclastic films., and to Charles Atlas for loaning me a copy of his film *Turning* prior to release. Thanks to Barbara Hammer and to film historian Ronald Gregg for reading key sections of this book and providing valuable insights.

Heartfelt thanks go out to my family for their unquestioning support and faith in this project. These include Frances and Mitchell Stevens, Kathleen and Lesley Lenkowsky, Margherita McMullen, Thomas Dougherty and Marsha Thomson Dougherty, and Patricia J. Swope.

THE IRREDUCIBLE I:
Space, Place, Authenticity, and Change

By Cecilia Dougherty

ATROPOS PRESS
new york • dresden

CONTENTS

Introduction

The Site of Change: Observation

> If there is one area where the achievement of
> consciousness comes into its own as a truly essential
> act, it is the realm of everyday life, where every passing
> instant reveals once again that the dice are loaded and
> that as per usual we are being taken for a ride.
>
> Raoul Vaneigem
> *The Revolution of Everyday Life*[1]

The achievement of consciousness occurs in the struggle, in the moments of daily life, for awareness of what sort of life is being lived. Making observations in the process of daily life is the initial step in the struggle for awareness. The first things that become noticeable to the observer are the connections of objects to the space they are in, to each other, and to the larger frame of the room, house, or landscape. One observes the space itself, what part of it seems to be in use and what part of it is not as differentiated; one also notices traces of what was once there – traces of paint or old signage, a tree stump, the uneven surface where pavement becomes cobblestone. We make these observations not as part of a scientific survey, but informally over the course of many realizations, memories, and associations that attach themselves to objects and places. Often these associations are not personal, nor are they necessarily impersonal or general, but are based on the significance placed there by the workings of consumerism. American popular culture, for example, no longer springs from the grassroots of

---

[1] Raoul Vaneigem, *The Revolution of Everyday Life*, trans. Donald Nicholson-Smith (London: Rebel Press, 2006), 11.

American daily life in an organic pastiche of things, gestures, music, and other aspects contributing to a common American sensibility. It springs from processes of consumerism such as trending, branding, and mass marketing, and it has taken over almost every sphere of daily life. Consumerism determines that our connection to daily life is second-hand; we must first submit to the re-creation of daily life for us by the corporation, and then we must forget that there is an authentic one waiting to be located and activated. But if the dice are loaded against us, as Vaneigem insists, we ought not be playing this game.

Corporate control of the space of daily life, including within the intimate space of each moment, makes everyone a subject of the corporation and prevents us from having an authentic relationship to our environment. Observation is the most basic act of resistance to corporate culture. The observer sees the space she occupies and becomes aware of the connections between herself and objects, people, events, etc.; she begins to construct a different geography and trace another history. She notices where her body ends and where everything else begins. This act of delineating the difference between the body and its surroundings, and therefore the self from everything else, is a tool for differentiating authentic space from corporate space, and for locating the space of the state as well.

Corporate space is the space of consumerism, and the space of the state is the space of authority, but consumerism is also a system of control. The function of the state regarding the population governed is to maintain a situation of control, a situation in which pathways to the mainstream are already mapped out, creating the status quo, a situation of cultural stasis. Creating a situation of stasis and control as the normal environment of everyday life results in the homogenization of culture and the regulation of daily life through routine. For the state, homogenization is a means of maintaining control through limitation, and for the corporation it is a way to control capital and the distribution of goods, to claim and exploit the earth's resources, and to control the conditions of human labor. The world as it appears now does not represent an unchangeable order of things; it represents systems of control. Locating authentic space is a beginning step first in identifying systems of control; secondly, it enables connections to be made between the state-corporate alliance and the individual and collective quality of life; and thirdly, it enables the subject to begin reclaiming his identity. The demarcation of the body from its surroundings opens a space for the realization that something else is possible. Change begins with resistance of individuals, and eventually groups and collectivities, to the demands and incentives of corporate capitalism. Resistance to consumerism is resistance to global corporatism.

I use the terms "subject" and "individual" somewhat interchangeably to refer to a person's present state of being, although these terms do not always have the same points of reference. Subjectivity is a position, a place from which the individual emerges into the social realm, but it is not a fixed entity. It is an articulation of the individual as she constructs her identity and is an articulation of the tendency of society to place the individual within a set of characteristics and expectations as well. Subjectivity had been a topic of a major cross-discipline dialogue in art, film, and literature during the 1980s and 1990s. The dialogue failed to discern the origins and value of specific subjectivities within their own communities or within a global community, however, but succeeded in changing the nature of representation and communal perceptions of difference. The conversations about identity suggested a multi-centered perspective, re-arranging the center-and-margins organization of the social into a model that more closely reflects the idea that diverse perspectives are engaged in the construction of the present moment, as an interchange, a give-and-take, rather than within the unequal relationships as prescribed by a social hierarchy based on race, gender, class, citizenship status etc. Identity politics, as it is called, succeeded in calling into question not the origins of specific identities but the origin of the political function of marginalization, and asserted that difference and diversity are effective measures against homogenization and control.

The basic work of identity politics began with an investigation of different bodies. The space of the body is not the same for everyone. In Western societies, as in the United States, people who have been classified as different, including entire groups and entire populations, are in particular relationships to their socio-political milieu based chiefly on their assigned difference. In order to be different, there must be an idea of sameness, or of the mainstream. For groups that have been marginalized and identified as being outside the mainstream, the space of the body is a heightened socio-political space. Gender, ethnicity and race, religion, aboriginal status, reproductive status, citizenship status, sexuality and patterns of loving, property ownership and states of homelessness all represent specific areas, for example, where the body of the individual may be legislated additionally. In other words, there are typical factors determining whether or not the individual may have more laws applied to him. Specific laws apply to entire populations that are given group classification that may or may not reflect the history of that group, but which always reflect the relationship of that group to authority. Some laws are written into a code while others are enforced through custom.

In her essay, "marginality as a site of resistance," bell hooks describes the everyday-ness of marginalization, and the everyday beginnings of resistance. Writing specifically about African-Americans, she states:

> Across those tracks was a world we could work in as maids, as janitors, as prostitutes, as long as it was in a service capacity. We could enter that world but we could not live there. We had always to return to the margin.

> There were laws to ensure our return. To not return was to risk being punished. Living as we did – on the edge – we developed a particular way of seeing reality. We looked both from the outside in and from the inside out. We focused our attention on the center as well as on the margin. . . . Our survival depended on an ongoing public awareness of the separation between margin and center . . . and on an ongoing private acknowledgement that we were a necessary vital part of that whole.

This sense of wholeness, impressed upon our consciousness by the structure of our daily lives, provided us an oppositional world view.[2]

hooks' statement describes the radicalizing influences of systematic identification of an entire population as racially marginal, who understand their oppression to be a group oppression. She states that acknowledgement of a racialized system was "private." However, it is the "structure of our daily lives" that impresses "an oppositional world view" on the private consciousness. The creation of an oppositional group consciousness begins in the private acknowledgement of oppression, at the level of the individual in assessment of the structure of the everyday. In America, racialism has been encoded in a system of laws, such as the former system of apartheid in the South, as well as in social customs, which affect aspects of behavior and mobility. The system of Southern apartheid is over, but crossing the line of customary social behavior continues to require tricky negotiations. W. E. B. Du Bois' major work, *The Souls of Black Folk,* has continuing relevance not only as historical record, but also in terms of his insight into the troubled association of African-Americans to the police and the criminal justice system, a relationship that has not changed significantly since the publication of his book in 1903. Modern policing remains heavily influenced by previously official systems of racial segregation, and law enforcement takes seriously its inherited responsibility to enforce the old social arrangements, where the behavior of people of color is always under suspicion, for example, and their myriad intentions are presumed to be primarily criminal. Even to assume the demeanor of innocence and the behavior of the status quo becomes suspect.

---

[2] bell hooks, *Feminist Theory: From Margin to Center,* (New York: South End Press, 1984), quoted in bell hooks, "marginality as a site of resistance," *Out There: Marginalization and Contemporary Cultures,* ed. Russell Ferguson and others (New York: New Museum of Contemporary Art, 1990), 341.

Resistance to oppression begins with awareness of the possibility of punishment, and of the specific relationship of the threatened body (in "private acknowledgement") to the socio-political environment within the moments of daily life. Laws affect different individuals and groups in the same location differently, and they either demand or prohibit actions at the level of mundane activity. Writer Georges Perec finds evidence of the consequence of different bodies within the same space when he describes the path he took in 1974, from his own room, hallway, stairs, building, street, and neighborhood, that lead to a doorway that showed evidence of his mother's presence, before she was transported to Auschwitz:

> First a single storey building with, on the ground floor, a doorway (blocked up); all around still traces of paintwork and above, not yet completely rubbed away, the inscription
>
> LADIES' HAIRDRESSER
>
> Then a low building with a doorway giving on to a long paved courtyard on several different levels (flights of two or three steps). On the right, a long single-storey building (giving in the old days on to the street through the blocked up doorway to the hairdressing salon) with a double flight of concrete steps leading up to it (this is the building we lived in: the hairdressing salon was my mother's).[3]

The state had created a differentiated space out of the collective space, based on Perec's mother's identity. Both Perec and hooks describe the phenomenon that Du Bois calls a 'double-consciousness,"[4] wherein an individual is able to see the whole situation, including the situation of exclusion and difference as well as the situation of the status quo – two types of space in the same location. Perec's writings and studies of space, which are

---

[3] Georges Perec, "The Rue Vilne," from "L'Infra-ordinaire," in *Species of Spaces and Other Pieces*, ed. and trans. John Sturrock (London: Penguin Classics, 1999), 214.
[4] W. E. B. Du Bois, *The Souls of Black Folk* (New York: Signet Classic, 1995), 45.

quoted and discussed throughout this book, contain instructions on how to shape a conscious awareness of where the individual body ends and where everything else begins; this becomes a tool for understanding the effects of the process of identification on the experience of daily life. Acts of observation, and the formation of individual and collective identity, take on a political function within a social realm structured on hierarchies of power and authority, based partly on categories of identity, and socio-economic stratification. Michel de Certeau claims that the corporation has marginalized everyone, alienating everyone from the production of culture by commoditizing culture itself, not only in creating a commodity culture that might exist beside or within an authentic culture, but in creating a situation where all culture is a product of corporate engagement. In this case, which Certeau claims is the situation of the present, everyone remains in the margins. Social injustice is not a social problem. It is an economic problem created by corporate activity and allowed or promoted by the state. Unjust systems such as the system of slavery in the Americas, and racially unbalanced systems of criminal indictment and incarceration, for example, are based in economics rather than in actual differences between populations. Social injustice is not a root cause of social problems, but is part of the business plan.

Corporations have no single fleshly body that exists in relationship to its environment the way humans exist in relation to ours. The corporation exists as an entity to which specific laws apply, and under certain laws in America, corporations have acquired the status of persons. These laws create a relationship of the corporate body to the environment in which the individual body is not a factor. The corporate body has no clear point of separation, no skin that separates it from its surroundings. The corporate environment is everywhere. The corporation makes decisions that affect the quality of the everyday life of large segments of society, taking control of the means of making a living as well as taking control of culture, of the way the contemporary is built and the way the built environment is utilized. Corporations enfranchise individuals and groups by providing them with buying power. The corporation is promiscuous, and will provide goods or invent a new range of products based on the buying habits of any of the categories of population, within a system of trending and branding that it has established to measure and control buying habits. Although it seems as though choices are being made, this is a closed system. The corporation has set up an inauthentic culture in which habitual consumption is the norm. In order to find some relief from consumer culture, the consumer must consciously "opt out" of the system that surrounds her. But corporate influence extends beyond the production of consumer culture. The corporation exercises control not only of the consumer, but also of governments, legislation, working conditions, ethics and value systems, landscapes and natural resources, ecological systems, and the international regulation of land use, commerce, and uses of the military. Corporations function like wealthy governments, on a transnational level across political borders and national boundaries.

It is necessary to begin resistance of global corporatism at the level of daily life, first, in order to reclaim possession of authentic consciousness, and then to be able to speak collectively through the diverse realities that constitute the collective quotidian. Theorist Félix Guattari claims that planetary survival itself is at stake. Understanding what is possible within the realm of the everyday requires an examination of space: living space, social space, physical space, and the space of representation. It is necessary to replace consciousness based on a hierarchical organization of society that depends on categorization, separation, differentiation, and the homogenization of culture, with an awareness of the presence and function of systems of interrelationship that represent an authentic construction of everyday life.

Although individual identity is always open to question and change, from within and without, subjectivity is the location of consciousness and a vital point of connectivity to a system that includes not only other individuals, but also collectivities, ideas, nonhuman participants, and catalysts of interactivity. The system formed by the interactivity of these elements represents the world as it actually functions, with or without state and corporate systems of control that conceal this functioning, and also opens pathways to a more just and balanced world. Subjectivities and collectivities are diverse, and relationships are complex and often contradictory. The content of alternate belief systems and radical ideologies that form through individual or collective experience, however, do not form the basic matter of these networks of resistance. The basic matter of networks of resistance is the fact itself of non-hierarchical connectivity. The system of non-hierarchical connectivity accommodates varied belief systems, cultural difference, contradiction and paradox. A non-hierarchical system of connectivity is not a structure or a means of categorizing; it is a system that merely describes connections and affinities. In other words, it changes continuously, representing the organization of elements as connections are formed. The reality of any situation is a measure of the influences that contribute to the situation and is not a closed circuit of cause and effect.

In reference to a networked model of reality, this paper discusses what can be called the "irreducible I," which is the experience of being an individual within the networked system, in a state that cannot be reduced to specific or permanent relationships to self, society, or place. Even at the level of DNA, which is not so much a marker of identification as it is one of change, the self is irreducible. In the intimate moments of the everyday there is revolutionary potential in negating a search for an essential core self and asserting, instead, one's irreducible identity.

Space and Place: Location

The irreducible I requires space. After discussing the importance of developing a consciousness of the everyday through observation within the intimate experiences of the everyday, this book examines the place of daily life. Space and place are defined and delineated in relation to each other and to the organization of space. Space itself is an entity without a concept. It may have ground, sky, air, or directionality, but it could signify anything or nothing until it acquires objects and markers of human activity. Space is also the area we travel through to go from one place to another. Small spaces exist between objects, and between buildings. Large and small spaces provide a reference for scale, and also for time, since larger amounts of space can be perceived in terms of the length of time it may take to travel from one point to another. Space and time are presented as inseparable elements of the same reality. Place is articulated space, whether by architecture or ritual, and represents the arena of the social. Place is where society is built. Human need occupies the center of our concepts of space and place, and both space and place change through time, in memory, and by use. Traces of earlier societies may not always reveal what a particular place may have signified to them, and in losing the memory of that significance the place changes, returning to its status as unspecified space, or acquiring a new use and new significance in another society.

Representational space is discussed in terms of the spatial sense that enables differentiation and categorization of ideas, traits and characteristics. Representational space is where a separation of specific elements of society into situations of sameness and difference occurs, and where the functions of identity within a common perception of society as a whole are determined. The irreducible I uses the space of representation to continually update itself. This involves not only a network of language, imagery, speech and sound, for example, but also the influences of the perception of self and other, based on aspects of society that govern representation. These include the establishment of behavioral norms, perceptions of racial and gender differentiation and the meanings these might have within other spheres of society. These latter aspects of representational space do not so much govern the representation of difference, per se, but govern the basic perception of difference. Representational space is where the concepts of the norm and the status quo are formed.

In the context of this writing the space of society is the organized space of the collective consciousness of groups, cities, and nations under specific governance or tradition, as well as the global networks of telecommunications. Society is formed on communication, interaction, trade, and culture; society is the space of human culture, whether that culture is authentic or corporate, just or unjust, extended over a large or small area, or even isolated. Society is the invention of human interaction. Society is also represented by the formation of "place" out of "space," the organization of space into zones of meaning and reference, the use of language and other forms of representation that communicate meanings, and references that facilitate the organization of space.

Non-places and interstitial space are the final fragments of this chart of space and place, both of which refer to actual physical space as well as cultural conditions and states of mind, but one type of space could be said to represent an escape from the other. I use the term non-places to refer to the architectural infrastructure of the globalized market place as well as the electronic spaces we enter on a routine basis. Non-places include international hotel and restaurant chains, supermarkets, and shopping malls as well as the familiar spaces of computer operating systems, software windows, and smart phone applications. "Non-place" is a term coined by anthropologist Marc Augé to describe architectural spaces that are devoid of regional references, not only in terms of design and materials, but also in terms of value systems. They are homogenized, familiar places, meant for temporary use rather than for settlement – places we pass through while traveling, or places where we stop briefly to rest, to conduct business, to go shopping. To architectural historian Hans Ibelings, what Augé calls non-places are the culturally neutral zones of leisure and business that signify the borderless sphere of global commerce. The non-place, whether it is physical or wired, is a connected place, and because our world has been completely mapped and our contacts are on a global scale, non-places are important ports of call.

Interstitial space has a vital role in the social realm as well. It is often unregulated and noncommercial, disconnected from the surveillance of authority and the constraints of scheduling. The term refers to time, occasion, and activity more than to a type of physical space, and it refers to escape as well as discovery. This is a place where time is one's own. The interstitial spaces of childhood and youth are different from those of adulthood. The term refers to activities such as art making, poetry, lovemaking, daydreaming, and partying – essential activities for maintaining perspective, and perhaps sanity, and for the expression of a mutable and continuously forming subjectivity. Interstitial spaces may be tiny zones of autonomy, or the entire milieu of creativity. They may be moments of chaos or moments of meditation.

The fields from which I draw information and inspiration include literature, film, journalism, popular culture, telecommunications theory, geography, sociology, critical theory, philosophy, anthropology, and architecture. The topics one field brings to the discussion cannot be raised except in relation to topics across the range of influences, each a specific facet of the same phenomenal moment. Therefore the study of aspects of space cannot be separate from the study of aspects of representation, or corporate influence on culture and the authority of the state. The glue that holds this analysis together is a mixture of environmentalism, feminism, thoughts on expertise and commonness, and the influence of identity politics. The silver thread that runs through this piece is a search for the processes that enable the expression of authentic identity and an experience of autonomy.

The writings of Perec were the initial inspiration for beginning this project. The essays in *Species of Spaces and Other Pieces,* can be checked against many common experiences of daily life. The study of the meaning of actions taken in situations in everyday life led to a study of Situationist practices and ideas about the relationship of the individual to the state, and of working conditions to the construction of consumerist culture. Raoul Vaneigem's *The Revolution of Everyday Life*, Jean Baudrillard's *Simulations*, and Guy Debord's *Society of the Spectacle* were influential texts and are referenced throughout this piece, and, like Perec's work, remain relevant today. Henri Lefebvre and Michel De Certeau's analyses of the relationship of space, and kinds of spaces, to consumerism were influential as well in terms of understanding the breadth of corporate influence on the construction of the spaces of daily life.

Journalist and activist Naomi Klein's writings about globalization provide eyewitness accounts to the sphere of the international anti-globalization movement, as well as insights into specific corporate strategies for controlling the space of daily living. Klein's writings have been paired with those of Perec, unlikely as it may seem, in order to connect the record of intimate experiences of daily life with organized campaigns against spectacular consumerism, ecological disaster, and the destruction of the local. Geographer Yi-Fu Tuan provides a thread, similar to that of Perec, which runs through this piece. Tuan's discussion of space and place in relation to the idea of home and homeland brings many of these disciplines together, providing a view of the practical necessity of human social relations and the establishment of a physical basis for culture.

Félix Guattari and sociologist Bruno Latour provide key texts that describe networks and systems that can be activated against the rigid structures of political and economic hierarchies, structures that many falsely believe to be naturally occurring social structures and the only ones we have within which to live. Guattari's *The Three Ecologies* is an explication of eco-systems that are currently out of balance – mental, social and environmental – and his writing is a passionate plea to restore balance on all levels. Guattari sites the ongoing emergency of women's poverty and oppression as having roots in the exploitative practices of globalization, and makes clear that women's lack of civil rights, sexual independence, educational rights, and level of autonomy equal to that of men in many societies is an indication of systems out of balance, a condition that effects individual psychologies as well as the health and strength of communities. The individual level is important and, as the term implies, all ecologies are interconnected. Latour's *Reassembling the Social: An Introduction to Actor-Network Theory*, is another key text, describing a world always in flux, never completely situated, and constructed as a series of possibly endless networks. Latour's theory of sociological practice has been adapted to a general theory of interconnectedness, and I adopt this perspective in both the form and the content of this writing.

I refer to the feminism of Luce Irigaray as well, although it is a very different feminism from my own. Irigaray, like Guattari, seeks balance, but in terms of a balance between what she considers to be the two distinct cultures of the masculine and feminine. Working together, towards a situation of the common good, and meeting over a "bridge of respect," would allow for both the expression of independent identities and the giving of mutual support in the creation of one unified realm of the social. Irigaray's radical feminine is powerful and complete in her self, but she is also firmly rooted in the social. Gender is not the construction of either society or of sexuality, but refers to actual bodies. This must be acknowledged and established within a collective space where neither dominance nor submission can determine capacity for interaction.

Avital Ronell's writings, interviews, and lectures have been influential in terms of the practice of theory – the need to perform and embody the actions one is thinking and speaking about, to test them out. Her work presents theses, questions, and observations that are to be reached and utilized from many facets, approached from different angles, each providing a different reflection of the observer and of the points in question. Ronell's questions about scientism, certainty, and experimentation, bring into focus the complex system of how knowledge is acquired; she examines this on the level of intimate moments of the acquisition of knowledge, as well as on the level of the public agreement by which knowledge becomes official. Ronell's denial of the usefulness of the concept of genius and the explicit usefulness of the concept of stupidity is a feminist gesture. Gendered bodies can introduce the value of stupidity as a negation of masculinist strategies for organizing the world by means that must exclude everything but the single answer, the fact that will provide an affirmation of the initial hypothesis. But testing can be used otherwise, as a "kind of humiliation," when new knowledge requires the "willing[ness] to rescind" that which is discovered to be false, "in service"[5] to political action.

Clear representations of the irreducible I can be found in the writings of Kathy Acker and Laurie Weeks, as well as in the films of Barbara Hammer and Charles Atlas. Both Acker and Weeks write from the position of attempting to embody and represent fractured and multiple subjectivities, telling stories through a narrator constructed of a multiplicity of voices. The person of the narrator remains fractured and multiple, but never falls apart and never congeals into a single idea of being, one that has a center and is properly named. Hammer is engaged in a very different quest from the construction of multiple female selves but her conclusion is the same: identity is not fixed for longer than a moment. It is authentic when it is able to express its necessarily superficial nature, an identity that skims surfaces; it finds itself inside of action, and changes within situations as well. Charles Atlas represents identity differently, letting the differently-identified subjects speak in the passionate vernacular of their own difference. His work introduces transsexual identity to the discussion of being and becoming, and relativizes identity as an act of making decisions based on factors routed in the social as well as the subjective to the point where these become the same thing. In this case, there is no bridge between the experience of the self and the experience of the social. What crosses over here is not only gender, but all assertions of identity and identification based in the body. It is not simply that persistent and deeply felt perceptions are what matter most, it is definitely the body that matters, but more than that, crossing genders asserts that the body cannot exist outside the realm of the social, in respect to the realm of all bodies.

Architect Teddy Cruz, artist and educator Ricardo Dominguez, and poet Gloria Anzaldúa provide a perspective that runs along nineteen hundred miles of the Mexico-U.S. border, where the

---

[5] Avital Ronell, Eduardo Cadava, and Jean-Michel Rabaté, "On Testing, Torture, and Experimentation: The Test Drive," Slought Foundation, March 15, 2006, http://slought.org/content/11317/ (accessed August 8, 2012).

transiting of identities – from south to north, and then back again many times over – is the commonest of occurrences. The U.S. Border Patrol has the duty to fix the border, to make it impenetrable and stop the migration that has been going on for generations. But the migrants, likewise, have a duty. Their duty is to keep the border zone as a space of continuous drifting of bodies, ideas, materials, money, language, and culture. They are a constant reminder that what America has taken from Mexico is only on loan. A permanent shifting of geographies from Mexican to American has never taken place and the migrants who come north for work, and go south again with money and supplies, keep this border fluid and open. The culture of the border is neither American nor Mexican, and like the people themselves, is a *mestizo* culture that absorbs the colonizer in order to prevent assimilation.

Tuan's thoughtful insights fill out the political space of border transit and give it a deep history, explaining that the most mundane aspects of attachment to place are the longest-held and the strongest. In the midst of research for this work, Occupy Wall Street erupted, bringing the occupation of land, space, and language into the forefront of national discussion. Encampments across a wide area of the United States de-territorialized the American landscape, rendering state borders superfluous, while regional and local policing became subject to global scrutiny, making clear the global nature of contemporary policing practices. As short-lived as this series of demonstrations was, it raised questions about the possibility of occupying, or re-occupying, already-occupied land. Native American activists responded to the Occupiers by providing indigenous perspectives on American activism and their own responses to the problems of corporate globalism. The work of Native activists John Paul Montano and Clayton Thomas-Muller give critical insight to the issue of whose land this might be, and who may claim it back again. The traditions of the colonists and their ancestors, and the value systems that determine their relationship to place, are vastly different from the traditions of the nations who existed here when the Europeans first landed. But no one has remained stuck in time. A simultaneous re-territorialization is recommended.

Donna Haraway has been, like Perec, an underlying influence on this project. Her negation of a dialectical approach to activism, science, social theory, and other models of interactivity creates an opening through which the opposing binaries of the past rush out, and a cross-species frame of reference rushes in. The bifurcated human becomes whole again; and furthermore, s/he is a willing participant in promiscuous exchanges with human, nonhuman, machinic and other agents for change – for mutation.

Subjectivities: Inexpert Iterations

The network model is one I adopt not only as a description of the interrelationship of elements of every kind that form within each moment, but also as the description of how this particular work came into being. As connections formed between topics within the large diagram of my discussion, it became useful to look at the network model itself and to see how this structure might apply to the writing of this work. The consideration of subjectivity and placement needed an already activated space for expression. Placing a high value on lived experience provides a thematic background for the work at hand, and the creation of a body of work in experimental video over a period of twenty-seven years rounds out my field of research by including a deep familiarity with the artistic process. This paper takes for granted, similar to Certeau's observation that everyone has been marginalized, that most aspects of society are politicized. A transformation has taken place in the process of research and writing, fortunately. The use of ideologies to examine identity formation and to fix ideas about social structures, even progressive social structures, became obstructive, while the value of form, or of continuous formation, as the creator of the content of the social realm became increasingly apparent. As I drifted away from ideological thinking to thinking about society as a process rather than a product, or as a container or structure for the organization of populations, I was able to approach the question of subjectivity, context, and space with tools that were themselves formed within the same system of affinities and connections.

Michael Anker's *The Ethics of Uncertainty: Aporetic Openings* is underscored by the refrain: "As something is coming to be it is always already becoming other."[6] This phrase sums up elegantly the function of time, place, event, and action that are fundamental to the perspective of this book. The ethics involved are social ethics. The responsibility to participate actively emerges from the opened pathways of possibility, within fields of uncertainty, in the formation of a shared future. The formation of a just society is a continuous process; it will not result in a finished product or a final contract between the members of a society and systems of authority. Ethics, within Anker's discourse, are not based on belief systems, but offer a kind of infrastructure for responsible decision-making within ongoing processes of becoming. Becoming is the state of being human, but it is also the state of things in general. Everything is always in the process of becoming something else, and this condition of continuous uncertainty is the foundation for social justice.

The subjective perspective becomes more interesting rather than less in a situation where change is the fundamental characteristic of being. Information gleaned in the intimate moments of the everyday is, likewise, more valuable rather than less. Information gleaned in the process of observing the everyday can be used to distinguish authentic reality from corporate culture, a fluid social realm from a static one, or the processes of change from those of spectacle. The spectacle is not merely that which occupies the mind or the consciousness of the spectator, or that which influences buying habits; it is effective in completely authoring and governing public as well as non-public space. Consumerism creates corporate space out of all space, and the individual who becomes the consumer is the subject of the corporation. Confessional writing, women's writing, writing from within the margins of society, the first person narrative,

---

[6] Michael Anker, *The Ethics of Uncertainty: Aporetic Openings,* (PhD diss., European Graduate School, 2009), 11.

and the inexpert and inexact statements of everyday people provide countless examples of how the process of change, becoming, and awareness occur in the intimate moments of daily life. The personal account is the basis for noticing and observing the interconnections of the elements of the everyday in the formation of a clearer picture of what may be happening collectively and globally. This book is dedicated to keeping the subject and her inexpert perspective in view, even as the focus ring must always be readjusted.

Borderlines and Migrations: Becoming

The act of making observations within the intimate moments of the everyday and opening our eyes to what is around us opens our consciousness as well. We not only see the familiar world of hierarchies and bureaucracies, categories and boundaries that was structured for us by our governments and by global commerce, but we also realize that it is possible to see through those structures and participate actively in a borderless network that is already in formation. The milieu for radical social action is motion itself. The subjective self, the I, is mutable. The mutable I is linked to others in multiple and simultaneous exchanges of ideas, objects, processes, biologies, information, machines, etc. The conversation is unfinished, decentered and multi-dimensional. This is the network we have within which to reclaim the space of the everyday. The network is a diagram of the interrelatedness of objects, actors and agents within the realm of the social. The network is neutral, but it enables the formation of meaningful content and meaningful connectivity within a decentralized and non-hierarchical complex of influences and actions. The structure of the network and the connectivity of content are what matters. Fixed ideologies and disconnected disciplines may tend to open up within the diverse range of influences that heterogeneous connectivity engenders. Charters, resolutions and completed missions fall short of the capacity of the network.

The space of the network is the space of daily life. In considering the concepts of space and place, it becomes clear that these concepts must be analyzed in terms of the subjectivities and collectivities that make them significant. The places where we live and where we spend time are, for the most part, places that have been overlaid with corporate significance, and designed for the purposes of authority and control in the most mundane, or the most extreme, manner. An analysis of space, in human terms, is an analysis of migration and transformation – of becoming something else.

Part 1: The Practice of Everyday Life and the Experience of the Present

The Space of the Everyday and the Intimate Beginnings of Change

The space of the everyday is the fundamental space of experience and event. The space of the everyday is intimate; it begins with the body and includes the environments of the body: beds, rooms, doorways, stairs, objects and walls. The space of the everyday is a shared space, and includes sidewalks, the street, the neighborhood, the city, its shops, schools and meeting places. The space of the everyday is created by the intersection of people, objects, events, actions and ideas; it is mobile, social, and transformative; it is relational, made up of inter-dependent elements; and it is always in the process of renewing itself. The space of the everyday is total, producing an ongoing string of influences that creates each moment. But the space of the everyday is not simply everything. It is specific, and an awareness of what it is, what it contains, how to navigate it, and how to distinguish it from its simulacrum, is necessary in order to retrieve the authentic aspects of both the subjective and the social realm from the grip of a global consumer culture that has been gradually mapped over it. The space of the everyday is a highly contested space, and the authenticity in question is not so much a permanent situation, but rather is a result of the interaction of autonomous elements created by interactive processes, in the moment.

In the fall of 1974, Georges Perec spent a weekend at the cafés near one particular Paris street corner observing and writing down what went on around him. *An Attempt at Exhausting a Place in Paris*, published in 1975, is a record of his observations. Perec's guidelines were simple: to record the details of the space, including interactions and events that were observable from his café table. He describes people's gestures, their demeanor, verbal exchanges and the directions in which they were walking or driving, as well as the makeup and flow of traffic, the model and color of automobiles, the route number of buses, the number of people sitting in them, the placement of shops, dogs, and people, noting the details that came to distinguish one day's experience of the place from the next. Nothing spectacular happens. The description of the place can never be finished, or exhausted, because it is always in flux, renewing itself continuously. Perec is a subjective observer. His laboratory is open and there is no control group. His record of small events and non-happenings is sometimes a simple list, or a series of descriptions with brief commentary. Punctuation is intermittent. One entry, for example, is a compilation of factors rather than events, creating the impression of a very active street corner:

Date: 18 October 1974
Time: 12:40 PM
Location: Café de la Mairie

tens, hundreds of simultaneous actions, micro-events, each one of which necessitates postures, movements, specific expenditures of energy:

conversations between two people, conversations between three people, conversations between several people: the movement of lips, gestures, gesticulations

means of locomotion: walking, two-wheeled vehicles (with and without motor), automobiles (private cars, company cars, rented cars, driving school cars), commercial vehicles, public services, public transport, tourist buses

means of carrying (by hand, under the arm, on the back)

means of traction (shopping bag on wheels)

> degrees of determination or motivation: waiting, sauntering, dawdling, wandering, going, running toward, rushing (toward a free taxi, for instance), seeking, idling about, hesitating, walking with determination[7]

Perec's descriptions are exercises in non-judgment and non-interpretation – exercises in empathy. His empathy is encrypted in the simplicity of each day's account and re-surfaces as the reader reconstructs the scene. The apparatus (sitting at a café) is set up (date, time, location) but its workings are hidden inside the process of listing (encoding) events/non-events. The text describes rather than interprets a scene, creating narrative without engaging in cause-and-effect storytelling. The reader accesses Perec's empathy by decoding the narrative: direct observation, depoliticized language, varied structure, and informal tone – these elements are instructions. She decodes the text literally and intuitively, rather than interpretively. She imagines the scene made up of mostly anonymous people (Perec occasionally meets an acquaintance) and their movements, based on the specifics that Perec has included in his account, and she mentally reconstructs the corner. The mundanity of the scene and the simplicity with which the elements of the place are enumerated belie their importance. The instructions being given to the reader are for activating the authentic aspects of a place.

Compare Perec's methodology, itself a protocol, with network theorist Alexander R. Galloway's description of the interpretive aspects of the Internet, from his book *Protocol: How Control Exists After Decentralization*:

> *Anonymous but descriptive.* The conflict between the total and the specific is palpable on the Internet. Each movement on the Net is recorded in myriad different locations (log files, server statistics, email boxes); however, the real identity of those movements is irrelevant. Demographics

---

[7] Georges Perec, *An Attempt at Exhausting a Place in Paris,* trans. Marc Lowenthal (Cambridge: Wakefield Press, 2010), 10.

and user statistics are more important than real names and real identities. On the Internet there is no reason to know the name of a particular user, only to know what that user likes, where they shop, where they live, and so on. The clustering of descriptive information around a specific user becomes sufficient to explain the identity of that user.[8]

In this case, conflict exists between objects and information, resolved by a series of nested protocols, the "common languages" of all networked computers. Protocols enable information to be carried back and forth, but are not concerned with the content of the information, which is the function of the user. The form delivers the content, which could be anything. For Perec, his manner of observation and the nature of the description it produces delivers the content of the street corner to the reader, regardless of what that content may be. Descriptive information in terms of the Internet amounts to keywords, clicks, links, page views, profiles, images, HTML, code and digital objects that use a logic that is both linear and non-linear, but which are not connected linguistically. Galloway describes it simply: "Digital objects are pure positivities. They are the heterogeneous elements that exist in what Deleuze and Guattari have called 'machinic' processes."[9] Objects are the result of processes, meaning they appear and disappear. Protocol does not create digital objects, but rather structures them. The conflict between the total and the specific is palpable in Perec's text, but perhaps Perec is writing less of conflict than of a correlation between the total and the specific. The process carries the content, but it also creates the content. Perec's process is to witness the reality of others by enabling memory (of the past), desire (imagining the future) and history (the continuity of events) to be not only confluent, but to be the same thing in any event. Moments of this confluence are recorded and empathy resolves the conflict between objects and information. The

---

[8] Alexander R. Galloway, *Protocol: How Control Exists After Decentralization* (Cambridge and London: MIT Press, 2004), 69.
[9] Galloway, 74.

reader follows the writing as though decoding the information of the street.

Perec's intention with *An Attempt at Exhausting a Place in Paris* is, "to describe . . . that which is generally not taken note of, that which is not noticed, that which has no importance: what happens when nothing happens other than the weather, people, cars and clouds."[10] Perec's account of the comings and goings of people, cars, and clouds in this one place in Paris is a surprisingly melancholy book. It leaves the reader with an unfocussed sadness, a feeling of being ill at ease, and a sense of loss. Perec's chronicle of his surroundings describes the relationship of the subjective self to everything outside of the self – the relationship between the workings of interiority and exteriority, not as two separate realities, each with distinct characteristics and links, but as phenomena coming together interactively and intuitively. Perec's small book may leave the reader feeling melancholy because it is a record of the struggle to enact the authentic via the practice of noticing and making connections, which is the struggle to reclaim the space around the body, and to discern the nature of the society within which we are situated. This practice marks the beginning of change.

The Infra-ordinary

What speaks to us, seemingly, is always the big event, the untoward, the extra-ordinary: the front-page splash, the banner headlines. Railway trains only begin to exist when they are derailed, and the more passengers that are killed, the more the trains exist. Aeroplanes achieve existence only when they are hijacked. The one and only destiny of motor-cars is to drive into plane trees. Fifty-two weekends a year, fifty-two casualty lists: so many dead and all the better for

---

[10] Perec, *An Attempt at Exhausting a Place in Paris*, 3.

the news media if the figures keep going up! Behind the event there is a scandal, a fissure, a danger, as if life reveals itself only by way of the spectacular, as if what speaks, what is significant, is always abnormal: natural cataclysms or social upheavals, social unrest, political scandals....

What's really going on, what we're experiencing, the rest, all the rest, where is it? How should we take account of, question, describe what happens every day and recurs everyday: the banal, the quotidian, the obvious, the common, the ordinary, the infra-ordinary, the background noise, the habitual?[11]

"The infra-ordinary," is Perec's term for the events and routines that comprise the experience of daily life. In his 1974 book of essays, *Species of Spaces and Other Pieces*, his essay, "*L'Infra-ordinaire*,"[12] quoted above, illustrates systems for the habitual questioning of the details of day-to-day living, which include things that we may routinely overlook as the spectacle of the extraordinary commandeers our attention away from what matters most. The fissure he writes about in terms of the spectacular event is the fissure created by consumerism, a crack in the continuity of a person's life. An emphasis on the spectacular, the new, and the extraordinary obscures objects and events in the present so we are not able to "take account of, question, describe what happens every day and recurs everyday."[13] The ordinary, as such, ceases to be "the bearer of any information"[14] in the present moment. Human agency is

---

[11] Perec, "L'Infra-ordinaire," in *Species of Spaces and Other Pieces*, 209.
[12] Perec, "L'Infra-ordinaire," first published in 1973 in *Cause Commune*, a periodical with which Perec was involved, along with his former teacher Jean Duvignaud and Paul Virilio. One of its aims was "To undertake an investigation of everyday life at every level, right down to the recesses and basements that are normally ignored or suppressed." This quote is taken from *George Perec: A Life in Words* by David Bellos, 492.
[13] Perec, "*L'Infra-ordinaire*," in *Species of Spaces and Other Pieces*, 210.
[14] Ibid.

affected because our attention is diverted away from real life and towards the gloss and shine that signify marketing, and in that process the market becomes the milieu for life, growth, learning, relations, and action.

Perec is not writing about finding or creating deep meaning so much as about witnessing and knowing – about information. Locating the meaning in writings as well as in observations requires interpretation; what is known is filtered through signifiers, intentions, needs, memories, history, fictions and desire – and then analyzed and formulated into a rational narrative, solidified, eventually becoming an account of the past. Information, however, exists in the present, in the lived moment, and is continuous and always changing. A witness exists in the present, as well, in the space and time of the thing observed. Perec returns to the question of the present: "But where is our life? Where is our body? Where is our space?"[15] Perec's question of where is our space assumes the unassailable right of the body to occupy space. The body is the primary environment and is both the subject and object of the everyday. The individual body is significant not simply as the basic subject-object of experience, but as a force of individual and collective agency. The body has a place in the present. The body, in place, has the ability to determine the significance of its location. Bearing witness, sending and receiving information, and signifying meaning are congruent states of the body within a fluid system of the continuously renewed present. Perec's space of the infra-ordinary is the space in which we can extricate ourselves, our bodies, from the milieu of the market.

Perec states, "What's needed perhaps is finally to found our own anthropology, one that will speak about us, will look in ourselves for what for so long we've been pillaging from others. Not the exotic anymore, but the endotic."[16] The endotic is that which is common, banal, routine, and at hand – the first thing to

---

[15] Ibid.
[16] Ibid.

meet the body of the observer. The endotic gives relevance to common things and can tell us not only what those things are, but who we are in relation to the things that are common. For Perec, the triviality and seeming futility of the objects and substances of everyday living, from the contents of someone's pockets to the bricks of houses and the tarmac of streets, indicates that the objects and spaces observed hold a key to the nature of one's life and open up the spaces of resistance. When Perec asks "But where is our life?" he is saying that we need to occupy our bodies and the space around them with a sense of awareness, or else there will be no challenges made to consumer culture and the authority that has fabricated the unbelievable new details of our lives. Perec states simply that there is a need to "question things," which is the beginning point of tearing ourselves away from the spectacle and operating in a new milieu of authenticity and action.

Perec's discussion is almost always about observing, naming, and questioning. In his writing on spaces and places, in describing rooms, hallways and staircases, in tracing the steps from his own bedroom to the door of his mother's former hairdressing shop, he illustrates how easily the pathways run from the routines of daily life to the control of all aspects of life. The mundane is remarkable and in examining and remarking Perec discovers the pathology that allows systems of authority to control daily life. In the 1940s, his mother, who was deported to Auschwitz in 1943, her hairdressing shop, and Perec himself as a young child were all threats to the state. By retracing the pathways from the space around his body in the present to the spaces of terrible oppression – from the spaces of the present to those of the past – he creates an expanded dimension of time that enables history and memory to reveal their relevant functioning in the present.

Perec's discoveries include the realization that the self is not a complete thing but is a process. His investigations are not primarily existential, but rather look further into the singularity of the self as a process of authentication. In his essay "Homo Generator: Media and Postmodern Technology," Wolfgang Schirmacher discusses the self as activity:

The first law of media is: *The self is the focal point.* This self is not the ego of domination or the subject of modern times but the activity of "caring for one's self." Taking care of oneself is now the activity of media. . . . The self is in no way satisfied by being apart and single. The self wants to overcome its separateness without losing its specialness. The self of media is an activity.[17]

Schirmacher continues the logic of the self as media activity by stating that the self has no "fixed outlook" or "secure space in society." The activity of the self is a creative one, both using and abusing the conventions of the status quo. This perspective encompasses the present as well as the future, but it is not a product of media technologies. Perec's self-in-process and Schirmacher's creatively activated self are autonomous, enabling observation and resistance from within an authentic, progressive, creation of the self. Technology has always been with us. Technologies of writing (Perec) and of communications (Schirmacher) are only two of the means by which systems of the self become evident. The protocols of the infra-ordinary transfer information from the milieu of the observer, be it physical space and the movement of people and objects there, or an ever-reconstituted electronic space.

Situationist Strategies: Re-Routing Avenues of Control

The Situationist International (SI), a group of artists, writers and theorists based chiefly in Paris from the late 1950s through the early 1970s, were intentional outsiders engaged in a critique of the homogenizing effects of modernity and the spectacular commoditization of contemporary society. Members included

---

[17] Wolfgang Schirmacher, "Homo Generator: Media and Postmodern Technology," in *Culture on the Brink: Ideologies of Technology,* Gretchen Bender and Timothy Druckrey, eds. (Seattle: Bay Press, 1994), 77.

Mustapha Khayati, whose persuasive 1966 pamphlet, "On the Poverty of Student Life," was intellectual fuel for the May 1968 protests and general strike in France, as well as Ivan Chtcheglov, who early on wrote of the necessity for urban dwellers to create a city that can be modified to their needs rather than the needs of governments and commerce. Other prominent Situationists were Guy Debord, Henri Lefebvre (for a brief time), Raoul Vaneigem, Jacqueline de Jong, who was publisher and editor of the journal *The Situationist Times,* and many others who came into and out of the discussions and conferences during the fifteen years of SI activity. The Situationists understood that a critique of daily life rendered the dominating power of the "single social form"[18] transparent, and would enable a collective imagining of daily life as a free and autonomous creation of the social realm. This would mean nothing less than a total upheaval within economic networks, which function now at an advanced pace and on a larger geographical scale than during the time of the SI. For the Situationists, daily life was the basic unit of revolution. Membership in the SI was mostly male, and they challenged the status quo in radical ways, yet were themselves unable to escape the confines and short-sightedness of male privilege; they were perhaps unable to critique it, or even to see beyond it, to understand its function as a controlling force, not only towards women, but towards the entire society.

Perec was not a member of the SI, but they share common perceptions about the need to explore the individual and collective spaces of the everyday in response to an enforced consumer culture. Debord, in his 1967 publication, *Society of the Spectacle,* the most well known and widely distributed Situationist text, writes: "In societies dominated by modern conditions of production, life is presented as an immense accumulation of *spectacles*. Everything that was directly lived

---

[18] Mustapha Khayati, "On the Poverty of Student Life," (1966) in Ken Knabb, trans. and ed., *Situationist International Anthology* (Berkeley: Bureau of Public Secrets, 2006), 423.

has receded into a representation."[19] This most startling statement claims that the spectacles under consideration not only dominate the representation of everyday life, but also colonize it and have turned daily life into a representation of the market. A new space of the everyday has therefore been created where the market controls the relationship of the consumer to goods, as well as that of people and events to most objects and spaces, to culture, including political discussions, acts of dissent and social reform. The common environment of the spectacle today has expanded since Debord's pronouncement. It is now inside the body as well, as processed foods, as illness and disease; it is in the mind as the detritus of branding, dreadfully inadequate education, pop-nationalistic sentimentalism; and it emerges in the shift of ethical standards to a value system borrowed from marketing practices. The spectacle influences affinities and the formation of communities as well, holding autonomy in ransom to networks of commerce. As in one of the hallucination sequences in David Cronenberg's 1983 film *Videodrome*,[20] where the protagonist, Max Renn (played by James Woods), inserts a VHS tape into his own gut in order to play it, we are playing the new spectacle with our bodies. The media guru of *Videodrome* is a character named Brian O'Blivion (played by Jack Creley), whose unsettling yet over-ripe symbolic gesture is to refuse to appear anywhere except as a televised image. The premise of the story is that the video screen is the retina of the mind, controlling the viewer through images that transport hypnotic messages directly into her subconscious brain.

But there is no longer a need for the television set. Countless tiny televisions and video cameras are carried in the pockets of the multitude as the standard devices and applications installed in cell phones and computers. Television is mobile and ubiquitous. Fantasy fiction writer and future-trends analyst

---

[19] Guy Debord, *Society of the Spectacle* (Detroit: Black and Red, 1983), Chapter I, 1.
[20] David Cronenberg, *Videodrome*, DVD. Directed by David Cronenberg, (Toronto: Canadian Film Development Corporation, 1983).

Bruce Sterling predicts that within twenty-five years the recording device itself will all but disappear. He imagines that our fingers, body movements, and retinas will constitute an "interface for computation," with the aid of an "absorptive surface that absorbs any photon [and will] send it out into the computational cloud."[21] A lens-less device – merely a *surface* – would be able to store information based on gesture and gaze alone, within a total wired society hooked into the über-expanded services of a web browser, such as Google. Editing could be accomplished by verbal command to call up files from within a streaming electronic matrix, which would turn data into video and audio on request. For Sterling, the near future is "a world of augmented, always-on, geo-locative interactivity. [The device is] a remote control for reality – not really a camera, just an interface toward the cloud."[22] Sterling's aggregator of the camera-less recording, Google, is a likely environment for this future trend, since Google is the most frequently visited search engine on the planet and the Google home page may be the most familiar Internet image worldwide. The upgrade from multiple recording devices to effortless, on command, recording-by-gesture would seem only natural to the Google-oriented global user. Schirmacher made a similar prediction more than ten years earlier, since this "always-on" world describes the native ecology of homo-generator, his creative/d, autonomous, in-process subject. Schirmacher states, "There is no dialogue outside media, and all the action takes place within. . . . Media

---

[21] Bruce Sterling, "Closing Keynote: Vernacular Video and Saffo's Law," Aku Aku, http://www.akuaku.org/2011/01/vernacular-video-and-saffos-law.html (accessed January 28, 2012). As of March 1, 2012, Google consolidated privacy policies across its platforms and services, automatically combining search and web surfing habits to compile "the mother of all profiles," according to Wired Magazine's online service, *Extremetech*. It would be just a hop, skip and a jump to not only be able to store, but also record on demand, bringing Sterling's prediction much closer than the twenty-five year time span he is giving this event. Google's new policy will make it easier for regulatory agencies worldwide to keep track of users as well, by watching their online activities as consolidated into one Google product.

[22] Ibid.

has to seduce and open up a field of action which has no goal
other than playing life, rearranging a never fixed lifeworld."[23]

Sterling's media-binge fantasy seems to be the end point in a
trajectory from Debord's thesis of the spectacle as the
replacement of reality with representation and the non-stop self-
promotion of the ruling order. The human-machine interface is
resolved in Sterling's scenario. The language of media is no
longer part of a separate dialogue, but is the language of the
human-human interface as well. While Sterling's future trend
depends on an unqualified submission to the authority of techno-
consumerism, it also depends on an active participation and
collective organization of wireless space, along with the
evolution of new relationships to both space and time. The path
of least resistance may lead us to fulfill his vision, but could we
possibly conceive of alternatives to being the subject and object
of a global centralized database? Is this scenario a possible end
point for Debord's nightmare?

Sterling seems to place the relevance of Perec's careful
witnessing in question as well, but the user is able to take a
systematic approach to an awareness of the details of the
telecommunications environment just as well as of the built
environment. And the body in the space of the everyday
continues to be the basic unit of resistance to the authority of the
state-corporate complex. As with Perec, there is no forward or
backward in Sterling's scenario. There is, however, the ability to
access past, future, and present in a networked space-time that is
porous and spontaneous.[24] Issues of what space and time become
in an interactive social network surface in contemporary
dialogues about consumerism and authority and these references
to interactivity are more than metaphors for the Internet. While
elements of both Schirmacher's and Sterling's predictions of a
universal media and telecommunications environment already

---

[23] Schirmacher, "Homo Generator: Media and Postmodern Technology," in
Culture on the Brink, 78.
[24] Ibid.

seem familiar, they suggest that a radical reordering of society is already taking place, based on functioning, non-hierarchical systems of interactivity in which individuals, groups, ideas, media, objects, and processes are drilling tunnels through and around the weighted hierarchies that feed the status quo.

Telecommunications will not make or break this process. The structure of the environment of the Internet is similar in aspects to the networked structure of an autonomous collectivity, but it was conceived and put into practice because a decentralized structure is a more efficient system of connectivity and is less vulnerable to attacks than a highly centralized structure. The above listing – people, ideas, processes – merely represents potential. The reality is much broader and inclusive, a vast interchange that has been the true function of the elements of our reality since the big bang.[25] The state-corporate complex controls a structure that it must inhabit along with the rest of us, however, and its performance and the image it projects of itself, are under the constant surveillance of the marketplace. Its performance and image are also in conflict with urgent political and social movements that are opening up within post-colonial, post-industrial, and post-dictatorship societies. The conflict is not between generations, as though a new generation would be any more immune to the power of mass marketing, the spectacle, or the mental incarceration of working without satisfaction than the old one is; we are all in conflict with the established order for the life-sustaining resources of the planet itself.

Khayati, writing in 1966, states that even though there is dissent within consumer societies, the response that successfully stifles dissent is reform from within the society. He writes, "What they fail to realize is that the banality of everyday life is not incidental, *but the central mechanism and product of modern capitalism.*"[26] Situationist strategies were designed to re-

---

[25] I am waiting for the physicists who recently proved the existence of the Higgs-Boson particle, which unifies everything, to confirm this theory.

[26] Mustapha Khayati, "On the Poverty of Student Life." This specific quote is from a translation of the essay by Donald Nicholson-Smith and Christopher

organize social space, including how the space can be perceived and opened up for continuing change. The strategy was not for improving the experience of life within the existing social order. Situationist strategies of *détournement, dérive,* pastiche, collage, psychogeography and *flâneur*-ism were enacted to loosen the hold on one's perceptions of assumptions about urban space, and they provided means for re-routing avenues of state and market control over the experience of the city. With a Situationist toolbox, a traveler or citizen might be able to map out and complete her *own* journey through a truly new space-time, rather than take the rutted route set up for her by the market and by the state; an individual might then be able to discern the space of his own body, movement, and orientation, and in doing so, begin to figure an authentic collective space.[27] The strategy of *détournement,* used prior to the Situationists by Dadaist and Surrealist artists, is the juxtaposition of unlike elements in the creation of a newly configured logic, or the uncovering of an already existing but hidden text or influence. "Any elements, no matter where they are taken from, can be used to make new

---

Gray, and differs from the Ken Knabb translation cited previously. Notbored.org, http://www.notbored.org/poverty.html (accessed July 19, 2012).

[27] The political essence of public space becomes clear when considering the space allocated to women. In San Francisco in the fall of 1978, I participated in the first Take Back the Night march and rally, a demonstration by several hundred women against the sexual violence that women experience routinely on the street at night. The march, which was most likely not organized with Situationist principles in mind, addressed the tradition of male domination of the public sphere. The march took place through San Francisco's "porn district" in a symbolic liberation of the district from the pornography industry and from the exclusion of women except as obscene subjects. The experience of being a woman walking down the street has not changed since 1978. An interesting if not disheartening side note is that men, too, are now completely sexualized by the advertising industry in a way that does not suggest male power so much as men's dependence on being successfully triangulated in the same subject-image-object configuration as women. For the advertising industries, the realization of gender equality occurred when maleness as well as femaleness was successfully exploited in order to sell a bottle of beer, a night on the town, or a spray of deodorant.

combinations,"[28] writes Debord and Gil J. Wolman in the 1956 essay, "A User's Guide to *Détournement.*" Paintings, photographs, films, objects, and places can be repurposed in order to disorient the artist or viewer, and set in motion an alternative set of associations.

Debord and Wolman state that, "If *détournement* were extended to urbanistic realizations, not many people would remain unaffected by an exact reconstruction in one city of an entire neighborhood of another. Life can never be too disorienting: *détournement* on this level would really spice it up."[29] But *détournement* apparently swings both ways, for a city-out-of-place is exactly what Rem Koolhaas and his architectural firm, OMA, have designed for Dubai. The Waterfront City project, as it is called, is to be a development of nearly one square mile of skyscrapers surrounding a central park, with a grid-like street pattern and the population density of Manhattan, built on an artificially constructed square island. OMA's partner in development, Nakheel Properties, describes the "masterplan" on OMA's website:

> Waterfront City in Dubai is a masterplan of possibly unprecedented scale and ambition, aiming to generate a critical mass of density and diversity in a city that has seen explosive growth in recent years but little cultivation of the street-level urban activity that most metropolises thrive on. The development consists of an artificial Island linked to four distinct neighbourhoods – Madinat Al Soor, the Boulevard, the Marina, and the Resorts – which together are twice the size of Hong Kong Island and yield a total floor space of 11.8 million [square miles] across various building types and programs. The masterplan takes an optimistic view of the future of urbanism and exploits two usually

---

[28] Guy Debord and Gil J. Wolman, "A User's Guide to *Détournement,*" in *Situationist International Anthology*, ed. and trans. Ken Knabb (Berkeley: Bureau of Public Secrets, 2006), 15.
[29] Ibid., 20.

opposing elements of 21st century architecture: the generic and the iconic.[30]

The Waterfront City project, whose "generic and iconic" designs were made public by OMA in 2008, is currently on hold, but when plans were announced in 2008, it created a buzz on architectural websites and forums. From "Parisian Girl," in reference to the models of the project posted online: "Nice renders bizzy ... This city is gonna rock!!! Can't wait to see construction begin on that island." Another posting, understated, simply anticipates completion: "2020."[31] Not every fan of architecture is enamored of the plan for Waterfront City, however. "Anonymous" writes: " Koolhaas has no conscience - issues that come up for me are about the desert environment (sustainability), architecture that destroys the history of a place, and the civil rights, wages and substandard housing of the construction workers. Doesn't the architect have a responsibility for any of these issues?"[32] This comment, written in 2008, suggests that Koolhaas is not practicing an authentic *détournement,* but has merely co-opted *détournement* for a project for one of Dubai's biggest developers, Nakheel Properties, which commissioned the design. Koolhaas has brought *détournement* inside the power structure that it was designed to resist. Since unveiling the plan, Nakheel has been badly affected by the global economic downturn, spurred on in part by runaway property development, and in 2011, the

---

[30] OMA Architects, "Waterfront City UAE Dubai,"
http://oma.eu/projects/2008/waterfront-city (accessed May 21, 2012).
[31] Skyscraper City, Forums, Skyscraper City,
http://www.skyscrapercity.com/showthread.php?s=602cee6ec0cda77f3d61c238b
fd4f7b0&t=604171 (accessed May 20, 2012).
[32] Comments to an article by Dianna Dilworth, "Koolhaas Unveils New
Waterfront City in Dubai," Architectural Record, March 12, 2008,
http://archrecord.construction.com/news/daily/archives/080312koolhaas.asp
(accessed July 19, 2012).

company, heavily in debt, was signed over to the Government of Dubai.[33]

In a pre-SI text, a 1953 manifesto entitled "Formulary for a New Urbanism," Ivan Chtcheglov discusses the relevance of architectural space in relation to a humanist urbanism. He describes Le Corbusier's work as having a "style suitable for factories and hospitals, and no doubt eventually for prisons," whose "conceptions of the world" are "ugly," and "squash people under ignoble masses of reinforced concrete, a noble material that should rather be used to enable an aerial articulation of space . . . His cretinizing influence is immense."[34] For Chtcheglov, a building is meant to articulate the space in harmony with its geography, geology, aspects of light and shadow, day and night, sound, and surroundings – to be in conversation with those elements, "modulating reality and engendering dreams."[35] The psychology of place is based on its history and geography; the possibilities for architecture are for modulating not only space, but also time, and for becoming a part of an "economy" of the "laws of behavior accepted by a civilization." Architecture is not to be an "cretinizing influence," but should be a "modulation expressing an ephemeral beauty . . . producing influences in accordance with the eternal spectrum of human desires and the progress in fulfilling them."[36] Chtcheglov's recommendation that the nature of architecture be in harmony with the nature of the culture in which it is situated, bases the idea of harmony on factors beyond aesthetics. These include social and individual need, proprioceptive advantage, and adaptability (modulation) of the building or complex to adjust to people's changing needs and uses; they also include environmental factors such as air, light, and permeability, rather

---

[33] Chen Zhi, "Rescue of Nakheel saves Dubai's image," Xinhuanet.com, May 15, 2012, http://news.xinhuanet.com/english/business/2012-05/15/c_131589789.htm (accessed July 19, 2012).

[34] Ivan Chtcheglov, "Formulary for a New Urbanism," in Knabb, *Situationist International Anthology*, 2.

[35] Ibid., 3.

[36] Ibid.

than formalist concerns and specialization within architecture as a design field. Architecture is not meant to produce monoliths. Architectural complexes are meant to be modifiable, mobile, and possibly portable, based on the needs of their inhabitants. Beauty in architecture is defined by the body's sense of the space that a building articulates, as well as by the potential, inherent in the design, for the structure to become a part of an ever-changing landscape by way of its ability to change with it. The desire for a modulating architecture carries within it the recognition that people, society, and civilizations are mobile entities.

Chtcheglov's conception of space is a concept of time and activity as well. His concerns do not end with a set of ideas about design and construction. The most important aspect of architecture is how it is used by the occupants, not in relation to a single structure such as a home, but in relation to the overall city plan; and not in terms of settling down, but quite the opposite. "The main activity of the inhabitants will be CONTINUOUS DRIFTING. The changing of landscapes from one hour to the next will result in total disorientation." Chtcheglov continues:

> Couples will no longer pass their nights in the home where they live and receive guests, which is nothing but a banal *social* custom. The chamber of love will be more distant from the center of the city: it will naturally recreate for the partners a sense of *exoticism* in a locale less open to light, more hidden, so as to recover the atmosphere of secrecy. The opposite tendency, seeking a center for intellectual discourse, will proceed through the same technique.[37]

The disorientation that comes from continuous drifting, like the disorientation of *détournement,* is an important element of the treatment of psychological space, not as the result of the experience itself of something new, exotic or unexpected, but as

---

[37] Chtcheglov, "Formulary for a New Urbanism," in Knabb, *Situationist International Anthology*, 7.

a route to a different understanding of a place based on wandering through it. A place for lovemaking may be more distant from the center of the city, for example, and intellectual discourse may occur in an opposite but equally suitable direction, but neither would necessarily take place at home. The connection being made here is that an activity, such as drifting, which is related to the history of human migration, defines the appropriate architecture. In some ways, this means that the architecture, the anatomy of a building, does not exist until its use is determined, and that determination is always temporary. Interstitial spaces emerge from the shadows and crevices as well, announcing possibilities for use of space that is always considered a default zone between two places.

In his 1955 essay, "Introduction to a Critique of Urban Geography," Debord observes that urban space is currently organized to encourage the development of habitual use of streets and neighborhoods, and to promote routine behavior based on limiting possibilities for use rather than providing space for a multiplicity of uses. He suggests a somewhat imprecise science, psychogeography, as a means to become aware of other possibilities for places, and for creating new uses for them. He writes:

> Geography . . . deals with the determinant action of general natural forces, such as soil composition or climatic conditions, on the economic structures of a society, and thus on the corresponding conception that such a society can have of the world. . . . The creation of a chosen emotional situation depends only on the thorough understanding and calculated application of a certain number of concrete techniques.[38]

These techniques include drifting through urban geographies in order to investigate the likelihood for creating a different emotional situation in a place where meaning had been

---

[38] Guy Debord, "A Critique of Urban Geography," in Knabb, *Situationist International Anthology*, 8 – 9.

previously defined by history, by police control of traffic and people's other activities, or determined by customary use. Drifting is meant to not only change navigational routes, but to add significance to a space. In a 2009 interview with Hans Ulrich Obrist, Vaneigem describes the function of psychogeography:

> HUO: My interviews often focus on the connections between art and architecture/urbanism, or literature and architecture/urbanism. Could you tell me about the Bureau of Unitary Urbanism?

> RV: That was an idea more than a project. It was about the urgency of rebuilding our social fabric, so damaged by the stranglehold of the market. Such a rebuilding effort goes hand in hand with the rebuilding by individuals of their own daily existence. That is what psychogeography is really about: a passionate and critical deciphering of what in our environment needs to be destroyed, subjected to *détournement*, rebuilt.[39]

In an article published in *Potlatch #1*,[40] Debord provides an example of psychogeography with the "Psychogeographical Game of the Week," directing readers to "choose a country . . . Build a house. Furnish it. Use decorations and surroundings to the best advantage." He instructs readers to choose a season, and a date and time, to host a cocktail party. "If there has been no error in your calculations, the result should prove satisfying."[41] Debord's style lacks some of the poetic quality and holistic sense of psychogeography that Chtcheglov, who imagines lovers and intellectuals reconfiguring spaces emotionally, brings to an

---

[39] Raoul Vaneigem, "In Conversation with Raoul Vaneigem," interview by Hans Ulrich Obrist, Eric Anglès, trans., E-Flux, May 2009, http://www.e-flux.com/journal/in-conversation-with-raoul-vaneigem/ (accessed March 12, 2012).

[40] *Potlatch* was a Lettrist publication of the mid-1950s.

[41] Debord, "A Critique of Urban Geography," in Knabb, *Situationist International Anthology*, 10.

understanding of it. But Debord's game is a guide for tearing down borders and boundaries, for situating architecture in a location best suited to human needs and geographical features, and for creating a temporary situation where abundance is a factor of use rather than one of accumulation. The game turns the tables on mass marketing: "We need to flood the market – even if for the moment merely the intellectual market – with a mass of desires whose fulfillment is not beyond the capacity of humanity's present means of action on the material world, but only beyond the capacity of the old social organization."[42] *Dérive* and psychogeography are tools for drawing other maps of the city, re-districting for zones of desire and fulfillment, and for setting up an economy based on sharing that is beyond the capacity of mass consumerism. Further in the same 2009 Obrist interview, Vaneigem discusses psychogeography as a still-viable method of resistance to taking back daily life from "the stranglehold of the market":

HUO: Which situationist projects remain unrealized?

RV: Psychogeography, the construction of situations, the superseding of predatory behavior. The radicality, which, notwithstanding some lapses, never ceased to motivate us, remains a source of inspiration to this day. Its effects are just beginning to manifest themselves in the autonomous groups that are now coming to grips with the collapse of financial capitalism.[43]

Transcending The Spell of Authority

There comes a moment of transcendence that is historically defined by the strength and weakness of Power; by the

---

[42] Ibid.

[43] Vaneigem, "In Conversation with Raoul Vaneigem," interview by Hans Ulrich Obrist, Eric Anglès, trans., E-Flux, May 2009, http://www.e-flux.com/journal/in-conversation-with-raoul-vaneigem/.

fragmentation of the individual to the point where he is a mere monad of subjectivity; and by the intimacy between everyday life and that which destroys it. This transcendence will be general, undivided, and built by subjectivity.[44]

Who is it that has the power to liberate zones of habitual use into an alternative-redistricting project of psychogeography? Is this the role of the resister and the revolutionary? Is it an act of desire? Does the action represent freedom granted to the self – that is, is it an authentic freedom? Perec's questions, "But where is our life? Where is our body? Where is our space?" resonate here, even as we begin feel the pull of the current of polymorphous town planning. In his introduction to *The Revolution of Everyday Life* (1967), Vaneigem writes that he is not trying to say anything new: "The only truly new thing here is the direction of the stream carrying commonplaces along."[45] A stream is an appropriate analogy for the place where individual life is lived within the collectivity of "commonplaces," making the collective the most ordinary location of the body, and drifting the most ordinary means of navigation through collective space. Having a fixed identity goes against the stream of collective benefit, and individual identity and subjectivity are changeable forces. The state and societal forces assign and re-assign identity to any person, class, group, etc. based on the priorities of maintaining the socio-political power structure, and these are meant to remain fixed within the social space created by the state. Haraway regards identity and its connective subjectivities as "permanently partial," necessitating "contradictory standpoints,"[46] what Vaneigem simply calls "roles." Our roles provide us with a place in the social hierarchy.

---

[44] Vaneigem, *The Revolution of Everyday Life,* 164.

[45] Ibid., 17 – 18.

[46] An inauthentic notion of identity, where identification becomes a deficit and can even be life threatening, is most readily observable in the instances of fixed identifications of gender and race as they operate within American social and political hierarchies. Haraway's quotations are from "A Manifesto for Cyborgs:

Vaneigem's analysis of the functions of subjectivity and collectivity within both an oppressive social order and a liberating collectivity, gives roles and stereotypes – that which enables others to recognize and respond to us – a vital function in a self-regulated dominant spectacle. People are separated and categorized, and re-integrated in the social hierarchy. This is how people come to identify themselves and each other, and categorization and stereotyping are essentially issues of representation. Access to roles, to having a role via identification, means access to the possibility of moving up in the social hierarchy, even as the roles alienate people from themselves and their authentic needs, histories, desires, etc. Regarding the function of roles, Vaneigem states:

> The role is a consumption of power. It locates one in the *representational* hierarchy, and hence in the spectacle: at the top, at the bottom, in the middle but never *outside* the hierarchy, whether this side of it or beyond it. The role is thus the means of access to the mechanism of culture: a form of *initiation*. It is also the medium of exchange of individual sacrifice, and in this sense performs a compensatory function. And lastly, as a residue of separation, it strives to construct a behavioural unity; in this aspect it depends on identification.[47]

The desire to be identified and identifiable, and to have a place in the social hierarchy, even a lowly place, is evidence of the effectiveness of the marketing of stereotypes as consumer trends, even within the trends and roles in use by the state's authority. In consumer culture, an assigned role may change or evolve depending on patterns of novelty and obsolescence. "The primary function [of the role] is always that of social adaptation, of integrating people into the well-polished universe of things."[48] Otherwise, they are unintelligible and cannot be

---

Science, Technology, and Socialist Feminism in the 1980s," in *The Haraway Reader* (New York and London: Routledge, 2004), 13.
[47] Vaneigem, *The Revolution of Everyday Life*, 132.
[48] Ibid., 134.

interpreted. One example of unintelligibility could be found in the reporting of news agencies and journalists when they first encountered participants of Occupy Wall Street demonstrations in the fall of 2011. Occupy's adherents operated outside the left-right dialectic to a degree where identifying opposition as well as support, in terms of reporting, became difficult. The terminology of protest, disorder, and free speech that the social order expects, allows, and turns into consumable product did not fit the situation. One image presented by news media was of a fractious group of ill-informed youth who had no leader, no platform, and no ideological conformity. Conservative Fox News commentator Aaron Klein, who claims to have been investigating Occupy Wall Street "instigators" for the past four years, looks for clues that would point in another direction, however, to a central organizing committee of people whose "millennial" ideologies seem to have congealed at some point around 1934:

> Behind the current Occupy Wall Street protests is a "red army" of radicals seeking no less than to provoke a new, definitive economic crisis, with their goal being the full collapse of the U.S. financial system, with the ensuing chaos to be rebuilt into a utopian socialist vision.

> The angry millennials pressing toward economic cataclysm are seasoned organizers of mass chaos aimed at provoking transformation.[49]

Fox News is commonly known for making claims of questionable legitimacy in order to promote a far-right editorial bias, but even within this particular framework, the commentator makes claims using standard fear-baiting language from previous eras, failing to comprehend the plain speech of the occupiers themselves. After quoting a practical summing up of

---

[49] Aaron Klein, "'Red Army' Behind Occupy Wall Street?" Fox News, October 25, 2011, http://www.foxnews.com/opinion/2011/10/25/red-army-behind-occupy-wall-street/ (accessed May 23, 2012).

Occupy events by Cornel West, who Klein quotes as saying, "It's impossible to translate the issue of the greed of Wall Street into one demand, or two demands. We're talking about a democratic awakening," and after calling the protests "a periodic renaissance" of "young people confronting a tired old regime,"[50] Klein persists in seeing only the patterns of identification that fall within those recognized by the language of the existing centralized power structure. "Provoking transformation," however, is exactly what is necessary for individuals and networks that want to enact change. Change is not available from within a culture of invasive and insidious consumerism, oppressive political and social hierarchies, and perceptions of behavior based on stereotyping. Methods to provoke change from outside the culture remain incomprehensible in this case, and actions, and even clear speech, are indecipherable. Identity is a valuable commodity. Any subject who claims her own identity outside the social hierarchy and refuses participation in the commoditization of herself, is taking steps to take her valuable identity off the market.

"Identity politics" has become a catch phrase, like "politically correct," for ideologies of the 1980s that are no longer a useful part of contemporary progressive dialogue. Identity politics was a dialogue that engaged and challenged the representation of women, queers, people of color, and others as they were most commonly created in popular consumerist culture, the arts, and language. In the 1980s and early 1990s, multi-culturalism and the politics of diversity caused cracks in the surface of the social hierarchy, forcing the signifiers – "African-American," "woman," "homosexual," "Chicano," "disabled," "Asian" – and their assigned counterparts into a public discourse on difference, equality, and respect. The dialogue was initially expansive and open but eventually became confined and boxed in by a new outcropping of more liberal stereotypes within popular culture. Obsessive defining and theorizing within academia, as well as curatorial strategies that sought to historicize representation of

---

[50] Ibid.

identity within the arts, further pushed the dialogue out of the public sphere into an area of expertise. Difference proved to be easily co-opted and turned into a consumer item, relegating those who were "different" back to the sidelines of the social order, where real power was in short supply. Multi-culturalism proved to be a fine location for the state to situate culture as food, ethnic dress, music, and traditional art as well; state institutions were able to embed the reality of a diverse society with diverse and intersecting needs into the dead zone of the "celebration" of many separate histories that seemed to find their end at an annual ethnic festival, enclosed in the space of the past and removed from public discourse. It took longer to acknowledge queer reality and allow for its equal representation, but queerness was, like all other information systems, finally cleaned up, legitimized and absolved of its oppositional potential.

The American Civil Rights movement has staged campaigns for inclusion, integration and assimilation into dominant culture from the 1950s onward; the movement for Black Power that emerged in the 1960s, was based on self-reliance, building a strong base of alliances, and portioning tasks to participants and allies ranging from providing breakfast for school children to overthrowing the American government. The feminist movement of the late 1960s and early 1970s, which was a reemergence of the politics of suffrage, equality, and citizenship, and which was further inspired by the civil rights movement, challenged patriarchal systems of female oppression. Conservative feminist campaigns sought equal power for women within the existing social structures. Radical women challenged the hierarchy on more specific issues of control: reclamation of the female body and female subjectivity, challenging the enormous networks of violence against women and the meaning of physical abuse in the social sphere, and examining the validity of the authority of heterosexuality in determining women's roles in all areas of life. Negation is the default mode for these identity movements. In her discussion about the difficulties of naming or categorizing oneself, Haraway observes that positive identity becomes negation in its broad socio-political context. A dialectic that establishes "us" and "them" is set up when affinity becomes an agent of exclusion in the search for foundational or true identity. Haraway refers to the writings of Chicana theorist Chela Sandoval, who has postulated a "model of political identity called oppositional consciousness." Sandoval envisions oppositional consciousness as a shared consciousness independent of the essences of identification:

> "Women of color," a name contested at its origins by those whom it would incorporate, as well as a historical consciousness marking systematic breakdown of all the signs of Man in "Western" traditions, constructs a kind of post-modernist identity out of otherness and difference.

> [Sandoval] notes that the definition of the group has been by conscious appropriation of negation. For example, a Chicana or U.S. black woman has not been able to speak as a woman or as a black person or as a Chicano. Thus, she was at the bottom of a cascade of negative identities, left out of even the privileged oppressed authorial categories called "women and blacks," who claimed to make the important revolutions. . . .This identity marks out a self-consciously constructed space that cannot affirm the capacity to act on the basis of natural identification, but only on the basis of conscious coalition, of affinity, of political kinship.[51]

The organization of conscious coalitions based on political affinity and working together across lines of race, class, and gender still confines these identities within the boundaries of the existing social hierarchy. Identity politics and politicized speech are not reflections of the set of minorities or women that they refer to, but are reflections of the system that has created minority and female as categories with specific characteristics and with specific limited amounts of power in society. The affinities are real, however, and coalitions create links between individuals and groups who may have formerly only understood

---

[51] Donna Haraway, "A Manifesto for Cyborgs: Science, Technology, and Socialist Feminism in the 1980s," in *The Haraway Reader*, 14.

each other's subjectivity in theoretical terms that may have been only remotely related to their own pursuit of justice. The possibilities of working together include the creation of spheres of shared subjectivity through lived experience. The watchful eyes of identity politics and political correctness are a mirror to exclusion, and in their simplification and overstatement of who and what is woman, Latino, queer, Asian, and differently-abled, have become disciplines in their own right, an essentialism that effectively challenges the essentialism of the social hierarchy. Until, that is, each is absorbed into the mainstream and exploited in advertising and marketing, thus being simultaneously included in mainstream consciousness and confined to the possibilities determined by branding. Being absorbed back into the system as alternatives to the mainstream is inevitable unless an effective model for building coalitions is revealed and utilized.

Vaneigem predicts the coming movement of the politics of identity by his insistence on self-realization as a necessary factor in liberation. Identity-based artwork and other forms of image-representation from the 1980s and 1990s insist that the process of seeing through the system of oppression begins with awareness of the body and its immediate surroundings. Representation from a multiplicity of perspectives opened up a cultural environment in which autonomous actors are able to work collectively within their communities and across networks of other communities. For Vaneigem, realizing authentic subjectivity is a creative process that leads to affinities rather than to the isolation and powerlessness of assuming roles within the hierarchy. The struggle for self-realization is the link between the individual and history. Transcendence is the making of history. According to Vaneigem, transcendence puts the subject in serious opposition to the ruling order:

Everyone finds himself at the centre of the struggle *in his daily life*. This has two consequences:

a) In the first place, the individual is not only the victim of social atomization, he or she is also the victim of fragmented power. Now that subjectivity has emerged onto the historical stage, only to come immediately under attack, it has become the most crucial revolutionary demand. Henceforward the construction of a harmonious collectivity will require a revolutionary theory founded not on communitarianism but rather upon subjectivity, a theory founded, in other words, on individual cases, on the lived experience of individuals.

b) Secondly, the extreme fragmentariness of resistance and refusal turns, ironically, into its opposite, for it recreates the preconditions for a global refusal. The new revolutionary collective will come into being through a chain reaction, from one subjectivity to the next. The construction of a community of people who are whole individuals will inaugurate the reversal of perspective without which no transcendence is possible.[52]

Vaneigem's "harmonious collectivity" sounds very much like Sandoval's oppositional consciousness based on affinity and political kinship. It is created within a non-hierarchical network. In this network, which is fluid and in a state of continuous change and renewal, individuals and groups come into and out of knowledge of each other, forming long or short-term affinities in a potentially endless stream of connectivity. This may sound similar to a model of the Internet, but this physical-world model pre-dates the Internet, and not only embraces diversity, but actually requires it in order to function as a meaningful network. Participants in the current global democracy movement, for example, retain their regional priorities while recognizing and benefiting from affinities beyond their political borders. Global telecommunications did not create the global democracy movement, nor will it homogenize users. Rather, human interaction has re-purposed social networking sites, created to cater to groups of friends and advertise goods and services based on the content of their posts, into sites for groups of activists who relate on a global scale. Subjectivities, then, are based in

---

[52] Vaneigem, *The Revolution of Everyday Life,* 166.

time and place, under a multiplicity of influences, and are neither diluted nor assimilated in cross-cultural/global telecommunications. Diversity, plurality, and a general coming into and going out of a universe of muck and potential are the current environment of political activism. Vaneigem calls for a "reversal of perspective," which is a collective process involving thousands of people who are activists or lurkers. Even the tangential participation of lurkers has value in terms of reversing the perspective provided by state and capital.

In order to construct a daily life based on more than survival, which Vaneigem claims is the reality of most who routinely work for a living, an inauthentic experience of life lived entirely within the system created for the worker, we must first reclaim the real space of the intimate. The worker, whose entire life has been appropriated by the economic system that owns his labor, is given just one choice for daily living: to fall under the spell of authority, to exist on the level of survival, which becomes, for most, the status quo. The intimate space of the everyday is the primary location of radical connectivity, however, where individuals can place themselves outside the architecture of their oppression. Connectivity pushes the person towards local and common spaces of an experience of the everyday based on connections and continuities rather than on authority and conformity. The "whole individual," through the "construction of communities," continues to the next event, building effective networks of resistance based on a collective reversal of perspective. In order to create an authentic event of conscious living, rather than accepting an existence of mere survival, the individual must reject all compromises with authority. She does not have to do this alone, however. Taking action against systems of control and forming a core of resistance includes more than an awareness of the mesmerizing effects of the spectacle and the problems inherent in a society overwhelmed by false representations of daily life. It also involves becoming an actor and a catalyst in a collective movement towards human autonomy.

The individual as represented in *The Revolution of Everyday Life*
comes into being on a continuous basis, continuously refreshed,
and relates to the collective in non-hierarchical networks of
perspective, action, and possibility. Multiple and fluid
subjectivities are part of Vaneigem's event of transcendence. His
prediction – that the "fragmentariness" created by the refusals of
many to comply with the meager standards of existence that they
were born into creates the space for rebellion on a global scale –
makes obvious sense in the age of telecommunications. The
whole world *has* been mapped. Now it is time to map
connections. Authenticity is the goal of daily experience rather
than a description or judgment of an individual's identity. It
allows for play within activity and for the experience of identity
that is not fixed, but rather is always coming into being. For
Perec, the answer to the question of where the body is may seem
to be bound up in questions of identity. But today more than
ever his methodology of constant surveillance and directing
one's attention to the connectivity of everything that happens in,
or passes through, the present moment breaks the spell of
authority. If one looks carefully, and objectively, one can see
clearly both the inside and outside of the social hierarchy. More
importantly, the focus on connectivity reveals that places and
spaces for the body, and the life lived, are always in motion.

In *Species of Spaces and Other Pieces*, Perec's account of
spaces and places, and the means of traversing them, is inclusive
to the point of describing the place of the page he is writing on
and the page as it appears to the reader. The intimacy of the
moment includes the reader. The essay entitled "Reading: A
Socio-physiological Outline,"[53] winds its way into the body of
the reader by describing how the reader's eyes move across the
words and gather the information, in a manner "like a pigeon
pecking at the ground in search of breadcrumbs."[54] Situationist
principles of daily life are embedded in "Species of Spaces," but
Perec's embedded politics speak of a political origin for daily

---

[53] Perec, "Reading: A Socio-physiological Outline," in *Species of Spaces and Other Pieces*, 174.
[54] Ibid., 176.

experience that is fundamental to the nature of existence in a more inclusive way than are the Situationist strategies such as *détournement, dérive*, pastiche, collage or psychogeography. In *An Attempt at Exhausting A Place In Paris*, he takes Situationist strategies to a conclusion that creates a deeply moving pathway to the real. The reader enters the place of the writing and of the scenes represented through a creative act of imagining the people, objects, events and the location of the café. All are ordinary enough. So then, how do Perec's unadorned descriptions create an emotional response? Does the reader visualize the space and imagine the longing it represents, or does the writer? In the afterward to the 2010 English edition, the translator, Marc Lowenthal, notes that this is primarily writing about space and time. He writes:

> Time, unarrestable, works against this project, though, and [Perec] is diverted from his observations by an effort to observe what has specifically changed in his field of view from one day to the next; seemingly nothing, but then again, yes . . . what will, in fact, eventually become everything. Every bus that passes, every person who walks by, every object, thing, and event – everything that happens and that does not happen ultimately serves no other function than that of so many chronometers, so many signals, methods, and clues for making time, for eroding permanence.[55]

Perec ignores the differentiation of subjective experience and objective account. This allows perspective to be created by the reader on the physical space of the page. The authentic experience of the place is not forced or expressed; it is revealed in a three-fold experience of intimacy, collectivity, and creativity. In creating a space-time that includes the history of a place in every new experience of it, Perec addresses the problem of narrative linearity as the method of writing history as a successive series of large events. He counters this most

---

[55] Marc Lowenthal, Afterword, in Perec, *An Attempt at Exhausting a Place in Paris*, 49 – 50.

obviously in a discussion of space that includes nothingness and it's "extension, the external...our ambient milieu, the space around us."[56] Not an empty space, but one that is in use, and subject, even, to playful re-arrangement, "a Métro in the heart of the countryside,"[57] for example. A simple act of what Debord may call "minor *détournement*" creates simultaneous awareness of what is present and what is possible.

One must see both as reasonable courses of action in order to see the present moment as it exists both inside and outside the structures in place that control perception and the ability – individual as well as collective – to create a future not based on survival but on living. By revealing the difference between what is and what is not, a society is able to imagine a course of action based on an awareness of the common matrix, and is able to know the present as always being in flux and under construction. The present moment, as described by and within an economic system that reduces people to a situation of survival, is not the basis for understanding either history or the present reality. The present moment, as inscribed within the current state-corporate system, is always taken up by the presence of authority – of corporate domination of time, space, resources, consciousness and the historical record; and of state complicity in enabling corporate dominance over the interests of the public, and in permitting corporate influence over public mandate in the state's relationship to the people. The infra-ordinary is life with all its related individual and collective connections within a reclaimed present moment. The reclamation of the moment begins in the first moments of perceptual endeavors. Perec: "This is how space begins, with words only, signs on a blank page."[58]

---

[56] Perec, *Species of Spaces and Other Pieces*, 4.
[57] Ibid., 5.
[58] Ibid., 31.

Corporate Interventions into the Everyday

In *No Space, No Choice, No Jobs: No Logo,* journalist Naomi Klein, writing 30 years after Perec, examines the contemporary conditions of autonomy, authentic experience, and the writing of history through an identification of specific state-corporate relationships as the structural underpinning of the systems of power. *No Logo* is also a study of the relationship of advertising to place and subjectivity, and the corporate alchemy that turns citizens into markets. In one passage Klein describes her own adolescent awakenings in relation to what amounted to a pointless search for a pathway to an unwritten future within an autonomous space of daily life:

> In our final year of high school, my best friend, Lan Ying, and I passed the time with morbid discussions about the meaninglessness of life when everything had already been done. The world stretched out before us not as a slate of possibility, but as a maze of well-worn grooves like the ridges burrowed by insects in hardwood. Step off the straight and narrow groove and you just end up on another one – the groove for people who step off the main groove... Everywhere we imagined ourselves standing turned into a cliché beneath our feet – the stuff of Jeep ad copy and sketch comedy.[59]

Klein's youthful expectation of being able to formulate her own path in life was based on a belief that her future was open – a future in which the autonomous subject is free to explore authentic terrains of the present as a way to build the future, a time and space not yet defined. This is the expectation of most middle class non-immigrant citizens of Western countries. The pathways available to such citizens always involve the consumer economy, as their expectations have been researched by industries whose sole product is information about the buying

---

[59] Naomi Klein, *No Space, No Choice, No Jobs: No Logo* (New York: Picador, 2002), 63.

habits of populations. The measure of social equality is the normalization of others as consumers. A trip to the future can be designed for any demographic. The space within which the expectation of a future filled with choice was nurtured was already a corporate space where the choices offered are all consumer choices. The future is locked down by brands and consumer trends, whose presence and influence privatize public space, turning it into a corporate space instead. A step off the groove, as Klein concludes, puts the explorer on another equivalent groove, taking her back into the role of consumer. The packaged adventure of possibility is a simulation of action and choice. Authentic space must be reclaimed and taken out of the consumer loop.

A recent example of the reclamation of privatized space can be found in the story of one Bedford-Stuyvesant, Brooklyn, community garden, which was created by the labor of volunteers forming a loose coalition of neighborhood organizations and individuals who lived in the area. The project was to reclaim a litter-strewn empty lot and turn it into an urban vegetable garden. The garden eventually became a beautiful social space, an urban farm, and a place where neighborhood youth could meet to learn about the earth, about plants, and about food. The people of Bedford-Stuyvesant, a large district composed of poor and working class families of color and lower-income whites, have established a network of at least twenty-seven gardens creating areas of natural beauty that enable urban dwellers to have a direct relationship with the earth and the experience of growing their own food in a neighborhood largely neglected in terms of city services. Privatization has crept back into one garden, however, whose caretakers have agreed to position a banner over its entrance advertising McDonald's restaurants in exchange for a $10,000 donation for tools, supplies for maintenance of the garden.[60] An advertisement for McDonald's

---

[60] This information is from a course in which I participated during the fall of 2011, entitled Food Justice, given by Brooklyn urban farmer and Food Justice activist Yonette Fleming. Fleming is vice president of the Hattie Carthan Community Garden in Bedford-Stuyvesant, Brooklyn.

over the entrance to an organic community garden privatizes the community space, claiming it for the McDonald's Corporation, and turns the garden into its antithesis. McDonald's becomes the new squatter. The irony of a global food company, which has been criticized for past practices of buying beef from ranchers who engaged in the often illegal and deadly destruction of rain forests in South America in order to raise cattle as well as for unfair labor practices, "supporting" a tiny community garden in a struggling Brooklyn neighborhood, illustrates how the community and the corporation become intertwined in small moments of a giant spectacle.[61]

The relationship of the individual to the spectacle is the same as the relationship of the individual to systems of survival. The issue of survival that Vaneigem brings to the discussion is obviously about more than psychological survival, personal fulfillment, or happiness. He writes:

> As we know, the consumption of goods – which comes down always, in the present state of things, to the consumption of power – carries within itself the seeds of its own destruction and the conditions of its own transcendence. The consumer cannot and must not ever attain satisfaction: the logic of the consumable object demands the creation of fresh needs, yet the accumulation of such false needs exacerbates the malaise of people

---

[61] As recently as 2006, after much criticism about the destruction of the Brazilian rainforest for the production of cattle and cattle feed, McDonald's ceased its Brazilian supply-line. Instead, it imports cattle from Australia and New Zealand, where they have exported the exact pattern of destruction of native forest for the raising of cattle and cattle feed. More information about McDonald's environmental policies can be found at McDonald's own website, at http://www.mcdonalds.com/ (accessed July 4, 2012). Other views can be found at environmental watchdog agency sites such as The Ecologist, http://www.theecologist.org/green_green_living/behind_the_label/941743/behin d_the_brand_mcdonalds.html (accessed July 4, 2012); and at the International Union of Food and Allied Workers website, http://www.iuf.org/cgi-bin/editorials/db.cgi?db=default&ww=1&uid=default&ID=47&view_records=1 &en=1 (accessed July 4, 2012).

confined with increasing difficulty solely to the status of consumers. Furthermore, the wealth of consumer goods impoverishes authentic life. . . . First, it replaces authentic life with *things*. Secondly, it makes it impossible, with the best will in the world, to become attached to these things, precisely because they have to be *consumed*, i.e., destroyed.[62]

Widening the lens a bit enables a perspective that links individual desire to nothing less than the increasingly evident destruction of the physical space of the world. McDonald's may seem like an easy target, the generic boogey-man, but the McDonald's death ray is still fully functional. It is aimed in two directions: at the never-satisfied consumer, and at the origin point of the production of the lie. In the example of the urban garden, the lie is directed at the visitor to the garden as well as at the earth's ecosystem in a suggestion of timelessness and stasis. With the McDonald's logo over the garden's entrance, there is no easy way back into the consciousness of the infra-ordinary. The process of coming into power must begin at an identical point of origin (e.g. rainforest, or community garden) where one finds neither the phantasm of spectacular consumerism nor the truth of exploitation, but the possibility of continuous agency to produce and develop a livable future on a global scale. The point of origin is local. Ethics are a communal underpinning for refusal and resistance; ethics are closely related to compassion in the individual and to diversity in the collective.

Morality, on the other hand, functions to create the fear of otherness by associating others with loss of control: crime, terrorism, unpredictability, unintelligibility, and opposition to the status quo. Violence results from moral zealousness as the herd instinct kicks in, in a gesture claiming self-defense. Nietzsche's writing on the herd is fitting and prescient. He states, "Herd instinct – Wherever we encounter a morality, we also encounter valuations and an order of rank of human impulses and actions. These valuations are always expressions

---

[62] Vaneigem, *The Revolution of Everyday Life*, 162.

of the needs of the herd: whatever benefits it most – and second most, and third most – that is also considered the first standard for the value of all individuals. Morality trains the individual to be a function of the herd and to ascribe value to himself only as a function."[63] The herd is not the community, but is the prevention of the formation of community. The herd runs in the same direction, even if it runs in a circle. For many, there is nothing between morality (the herd) and perversity (the autonomous individual within the common). For those outside the morality of the herd, perversity must be virtue, while autonomy is a kind of loneliness that finds relief in the realization of what is possible for the self and for others outside the system. The herd runs on the fear that, through affinity and interaction, an authentic community will arise. Commitment to the herd may foster a sense of security in the individual, but it belies the danger of complete reliance on the status quo, including the danger of violence.

The extraordinary occurrence tests the herding mechanism to confirm its effectiveness as a control measure. The test is a matter of confirming the authority of economic and political hierarchies that create the system of the herd and that alienate or violate authentic subjectivities. In a 2011 lecture at the European Graduate School, Avital Ronell discusses testing as the abomination of "the what is." The "what is" is the open-ended reality of the everyday. She states that within the situation of the test, "You're now in the realm of the hypothetical, that which does not have stable grounding, but becomes some sort of movement of erasure or self-erasure or, possibly, destruction. Testing is related to destruction."[64] Ronell asks, "What is the absence of a test? Can we even imagine a non-testing ground, a

---

[63] Friedrich Nietzsche, *The Gay Science: With a Prelude in Rhymes and an Appendix of Songs*, trans. Walter Kaufmann (New York: Vintage Books, 1974), 174.

[64] Avital Ronell, "Test Drive: The Test, and Testing," lecture at the European Graduate School, Saas-Fee, 2011. This lecture can be viewed online at http://www.youtube.com/watch?v=nvR4cKYzuxc (accessed April 16, 2012).

non-proving ground?" These questions pry open the case against the norm of emergencies punctuated by monotony, fear of difference (difference, in order to not terrify, must be planned and marketed), and the closing of portals and ways out that the system generates in its subjects.

In *Simulations*, Jean Baudrillard writes of consumerist culture as not only a false popular culture, but as a test of the consumer by the products themselves. In discussing popular films, he sites Benjamin from "The Work of Art in the Age of Mechanical Reproduction," who analyzes the film apparatus and the relationship of the camera to the actor in terms of testing:

> The expansion of the field of the testable which mechanical equipment brings about for the actor corresponds to the extraordinary expansion of the field of the testable brought about for the individual through economic conditions. Thus, vocational aptitude tests become constantly more important. What matters in these tests are the segmental performances of the individual. The film shot and the vocational aptitude test are taken before a committee of experts. The camera director in the studio occupies a place identical with that of the examiner during aptitude tests.[65]

Baudrillard continues: "Film no longer allows you to question. It questions you, and directly. The role of the message is no longer information, but testing and polling, and finally control ("contra-role," in the sense that all your answers are already inscribed in the "role," on the anticipated registers of the code)."[66] The message is constructed by a code (Vaneigem's "role" and "identification"), which carries the content. The content of the communiqué from the apparatus to the audience/consumer has been tested many times before it makes an appearance. It consists of narrative formulas from within which the

[65] Walter Benjamin, "The Work of Art in the Age of Mechanical Reproduction" (1936), quoted in Jean Baudrillard, *Simulations* (Los Angeles: Semiotext(e), 1983), 118 – 119.
[66] Baudrillard, *Simulations,* 119.

emergencies and chaos of uncertainty speak a dumb message to the consumers, who de-code the message via their familiarity with its premise, trajectory, intended effect, and denouement, automatically reversing the process by which the narrative is constructed. These narrative strategies work in entertainment media, definitely, but in all aspects of marketing as well. One typical consumerist narrative, for example, places highly processed foods at the center of the discussion: control or guidance of children is encouraged through the simple silencing power of sugar, and the massive and costly system of processed food invention, production, distribution, and marketing is presented as a more timely route to dinner than simply buying produce, cutting it up, cooking it and eating it.

Other narratives surrounding the most clichéd pop music or clothing fixations create a group dynamic around consumer products, many of which are placed directly in front of youth. Youth marketing reaches those who live in poor communities, too, where belonging to the status quo via consumer products may ease the stress of being marginalized by poverty. Even if poverty is not an issue, the pressure to be identified with what is new and contemporary is sometimes overwhelming for young people. Advertising targets youth specifically, keeping tabs on youth culture, watching closely for trends that may be exploited and sold back to them. In *No Logo,* Klein writes:

> After almost a decade of the branding frenzy, cool hunting has become an internal contradiction: the hunters must rarefy your "micro cultures" by claiming that only full-time hunters have the know how to unearth them. [Corporate consultant] Sputnik warns its clients that if the cool trend is "visible in your neighborhood...it's too late."...And yet this is demonstrably false; so-called street fashions – many of them planted by brandmasters like Nike and Hilfiger from day one – reach the ballooning industry of glossy youth-culture magazines and video stations without a heartbeat's delay. And if there is one thing virtually every person now

knows, it's that street style and youth culture are infinitely
marketable commodities.[67]

Trends are a measure of how well a society's youth have
absorbed the values of the corporation. Youth are an easy target
for advertising; brand loyalty and product consumption are the
markers of rebellion against parents and authority figures, and
elevate peer group status. Youthful rebelliousness is no longer
part of the tradition of coming of age, but now results from the
careful staging of a series of trends. The youthful targets, who
are often impatient to strike out on their own, even if only
symbolically, are quick to submit to the delusion of difference
from the previous generation's relationship to history, objects,
and popular culture. By branding an image, the corporation is
able to send out legions to disseminate logos and styles that refer
directly back to consumerism itself. The space of growing up
has been privatized by corporations, which attach their labels,
products, and claims on public space to everything, but
especially to the intimate experiences of growing up. Youth and
street culture are a part of the general space of the corporation.
Behind the cool hunters and branding are the factories – many of
them in China, Mexico, Pakistan and other places where labor is
cheap and the workers are like machines, in perpetual survival
mode. The trip through the economic foundation of trendsetting
is definitely not a safe one. The language of the street is
globalized by the economy of outsourcing and brought home
again by selling it back to the youth culture that inspired it, the
machine at the other end of the process.

Perhaps this is how the story is meant to end. It is difficult to
make history within the confines of the state sponsored
corporate control system, or to know what our lives are like
outside a branded space of for-profit daily life. The historical
record creates order and a sense of destiny out of the chaos of
war, colonialism, migration, and nation-building; the vital
information about daily life, and the history of thought and
expression, are topics for further research but have little

---

[67] Klein, *No Space, No Choice, No Jobs: No Logo*, 80.

influence on the historical record of global domination. Academia reforms the record by creating disciplines such as African-American History, Women's Studies (supplanted further by Gender Studies), Asian Studies, and other identity-based focuses, taking living history out of communities and cementing it within institutional pedagogy. The reforms are a reaction to the creation itself of history as the provenance of the patriarchy, but the reforms are ineffective outside the academy. Additions to the discipline do not challenge the foundational authority of the state, which determines which aspects of lived reality are relevant, but rather merely attempt to offer additional histories of marginalized perspectives, keeping the marginal status intact. The reality in the field is that the drive for economic power is the same as the drive for political power, and it is within the economic system that an official history is constructed to validate the system whose story it tells.

The Polyglots of Globalism

Authenticity, capitalism, assigning a market value to everything – can everything actually be adjusted to a market value? Or can a network of radical subjectivities, connections, and collectivities zero out the market value via other currencies and channels of resistance? If that is possible, where, exactly, would this paradisiacal resistance network be located, and how does one connect? Bruce Sterling's methodology for predicting future trends is to list a few of the major events, figures and ideas of twenty-five years in the past, extrapolate a current that seems to be moving through them, and use this current as the foundation for imagining a point ten years in the future. Corporate trend-spotters use similar methods by congealing the basic elements of a trend that is just beginning to show up on the street, for example, and then packaging and presenting it as the public face of a particular social group. A trend can become fashion, a style, or a lifestyle, and is marketed internationally. By the time the marketing of a trend hits the street, however, the trend-spotter is busy looking for what comes next based on how those who identify with the trend begin to use it, altering it in their everyday lives. Sterling watches trends in politics, art, technology, and language – signifiers of the broader culture, within a timeframe that is long enough to show a distinction between marketing trends and a cultural pattern.

In a series of lectures given at the European Graduate School in 2009, Sterling used print media and its infrastructure as a sample study in obsolescence and global networking to discuss the trend in paperless media. He created a flowchart showing how top-heavy industries disappear in technological aspects of globalism that are oriented to, and in many ways defined and invented by, the user. Literature as a language-based national form of communication solidifies national sentiment; society, however, is polyglot in nature.[68] Vernacular means of everyday communication, such as texting, streaming video, file sharing, social networking, cloud computing, and net piracy create information chains that bypass the slow, complex and expensive modes of paper and ink based means of promoting and distributing literature. The global vernacular is the language of technology as well as of text, an "electronic Creole" and "an emerging sub-language."[69] If literature frees language, the vernacular escapes it. The Internet is obviously a big player in global publishing, and the emerging global consciousness has a role in how the Internet evolves as an information source. Since it is faster and easier to put more material online at very low cost than to publish books or magazines, publishing online "empowers a lot of niche writers, and with it comes niche audiences and niche culture." According to Sterling, the literary canon is eventually destroyed and literature loses its power as a nationalizing social glue. Acquisition of material is decentralized, audiences are fragmented and lost to niches, and previously stifled voices are freed in a torrent of non-literary texts, websites, and blogs. The relationship is not a literary

---

[68] The term "polyglots of globalism" is taken from my notes on Bruce Sterling's 2009 European Graduate School lectures and is attributed to Sterling.

[69] Additional quotes in this section are from Bruce Sterling's seminars at the European Graduate School, June 2009.

relationship, but is "sub-literary textual expression."

The drivers are algorithms and social media – machine-generated information and a machine-mediated, crowd-sourced editing process – which are networked, ongoing (tumbling), sometimes self-regulating, and global in scale and participation. Wikipedia, the online user-generated encyclopedia is one example of an internationally self-regulated crowd-sourced editing project.[70] Convergence culture, which is the culture of the flow of information through telecommunications, is online media's distribution network. The audience is nomadic (the information flow can be relayed to and from any connected point) and shares information in the form of text, comments, sites, images, clicks, video, and code, as well as collecting the same "searchable, track-able and linkable merchandise."[71] Much of what is collected online stays there. The stability of convergence culture is not in the technology, but in the cooperative and performative process of being author and audience at the same time. The culture has a horizontal exchange structure and is borderless as well as timeless, situated as process rather than object. The information need not be valuable, but the process, which obliterates the distinctions between various formats of media, *is* valuable. The convergence is social rather than technical, and its value is political as well as social. Sterling states that it is "hard to make affirmative all-enhancing political statements when the dialogue is so mixed up." Likewise, it is difficult to control the sources of the dialogue and its content when it is so mixed up, but the politics are not situated in the dialogue. The polyglot nature of the dialogue destabilizes the centralized authority of governments to control media content, and replaces it with a non-hierarchical stream of connectivity that is local at its source, and remains local in its

---

[70] The term "wiki" is from the Hawaiian language and means "quick" or "fast." Ward Cunningham, the developer of the first wiki software, first applied the term to Internet applications. "Wiki," *Wikipedia*, http://en.wikipedia.org/wiki/Wiki (accessed May 25, 2012).
[71] Sterling, European Graduate School, June 2009. The following quotes on this page are taken from the same source.

content, while becoming global as it enters the telecommunications network – "machines driving other machines, machines being driven by other machines, with all the necessary couplings and connections."[72] Access is anonymous. Identification takes work. As Alexander R. Galloway reminds us, the Internet was designed as part of the American military defense system to provide a decentralized communications circuit that would continue to function if physical military bases were attacked. It was meant to survive a nuclear blast. If part of the system were to be knocked out, others would remain operational. It was designed as a distribution network and did not represent a chain of command – it was not top down, nor was every point on the network connected to only a central hub. The American military recognized a structure that was already the basis for the connectivity of many objects, elements, and actions previously considered unrelated, or having distinct sources and pathways through their specific processes.

Galloway uses Gilles Deleuze and Félix Guattari's rhizome theory to describe the distributed network:

- Not about "genetic axis or deep structure"

- Decentralized – having no central point of automation or control

- Rhizomatic in structure, with many autonomous nodes

- Heterogeneous and connective, connecting any point to any other point

- Connections are neither linear nor hierarchical

- Composed not of units but of dimensions

---

[72] Gilles Deleuze and Félix Guattari, *A Thousand Plateaus*, trans. Brian Massumi (Minneapolis: University of Minnesota Press, 2009), quoted in Noah Wardrip-Fruin and Nick Montfort, "From A Thousand Plateaus," in *The New Media Reader* (Cambridge: MIT Press, 2003), 406.

- Multiple and asymmetrical

- It is short-term memory, anti-memory, without organizing memory

- A non-signifying system

- Always a milieu, never complete

- Any part of the network is as large or small as its parent network

- There is no chain of command

- Routes are varied and are not predetermined

- If parts of the network are destroyed, surviving parts retain continuity[73]

Galloway states that the distributed network, which describes Deleuze and Guattari's rhizomatic universe as well as the Internet, "is part of a larger shift in social life. The shift includes a movement away from central bureaucracies and vertical hierarchies toward a broad network of autonomous social actors."[74] It is not clear if Galloway's social actors are instigators of action or are subjects of ongoing actions, connected to the stream. Within sociologist Bruno Latour, John Law and Michael Callon's Actor-Network Theory (ANT),[75] the actor is part of an already-existing system. Bruno Latour writes, "By definition,

---

[73] Alexander R. Galloway, *Protocol: How Control Exists After Decentralization.* This list is a distillation of ideas from the first chapter of the book entitled, "Physical Media." The terms "genetic axis" and "deep structure" are Galloway's quotation from Deleuze and Guattari, *A Thousand Plateaus: Capitalism and Schizophrenia* (1980).

[74] Ibid., 32.

[75] Actor-Network Theory is a theory of the study of social science developed in the 1990s by Bruno Latour, John Law, Michael Callon and others that maps the relationships between physical things, methodologies and concepts, with particular disregard for anthropocentric perspectives on the nature of experience.

action is *dislocated.* Action is borrowed, distributed, suggested, influenced, dominated, betrayed, translated. If an actor is said to be an *actor*-network, it is first of all to underline that it represents the major source of uncertainty about the origin of action – the turn of the word 'network' will come in due time."[76]

The social aspect of being an actor in an actor-network is being an active agent in the network as it is continuously constructed in the present moment. "The social," as Latour discusses, "is not yet made,"[77] and the uncertainty that Latour discusses above is indicative of the process. The social is a process rather than an object or a factor within a situation. The social, regarded as a factor, for example, might include things such as bad parenting, a gradual introduction to drug use, or, on the more positive side of things, a good education. These factors may influence individual behavior and perspective, or a person's presentation of herself in the social realm, but they do not alter how the social realm is constructed.

Both the actor-network and the rhizome models include interactions and means of participation that are based on existing networks of agents, forces, and processes engaged in a permanently unfinished, multi-dimensional conversation. The Internet does not fit either model, however. While functioning to make connections across horizontal axes between separate non-linear points of origin, the Internet is based on a hierarchy of protocols. As a metaphor for the polyglot of globalism, the Internet makes the natural connectivity of everything apparent within its own language. As a real tool that plugs into already existing networks, it renders linkages legible and is part of the actor-network, all the same, a nodal point in the rhizome. Computer code and protocols are mutable – they can always be rewritten. New languages replace the old with new functions, or with new adaptations of existing functions. Hypertext transfer protocol, for example, converts a page of plain text into a

---

[76] Bruno Latour, *Reassembling the Social: An Introduction to Actor-Network Theory* (Oxford and New York: Oxford University Press, 2007), 46 – 47.
[77] Ibid.

window that has color, images, audio, video, animation, specific placement, scale, and click-able links. Protocol is a universalizing system, a strategy for organizing connections where addresses, destinations, and routes matter; but content does not matter. The Internet is one nodal point, one actor in the network.

Lest this optimism about the advantages to Internet connectivity within a rhizomatic system of globally connected points be simply a bit of blue-skying (Sterling's term to indicate boundless optimism) about the possibilities for the Internet, and in order to avoid a dialectic of comparing all that is possibly "bad" about the Internet with all that seems to be "good," it may be worthwhile to abandon the push-pull argument of meaningful content and meaningful connectivity and to analyze them as inseparable elements of the same phenomenon. The next generation Internet will be web 3.0, the semantic web, a universal and pervasive mobile telecommunications service that integrates as many everyday objects and devices as possible, and which has the capacity to make interpretive decisions about information. Separate applications for separate functions, such as a weather application, global positioning, language translation, and currency conversion, for example, will no longer be necessary. All requests will be answered within the same network of everything. Bruce Sterling's prediction of a Google-based total video authoring capacity seems much less a fantasy than a not-so-distant point in the future, as one looks in the direction in which communications technology is already headed.

In 1970, the poet and musician Gil-Scott Heron, who died in 2011, recorded a song called "The Revolution Will Not Be Televised." The lyrics were tied specifically to advertising jingles, soap opera plots, national politics and the war in Vietnam, and were addressed to African-Americans:

> You will not be able to stay home, brother
> You will not be able to lose yourself on scag
> Or skip out for beer during commercials

...Green Acres and Beverly Hillbillies and Hooterville
Junction
Will no longer be so goddamned relevant
And women will not care if Dick finally screwed Jane
On Search for Tomorrow
Because black people will be in the street looking for a
brighter day

The revolution will not be right back
After a message about a white tornado, white lightning, or
white people
You will not have to worry about a dove in your
Bedroom, a tiger in your tank, or the giant in your toilet
bowl
The revolution will not go better with Coke
The revolution will not fight the germs that may cause bad
breath.
The revolution will put you in the driver's seat

The revolution will not be televised, will not be televised,
Will not be televised, will not be televised.
The revolution will be no re-run, brothers,
The revolution will be live[78]

In 2011, anyone with Internet access was able to witness popular
uprisings against corrupt governments in the Arab world as they
were happening. Using technology is not activism, but the
enormous desire for a global awareness from anonymous live
witnesses, and the enthusiastic reception by a global audience of
anonymous remote viewers, created value from an interstitial
space between live action (revolution) and active viewing
(support). The Arab Spring was not televised. However, it was
transmitted. Twitter, Facebook, blogs, and YouTube were many
minutes ahead of even the best news organizations. The social
networkers involved in the uprisings were in the street, as Scott-
Heron says they must be. The Occupy Wall Street actions that

---

[78] Gil Scott-Heron, "The Revolution Will Not Be Televised," *Small Talk at 125th
and Lenox*, RCA B000005MLX, 1995.

followed in the fall of 2011 represent a horizontal movement of information, but also of action. The Internet is coming to represent an unfixed approach to the inclusion of ethics into building policy as technology gets closer to intentionality. But it is still a service, a tool, and not an action. The revolution must be live. The Arab Revolutions of 2011 were not only a call to action but were action itself. They inspired people on a global scale to regard their own relationship to authority. The phenomenon known as the Arab Spring exists now as part of the global consciousness of revolutionary activity and inspiration. It belongs to world history, but it belongs specifically to the history of political revolution.

In August 2011, there were several days of rioting in London following the police shooting of a young man, Mark Duggan, who was suspected by police of possessing a gun. Duggan's family organized a peaceful protest march in London's Tottenham district, but within hours Tottenham had become the scene of rioting, and eventually the riot spread to other parts of London and to other cities as well. Rioters, peaceful marchers, witnesses and police were all using social media to report events, to organize further demonstrations, to learn each other's whereabouts, and identify participants by their Facebook and other social media postings. Around the same time, masses of people in Spain, Greece, Italy and Russia took to the streets over issues of government and financial sector corruption and economic hardship. By the fall of 2011, Occupy Wall Street began to form and took up what appeared to be a global common thread of people speaking out against injustice. From the Occupy Wall Street website, a "Modest Call to Action" was proposed:

A Modest Call to Action on this September 17th
Posted Sept. 17, 2011, 9:46 p.m. EST by OccupyWallSt

This statement is ours, and for anyone who will get behind it. Representing ourselves (not the movement as a whole), we bring this call for revolution.

We want freedom for all, without regards for identity,

because we are all people, and because no other reason should be needed. However, this freedom has been largely taken from the people, and slowly made to trickle down, whenever we get angry.

Money, it has been said, has taken over politics. In truth, we say, money has always been part of the capitalist political system. A system based on the existence of have and have nots, where inequality is inherent to the system, will inevitably lead to a situation where the haves find a way to rule, whether by the sword or by the dollar.[79]

Occupy Wall Street was originally coordinated to protest the control of the American government by the financial industries. People, individually and collectively, began to link the machinations of the global financial industry not only to the economic hardship encountered in their daily lives, but also to a pattern of environmental destruction linked to globalized industry, to racial inequity in law enforcement, the reduction in public services on the local level, higher costs for education, and, basically, the reduction of life to mere survival, as Vaneigem expresses it. Conflicting ideologies and contradictions emerge in the space of dialogue, but the common threads of dialogue within Occupy carried messages that could be understood and accepted widely as well, such as democracy, freedom of expression, freedom of assembly, and economic justice. But the most lasting events of 2011 are still the Arab Spring uprisings, which have resulted in new democratic processes in countries where the people have overturned totalitarian governments. Social networking enabled entire populations to become visible to each other for the first time in ways that were largely uncensored. It was possible to observe moments of the day-to-day lives of people on the other side of the world who were engaged in violent battles against oppressive governments, and to send out messages of support as

---

[79] Occupy Wall Street, "A Modest Call to Action on this September 17," Occupy Wall Street, http://occupywallst.org/article/September_Revolution/ (accessed February 10, 2012).

well. The space we were witnessing was the same space of daily occurrence, only this time it was also a space of revolution. The space of daily occurrence is a contradictory space, a contested space. In the space of the ordinary, whether it is occupied by revolution or by routine, the network of resistance is the same as the network of everything else. It is in these spaces, and not in the space of ideology, that affinities form. Data moves across connections, made in real time and space, sent out in the languages of the local and received in the polyglot of the global.

Part 2: Space and Place: The Radical Quotidian

Space

Space is a physical entity with properties: gravity, fields of light and magnetism, a carrier of sound waves, a medium for electricity, and a close associate of time. Even as a physical entity, it is considered intangible, however. It seems unobservable and empty, non-locatable unless there is an object or a place of reference in the space. Space is considered to be an ahistorical entity, in the service of objects and places, a container for things and a ground from which a recognizable place is built, or from which a place grows. Space connects objects, and enables movement. Within language and common configurations of place and movement, this is most often true. Within a more specific observation of relations, this is not so true. In an article published in 1935 and titled "Mimicry and Legendary Psychasthenia," sociologist Roger Caillois writes about what he calls the problem of distinction that extends to the distinction between a person and his surroundings. In discussing observations of the relationship of schizophrenia to spatial awareness, the question of distinction ultimately becomes a property of the body in space.

> From whatever side one approaches things, the ultimate problem turns out in the final analysis to be that of distinction: distinctions between the real and the imaginary, between waking and sleeping, between ignorance and knowledge, etc. – all of them, in short, distinctions in which valid consideration must demonstrate a keen awareness and the demand for resolution. Among distinctions, there is assuredly none more clear-cut than that between the organism and its surroundings; at least there is none in which the tangible experience of separation is more immediate. So it is worthwhile to observe the phenomenon with particular attention and, within the phenomenon, what is even more necessary, given the present state of our

knowledge, is to consider its condition as pathology (the word here having only a statistical meaning) – i.e., all the facts that come under the heading of mimicry. . . . for example with the invariable response of schizophrenics to the question: where are you? I know where I am, but I do not feel as though I'm at the spot where I find myself. To these dispossessed souls, space seems to be a devouring force. Space pursues them, encircles them, digests them in a gigantic phagocytosis. It ends by replacing them. Then the body separates itself from thought, the individual breaks the boundary of his skin and occupies the other side of his senses. He tries to look at himself from any point whatever in space. He feels himself becoming space, dark space where things cannot be put.[80]

In the case described by Caillois, one has the sense that it is the space that moves through the body and not vice versa. The simple question of "where am I?" posed to a person suffering from schizophrenia may provide an answer that describes the reality that scientists are just now discovering, but the question remains for every object in space – where does the object end and space begin? The theory of space moving through a body in motion rather than a body delineating space by walking through it has been proposed by mathematician and biologist Alan Rayner, who suggests that there is no tangible boundary between space and the objects in it. If this is true on the level of quantum physics, it may be true, period. But does it mean that we – humans and nonhumans – are capable of experiencing this non-distinction as space moves through us, or are our perceptions attuned to distinction, separateness and completeness of body and object in respect to the space around it? Caillois calls this perception "pathology." Rayner and particle physicists call it the underlying unity of the natural world.

---

[80] Roger Caillois, "Mimicry and Legendary Psychasthenia," originally published in *Minotaure, 7*, 1935, and published online at Generation Online, http://www.generation-online.org/p/fpcaillois.htm (accessed March 10, 2012).

Architectural historian S. Giedion, in *The Eternal Present: The Beginnings of Art*, compares contemporary representations of space with human conceptions of space in prehistory, specifically looking at spatial awareness as represented in Paleolithic drawings and paintings, and emphasizes that a specific sense of space is evident from the work of this era. Giedion himself regards space as an intangible entity, one that can be perceived, yet is infinite and invisible and, based on his study of Paleolithic art, claims that societies that produced this art prioritized space over time. Space becomes visible in the presence of architecture, which "confines emptiness" in the creation of form out of space. From complex systems of "lines, planes, massiveness, proportion, form," [81] a single entity is perceived, namely a place. The perception of a single entity from a wide diversity of elements – the recognition of a place, which brings with it memory and emotional experience – is the result of human ability to create an abstract sense of place from the sphere of the physical. The urge to express this experience graphically, as in Paleolithic cave drawings for example, shows that the human "takes cognizance of the emptiness which girds him round and gives it a psychic form and expression."[82] One perception, and likely misconception, of prehistoric art, popular from the mid-1800s to the mid-1900s, is that it lacks spatial awareness and compositional unity.[83] Giedion's point, however,

---

[81] S. Giedion, *The Eternal Present: The Beginnings of Art* (Washington: Pantheon, 1957), 515.

[82] Ibid.

[83] Ibid., 516 – 517. Giedion presents references to several nineteenth and twentieth century paleontologists and art writers expressing a theory of art contemporary to those decades that considered representational art, especially "realist" art, to make the most sense within a unified field of scale, proportion, and direction. The images of animals in prehistoric art, although often rendered with an accomplished realism, seemed most often to have a random placement and complete disregard for a sense of timing, spacing, and figure-to-ground relationship. One very interesting aspect of Paleolithic murals is that the imagery suggests an idea of time as simultaneous rather than as a linear progression of events. Werner Herzog's 2010 film, *Cave of Forgotten Dreams*, about the Chauvet Cave in southern France, for example, reveals paintings of animals placed in the same part of the cave, with one drawn on top of another but painted 5,000 years apart. This fact causes the question of a contemporary or modern experience of time to practically jump out of the screen: what exactly is our

that an era's "space conception" is "the graphic projection of its attitude towards the world,"[84] holds true. Compare Giedion's conclusion with Debord's statement, "This is the principle of commodity fetishism, the domination of society by 'intangible as well as tangible things.' Which reaches its absolute fulfillment in the spectacle, where the tangible world is replaced by a selection of images which exist above it, and which simultaneously impose themselves as the tangible *par excellence*."[85] Debord situates the spectacle that is commodity culture in both space and place; space is represented in his statement by "intangible things," and place is the realm of tangible objects. That the intangible is also a thing renders space more presence than absence. Images exist simultaneously in the tangible and intangible spaces of society.

In his 1974 treatise on space, *The Production of Space,* Lefebvre includes a discussion of what he calls a "philosophy of space" that occurs within mathematical theories as well as within non-Euclidean geometries. A philosophy of space includes the concept of infinity, which may map "invented" spaces, and hypothesize x-number of dimensions, for example. Lefebvre observes that the measuring and mapping of reality and reality itself are separate realms, and the idea of "mental space" has developed into the notion of a transitional space between logic and human mental capacities, on the one hand, and nature and practice, on the other. In semiotics, the transitional space is a mental space, or a space of knowledge, which is generalized. The space is pre-existing, in a way, and the subject takes that space in an assertion of her subjectivity – she enters the space of knowledge or theory. Lefebvre's critique goes beyond French semiotic theory and examines the problem of the metaphor of space as a way for identifying a real person within a real

---

atomic clock measuring? Is it time? The conflations of time, space and image that appear on the cave wall provide a glimpse of a different yet sophisticated awareness of how time and space work together in the long era of the Paleolithic art world.

[84] Ibid., 518.

[85] Debord, *Society of the Spectacle,* Chapter II, 36.

situation. By virtue of the "space" metaphor, the person and her situation remain in an unspecified relationship to the whole. "Consider how cognoscenti talk of pictorial space, Picasso's space . . . or the space of *Guernica*. Elsewhere we are forever hearing of architectural, plastic or literary 'spaces' . . . Specialized works keep their audience abreast of all sorts of equally specialized spaces: leisure, work, play, transportation, public facilities – all are spoken of in spatial terms."[86]

Mental space becomes the space of meaning, understanding, and imagining; it divides practices and categorizes experience. Lefebvre suggests that within this logic, theoretical space and ideological space promote the ideas of the dominant class, as hierarchies are easily conceptualized within divided levels of experience. The question becomes, do ideas themselves produce mental space? Mental space, ideological space, and theoretical space are all concepts based in metaphor, but an actual space wherein these concepts exist as objects, however much it can be visualized, does not exist. Theoretical practice, the production of ideas, and the attempt to understand and communicate or write the nature of the relationship of things may find its place, and function more specifically, within a network that includes idea, history, material, time, and subject.

Latour examines the notion of inside and outside as a concept that uses a planar metaphor for how space is traversed and how objects are connected, rather than as a description of physical reality. The idea of mental space as a parallel to physical space creates a metaphor of inside and outside. The network of ideas, however, has no inside or outside, it has only connections. Latour places signs and symbols, "entities and actions," within the milieu of association, in which they may take any shape. Experience and the present are discussed in terms of coding and recording, set against all "a-priori reductions."

---

[86] Henri Lefebvre, *The Production of Space*. trans. Donald Nicholson-Smith (Malden, MA: Blackwell, 1997), 7 - 8.

> AT [Actor-Network Theory] is a method to describe the
> deployment of associations, like semiotics is a method to
> describe the generative path of any narration. It does not say
> anything about the shape of entities and actions, but only
> what the recording device should be that would allow
> entities to be described in all their details. AT places the
> burden of theory on the recording, not on the specific shape
> that is recorded. When it says that actors may be human or
> unhuman, that they are infinitely pliable, heterogeneous,
> that they are free associationists, know no differences of
> scale, that there is no inertia, no order, that they build their
> own temporality, this does not qualify any real observed
> actor, but is the necessary condition for the observation and
> the recording of actors to be possible.[87]

Within the actor-network, humans, objects, and ideas are in
continuous interaction in the creation of the present. Inside and
outside, mental space, spiritual belief, action and place, for
example, are elements in flux. A being is not so much always in
a state of becoming, but being and becoming address a continual
presence of the object and its state of perpetual reconfiguration,
based on the ever-renewed configuration of the network of the
present. Mental space, emotional space, and theoretical space are
equalized as metaphors for being in the present. Production of
these types of spaces occurs in interaction; it is a relational
activity. The network functions as long as its elements continue
to interact, giving both the elements and the network agency in
the physical world. Agency occurs when entities become actors.
Latour writes, "Actors are not conceived as fixed entities but as
flows, as circulating objects, undergoing trials, and their
stability, continuity, isotopies [have] to be obtained by other
actions and other trials."[88]

---

[87] Latour, abstract for a paper: "The Trouble With Actor-Network Theory," CSI-
Paris/Science Studies-San Diego, 1990, http://www.cours.fse.ulaval.ca/edc-
65804/latour-clarifications.pdf (accessed March 9, 2012).

[88] Ibid.

In her 1985 "Cyborg Manifesto," Donna Haraway borrows from Actor-Network Theory in identifying the milieu of the contemporary as information, stating that she "argue[s] for a politics rooted in claims about fundamental changes in the nature of class, race, and gender in an emerging system of world order analogous in its novelty and scope to that created by industrial capitalism; we are living through a movement from an organic, industrial society to a polymorphous, information system – from all work to all play, a deadly game."[89] Haraway proposes a change from global hierarchies of power and interrelationship to a society based on networks and simultaneity, in which ideologies and objects emerge together in interaction. In her "Informatics of Domination,"[90] she notes the replacement of the idea of "representation" with that of "simulation," and the nature/culture dichotomy with overall "fields of difference." The proposed change of framework is critical in bringing concepts from feminism and identity politics – especially undervalued personal, autobiographical, and confessional narratives and the experiential knowledge of the powerless – into this field of difference. This recognition enables interpretation and inclusion to occur outside metaphorical references that may skew perception. The new visual and contextual configurations that have arisen from these disciplines concerning subjectivity and identity become active in the non-hierarchical network of political and social agency. Legitimacy is assumed, or acquired, within the network, and the stories of the commonplace of oppression reveal the function of the violence of inequality and denial of agency to certain subjectivities within the sphere of everyday life. In *The Practice of Everyday Life*, Michel de Certeau states that "Everyday [stories] traverse and organize places; they select and link them together; they make sentences and itineraries out of them. They

---

[89] Donna Haraway, "A Manifesto for Cyborgs: Science, Technology, and Socialist Feminism in the 1980s," in *The Haraway Reader*, 20 – 21.
[90] Ibid., 20 – 25.

are spatial trajectories,"[91] denoting the spatial aspect of narrative practice.

> Every story is a travel story – a spatial practice. For this reason, spatial practices concern everyday tactics, are part of them, from the alphabet of spatial indication ('It's to the right,' 'Take a left'), the beginning of a story the rest of which is written by footsteps, to the daily 'news' ('Guess who I met at the bakery?'), television news reports ('Teheran: Khomeini is becoming increasingly isolated . . . '), legends (Cinderella living in hovels), and stories that are told (memories and fiction of foreign lands or more or less distant times in the past). These narrated adventures, simultaneously producing geographies of actions and drifting into the commonplaces of an order, do not merely constitute a 'supplement' to pedestrian enunciations and rhetorics. They are not satisfied with displacing the latter and transposing them into the field of language. In reality, they organize walks. They make the journey, before or during the time the feet perform it.[92]

In this case, the social aspect of lived space emerges from the use of universalizing metaphors that are formed into descriptions and narratives, as though the experience of the body in space and the proprioceptive sense, without the use of metaphor, were inadequate for the job, as though we are unable to read the social codes or the physical aspects of a place.

The individual experience of the body in space is formed relationally and communally, and is always in a state of becoming. The pathways of consumer culture occur in a space constructed by both a corporate agenda for profit and a government agenda for control. Anyone who steps outside his main role as worker/consumer and develops a conscious awareness of the field of difference, the field that does not

---

[91] Michel de Certeau, *The Practice of Everyday Life*, trans. Steven Rendall (Berkeley: University of California Press, 1988), 115.
[92] Ibid., 115 – 116.

belong to the corporation or the state, is marginalized. The awareness that lived space is produced, however, provides a root-level consciousness of life on the ground; codes for consuming and codes for state authority continue to be visible, but a shift occurs in the field of difference created by the cognition of space in terms of stories and the codes of lived experience. In the space of consumerism, which is everywhere, individuality is a necessary fiction. Each individual is alienated, the common is subverted and made over in the image of the corporation and the state, and homogenization of desire and of the ordinary occurs. Within the field of difference, the constant state of re-creation and differentiation in lived space is perceivable, enabling the formation of a living dialogue.

Place

Place seems to offer the possibility of solid reference, and unlike space, which must be enacted, a discussion of place brings us down to earth, as it were. Place is physical, identifiable, familiar, object-based – things, substances, architecture, towns, roads, fields, and mountain ranges. But is it rivers as well? Geographer Yi-Fu Tuan writes that places are delineated territories, "centers of felt value where biological needs, such as those for food, water, rest, and procreation, are satisfied."[93] Tuan's definition applies to humans as well as nonhumans, but for humans, what quality makes a place specific? What occurs when a space becomes a place? Some may consider a space to be an undifferentiated area, lacking qualities that we can decipher or recognize until objects, architecture, or a walk through articulates it – until it is used. Places may lack coherence, and may act as spaces until our repeated or habitual presence renders them meaningful, individually or collectively. The anthropocentrism of human intuition about place is most likely based in our shared social

---

[93] Yi-Fu Tuan, *Space and Place: The Perspective of Experience* (Minneapolis: University of Minnesota Press, 2008), 4.

needs. Our chances of survival increase when we are able to make sense of the signifiers of a place, whether they point to the natural or built environment. Tuan defines space simply in terms of movement from one location to another, in terms of movement *through*. The body makes the connections as it moves through space from place to place, or as it moves from object to object. Space and place exist on an intimate as well as a grand scale, and a body's movement describes space as distance or as time in relation to place – how far can I throw this ball? how long does it take to get from Dublin to Cork?

Place is a configuration of space. How do space and place become different concepts or entities? When can they refer to the same thing; when do they overlap, mapped one on top of the other, or interact more fluidly, as interchanging entities, related in conversation, not the same and not different? Is a place really meaningless until defined by human activity? Certeau considers space to lack definition until human interaction renders it meaningful:

> In relations to place, space is like the word when it is spoken, that is, when it is caught in the ambiguity of an actualization, transformed into a term dependent upon many different conventions, situated as the act of a present (or of a time), and modified by the transformations caused by successive contexts. . . . In short, space is a practiced place. Thus the street geometrically defined by urban planning is transformed into a space by walkers. In the same way, an act of reading is the space produced by the practice of a particular place: a written text, i.e., a place constituted by a system of signs.[94]

It seems obvious that the distinctions are necessary in semiotic, political, conceptual, or narrative uses. But distinctions become useless in scientific practice, where space and place are inseparable entities at a quantum level. It seems most logical to

---

[94] Certeau, *The Practice of Everyday Life*, 117.

consider their sameness and their difference not as opposites, but as being relational in terms of presence and reconfiguration. Emptiness may be openness, for example, rather than a void, a negative, or nothing. Objects and locations change through time; stability is a delusion. Certeau's eloquent description of the "space" of the word becoming the "place" of the text through actions of writing and reading is the beginning of his exposition of the contest between space and place in linguistic metaphors.[95] As writing and reading identify the actor, the text becomes an actant. Text, ideas, readings and mis-readings alike find their place in the network. Writers speak of text as a physical body on the page, and the page itself as a place of writing. The intentions of the writer – to tell a story or to express an idea, emotion, opinion, etc. – are in addition to what happens in the act of writing.

Situationism looks for the spaces in places. Situationist practice manipulates concepts of place by changing how the body moves through a place, realigning the habitual use and perception of a place by practicing extraordinary methods of moving through space. This practice breaks down previous socio-political designations regarding what a place is and what can occur there, and it opens it up for the creation of something else, of an elsewhere. The Situationist strategy of *dérive* is the practice of creating an elsewhere, an authentic place found within the contours of a given urban place, for example, by means of an aimless or unconscious changing of direction, a wandering through spaces that connect one location to another. The goal is to discover or create a new experience rather than to reach a destination. A new experience occurs when a new place emerges from a pre-existing one, through social practice in dialogue with existing social norms. The space of the city is mapped into specific places, not only by the inhabitants in their daily tasks, but also by the state, which designates the routes by which those tasks are to be accomplished by maintaining a system of streets,

[95] Chapter IX, "Spatial Stories," in Certeau's *The Practice of Everyday Life* discusses the distinctions between space and place, many of them in terms of metaphor, syntax, narrative, expressions, and grammar.

roads, and rules of navigation. The regulation of streets, for example, renders aspects of a place invisible or indecipherable if these aspects fall outside those already established for social control. An authentic experience of place is thwarted, as well, when it becomes an environment of consumer capitalism. The environment of consumerism is a place shaped by the needs of corporations. It is called into being by advertising and marketing campaigns that engage in a repeated and renewed mapping over of authentic popular culture with an inauthentic consumer culture in the places of everyday living.

The poetics of *dérive* evoke a child's use of place. Children find routes by wandering, by creating shortcuts, and disregarding the rules of property ownership and the practicality of already designated routes. Children rearticulate place through fantasy as well – trees become houses, piles of snow become forts, an abandoned shack or barn becomes an adventure through time. Play and storytelling are strategies for locating authentic places beneath the marked, legislated, regulated, and consumer space of the quotidian. At a certain age, children forget to look for unregulated space and begin to act like grown-ups, conforming to less inspired standards of imagining the world.

The current fad of *le parcour* is a strategy similar to *dérive*, requiring a level of athleticism, however, that makes these journeys chiefly for the young and the fit. *Le parcour* is a practice of moving through an urban or natural landscape by the most direct possible route and it usually involves climbing walls, jumping over barriers, and leaping from rooftop to rooftop. The given landscape or cityscape becomes an obstacle course and established routes and paths become useless. The practice is often illegal, since it pays no heed to the rules of private property or the assigned use of public property; in terms of social interaction or performance of a social space, it destroys an habitual performance of the body through the collective space (such as walking along paths, being considerate of the presence and proximity of others, using a civil speed of movement, making no sudden or jarring movements) while it creates an entirely new perception of place. Practitioners of *le parcour*, called *traceurs*, perform a critique of the *flâneur,* whose slow and purposeless strolls nonetheless paved the way, conceptually, for an alternative to state sanctioned routes and methodologies of the body in the collective space. Speed is important in *le parcour,* making the *traceur's* illegal interventions momentary. Space is not occupied, but is traversed in the creation of new routes through previously unspecified places, and also in the unfixing of the authority of ownership and law over physical places in the public realm as well as in the creative imagination.

The Organization of Physical Space

Physical space is organized by its inhabitants, who first take measure of the interaction of elements such as gravity, motion and time, planetary forces (night and day), and climate. In a purposely-organized physical space, life can be sustained, and ecologies, both technical and natural, develop. Physical space is the location of objects, bodies and ground and is the plane on which space and place are constructed in the development of a society. The experience of physical space is enabled through the experience of time, a coexisting and inseparable element. Together, they form the conditions of the present, conceived within the realm of the social. In *Space and Place: The Perspective of Experience,* Tuan states that the experience of space and time together is revealed in the terms we use to articulate it:

> The experience of space and time is largely subconscious. We have a sense of space because we can move and of time because, as biological beings, we undergo recurrent phases of tension and ease. . . .When we stretch our limbs we experience space and time simultaneously – space as the sphere of freedom from physical constraint and time as duration in which tension is followed by ease. . . . Length is commonly given in time units. . . . The passage of time, conversely, is described as "length.". . . Daily living in modern society requires that we be aware of space and time as separate dimensions and as transposable measures of the

same experience.[96]

Tuan references the work of linguist Benjamin Lee Whorf, an expert in native languages from the American Southwest, who, in the 1950s, mapped traditional Hopi spatio-temporal experience from a sense of the relationship of space and time to two realms of reality, "manifested (objective) and manifesting (subjective)." The manifested realm includes the "historical physical universe," and the present as well as the past. The manifesting realm is the realm of the mind, of desire, and of the future, occupying worlds above and below the plane of the manifested realm. In Hopi spatio-temporal perception, objective and subjective realities are perceived as two realms, like circles on perpendicular axes, which meet at two remote points, creating a "borderland" where the distant past and the distant future come together in the timeless space of mythology.[97] Perhaps the distinctions attributed by Whorf and Tuan to a traditional Hopi sense of space could also be thought of as the difference between space and place.

The timeless space of mythology is equivalent to Certeau's consideration of narrative as a spatial practice in which stories organize the space ahead of the journey of the human traveler. According to Certeau, narrative structures have a "spatial syntax." He is not referring to the joining of perception and mythology, the place where time and timelessness meet within a pre-capitalist economy, however, but about the joining of the experience of space by the forces of consumerism. He writes, "Narrative structures have the status of spatial syntaxes. By means of a whole panoply of codes, ordered ways of proceeding and constraints, they regulate changes in space (or moves from one place to another) made by stories in the form of places put in

---

[96] Tuan, *Space and Place: The Perspective of Experience*, 118.
[97] Quotations in this paragraph are from Benjamin Lee Whorf, "An American Indian Model of the Universe," *Collected Papers on Metalinguistics* (Washington, D.C.: Foreign Service Institute, 1952), 47 – 52, in Tuan, 120 – 121.

linear or interlaced series."[98] Stories provide pathways and create a trajectory for the traveler so that the experience of a place requires the subject, the traveler, to complete a narrative of the experience written in each fragmented moment of consumption. "[Consumption] is devious, it is dispersed, but it insinuates itself everywhere, silently and almost invisibly, because it does not manifest itself through its own products, but rather through its *ways of using* the products imposed by a dominant economic order."[99] For Certeau, "place" is the constructed and ordered space of the state, where spatial narratives are written and waiting to be fulfilled by the traveler. Spatial practice is the completion of the narrative.

Resistance to the narratives of consumerism may be accomplished by using spatial narrative to create one's own story of the space, even if it means using the language of consumerism. When the traveler creates her own trajectories, forming "unforeseeable sentences, partly unreadable paths across space,"[100] the pre-existing consumer code is given a new syntax, and makes different kinds of connections in terms of the subject's own stories. Certeau uses the example of the forced adoption of Spanish culture, specifically the Catholic religion, by the conquered indigenous people of South America as a method for refusing to assimilate rather than as a capitulation to Spanish authority. The indigenous people made use of Catholic ritual, myth and iconography differently from what the Spanish colonizers had written into the code of Catholicism by absorbing it into an existing belief system. "Their use of the dominant social order deflected its power, which they lacked the means to challenge; they escaped it without leaving it. The strength of their difference lay in procedures of 'consumption.'"[101] The indigenous people created a space for the new religion within the story of their own mythologies and the practice of their own rituals; they escaped assimilation without having to leave the

---

[98] Certeau, *The Practice of Everyday Life*, 115.
[99] Ibid., xii – xiii.
[100] Ibid., xviii.
[101] Ibid., xiii.

place, and their relationship to the place remained intact.

Certeau distinguishes place from space by the forces that activate each realm. Space is articulated and performed, and is the arena of the user; place is a plane, an organized area. The organization of place relates to power structures and represents the situation that most are born into. This distinction between space and place situates the human at the center of both the experience of space and the construction of place. The time factor inherent in Certeau's spatial narratology, as in the traditional Hopi spatio-temporal configuration, puts the spatial narratives of place (narratives of authority, history and identification) in the present as it is on its way to becoming the past; the time factor allows a person to activate a place, creating a space (narratives of subjectivity, identity, intention) in the present as it moves into the future. The power struggle between the state and the subject is represented in terms of space use and the organization of place, a struggle between authenticity and authority. This struggle is founded on factors, conditions and constituent parts that belie the fact that the person, as part of her own environment, even in situations of oppressive state control, is in a continuous state of free association not only with others, but also with objects, ideas, memories, legal systems, consumer codes, and any other number of elements that configure the moments of the present.

The state organizes physical space into objects and systems that are a spatio-temporal zone of control. The state uses its authority to legislate on matters of noise, garbage, graffiti, streetlights, playing musical instruments, begging, walking, and driving, for example. It also legislates access to private property, and who may and may not practice violent behavior and to what extent, which in the United States depends on a separate set of laws for each of the fifty states. In the United Kingdom, anti-social behavior orders (ASBOs) establish all public space as a policing zone, permitting the surveillance of all youth activity and the restriction of public behavior perceived as threatening or offensive, though not necessarily illegal. Reports of anti-social behavior are not taken lightly and may result in incarceration for the accused. Both the *flâneur* and the *traceuse* present challenges to rules about maintaining a properly civic-minded public presence in places where the law designates behaviors and boundaries; the *flâneur*, or drifter, challenges by intention and purpose but the challenge may go unnoticed, and the *traceuse* by a more aggressive relocation of the trajectory of the journey. In both events, the journey is specifically not a completion of the narrative organization of the space ahead of the journey. There is only the journey, and in it, the formation of another place.

The human element in the question of the organization of space is anything but fixed. Both space and place are always in flux, their constituent elements – human and nonhuman – in a process of association that is additive, subtractive, informative, changing, and temporary. The process, however, is not reductive. This is a description of authenticity without essentialism, of identity without identification. The power of the state functions as an element in this picture of a relational construction of reality as well. The authority of the state, and of the corporations that influence the decisions made by the state, are fictions that may be considered the basic ground, the place where the story is written. But they are still fictions, and we can move outside of them. Knowledge of the street is collective as well as intimate. While some aspects of the relational system are random, chaotic and accidental, others depend on specific human action and interaction – a reorganization of space – if challenges to the status quo and to unsuitable political and economic systems are to begin to be effective.

Perec was neither *flâneur* nor *traceur*, but his observations and writing represent movements into the interstitial areas of both public space (neighborhood) and private space (home). All spaces and places are politically charged. There may be activities in a space that are not specifically political, but there is no human actor who escapes the political realm. Perec's suggestion for the human actor is to question "bricks, concrete, glass, our table manners, our utensils, our tools, the way we spend our time, our rhythms. To question that which seems to have ceased forever to astonish us." This is not a suggestion to merely think about the mundane, but to interrogate it. He writes:

> Question your tea spoons.
> What is there under your wallpaper?
> How many movements does it take to dial a phone number? Why?
> Why don't you find cigarettes in grocery stores? Why not?
> It matters little to me that these questions should be fragmentary, barely indicative of a method, at most of a project. It matters a lot to me that they should seem trivial and futile: that's exactly what makes them just as essential, if not more so, as all the other questions by which we've tried in vain to lay hold on our truth.[102]

An investigation like the one Perec suggests yields the origins of common things – their spaces and substances; it diverts attention away from the spectacle and locates a connecting stream linking objects, events, and intimate realities of the everyday. Uncertainty is a part of every interrogation and each interrogator may come to a different understanding of the moment in question. Uncertainty is part of what unseats the authority of consumerist consciousness and the invisible hands of state and corporation that guide our gestures, movements, plans and routes through daily life. The certain future, the certain conclusion, the certain result belong to the story that is already in place. The uncertain aspect of space, place and interactivity belong to a story that has not yet been completed, and which is being created by many actors, human and otherwise.

Latour's Actor-Network Theory, as utilized by "sociologists of association,"[103] relies on understanding the uncertainty of the

---

[102] Perec, "Approaches to What?" in *Species of Spaces and Other Pieces*, 210 – 211.
[103] "Sociologists of association" is Latour's terms for practitioners of Actor-Network Theory, as opposed to "sociologists of the social," his term for social scientists who practice a traditional sociology of cultural, global, familial, psychological and other foundational forces that provide a cause-and-effect

social sphere to guide a more precise method of observation. He writes:

> It is precisely because the social is not yet made that sociologists of associations should keep as their most cherished treasure all the traces that manifest the hesitations actors themselves feel about the 'drives' that make them act. . . . This is why we should paradoxically take all the uncertainties, hesitations, dislocations, and puzzlements as our foundation. . . . Here again, as soon as the decision is made to proceed in this direction, traces become innumerable and no study will ever stop for lack of information on those controversies. Every single interview, narrative, and commentary, no matter how trivial it may appear, will provide the analyst with a bewildering array of entities to account for the hows and whys of any course of action.[104]

Latour's description of a seeming paradox – that uncertainty creates the foundation, and answers to questions about social space occur in the minutia of interaction and intention rather than within a large framework of models of the social, which may then be applied to a number of specific situations – is no paradox at all. Political and social space is allowed to interact and exchange information freely within subjective space, and to sometimes be identical. Uncertainty is a function of the organization of physical space.

The human actor may choose to enter an arena of heightened political activity, arenas of violence, transgression of custom or religious law, for example, participating in a charged event or changing the dynamic of the political space by using it and existing in it differently from the pre-written narrative. This causes change in more than the individual actor, throwing the

---

framework for understanding the relationship of groups or individuals to a pre-formed and defined society as a whole.

[104] Latour, *Reassembling the Social: An Introduction to Actor-Network Theory*, 47.

intimate into the political, and bringing new consciousness into play. In such situations, transgressions become moments, or even patterns, of resistance. A well-known example can be found in Rosa Parks' refusal, in Montgomery, Alabama, in 1955, to give up her seat on a public bus to a white rider and thereby create a unified public space of riding the bus where there had previously been a public space bifurcated along lines of skin color. Rosa Parks was not acting alone. Her transgression, crossing over to another way of being in public, was planned in advance by the N.A.A.C.P., an organization that she was active in, as a means to spark the Montgomery bus boycott. While the singular genius and the lone hero are characters belonging to a defunct mythology, the community, the network, acts together in a great many moments of crossing over. The singular and often courageous actor performs, and is backed up by people, opportunities, communities, histories, and encounters that push the moment forward. The knowledge and intentions must be brought into physical space in the form of a person or an object and an action. In this case, the intimate act of refusal changed the political balance of the already politicized/racialized space.

In *Non-Places: Introduction to an Anthropology of Supermodernity* (1995), anthropologist Marc Augé refers to place as "anthropological," as "place in the established and symbolized sense.... We include in the notion of anthropological place the possibility of the journeys made in it, the discourses uttered in it, and the language characterizing it." [105] Space, on the other hand, would be hard to characterize outside its relationship to the body, motion, and time. For Augé, space is the "non-symbolized surfaces of the planet," referring to "unnamed or hard-to-name places." [106] Places are organized by their history and an attachment to events. Physical space, lived space, is both space and place. The human being is at the center of this delineation. Do animals experience a spatial relationship to the earth as well? Perhaps they have no equivalent experience to

---

[105] Marc Augé, *Non-Places: An Introduction to Supermodernity* (New York: Verso, 2006), 81.
[106] Ibid., 82.

"anthropological place." The symbolized sense of Augé's places, which refers to the human functions of language, memory, history and personal attachment, is similar to certain aspects of animal life – an animal's territory, den, breeding ground, pack, nest etc. – related to the animal's priorities to survive and to reproduce, making an equivalence between human effort and will and animal instinct and drive. Tuan states that animals do have a specific relationship to place: "Recent ethological studies show that nonhuman animals also have a sense of territory and of place. Spaces are marked off and defended against intruders. Places are centers of felt value where biological needs, such as those for food, water, rest and procreation, are satisfied."[107] This may seem obvious, but it advocates a decentered view of even delineated spaces. Perec offers a way out of this distinction between space and place by his enactments of deep investigations of the space of the body and its extension into buildings, the town, and the page as well, so that spaces and interstices are activated and have value. For Perec, the space of the page is a physical space and the text that inhabits it creates the place of writing.

Narrative organizes space, separating the space of human consciousness from other types of space; official narratives anchor meaning and assign use to physical places, while autobiographical and first person narratives offer forms of knowledge of place that create meaning and assign additional uses to physical space. The personal story provides a viewing platform for the continuum of history. Intimate knowledge gained from personal experience attests to the profound uncertainty of situations, and challenges a fixed view of history and of the present. Taking the personal story out of an understanding of history, and of the interrelatedness of things, catapults this privileged knowledge into a realm of abstraction. The form of abstraction, in this case, is alienation of intimate experience from collective knowledge. Certeau illuminates the value of personal experience in his discussion of marginality as a

---

[107] Tuan, *Space and Place: The Perspective of Experience*, 4.

function of consumerism instead of as one possible aspect of subjectivity:

> Marginality is today no longer limited to minority groups, but is rather massive and pervasive; this cultural activity of the non-producers of culture, an activity that is unsigned, unreadable, and unsymbolized, remains the only one possible for all those who nevertheless buy and pay for the showy products through which a productivist economy articulates itself. Marginality is becoming universal.[108]

If everyone is marginalized, how is non-marginalization represented? Class, race, gender and other designations refer to a relationship to the mainstream, but according to Certeau, the authority of consumerism marginalizes all groups, which is what they have in common. Certeau does not mean that social groups are becoming homogenous, however, but that they are homogenized as consumers. Each group may relate to the identical marketing strategy differently, depending on its members' status or relationship to social and political hierarchies. Certeau provides the example of the immigrant worker who is, like everyone else, a target of marketing, but who may read specific signs differently and in the different reading, be able to enact a "polemical analysis of culture,"[109] possibly uncovering the politics of consumerism as it operates in the situation. Like the indigenous people of Latin America who absorbed Catholicism into their own rituals, the contemporary migrant worker, in his reinterpretation of consumer culture for example, may represent a point of resistance rather than a point of assimilation. In terms of marginalization, the migrant has marginalized the new culture.

In *Supermodernism: Architecture in the Age of Globalization*, Dutch architecture historian Hans Ibelings makes a claim for globalization as a tool for collapsing both time and space within an international economic system. Ibelings' *Supermodernism* is

---

[108] Certeau, *The Practice of Everyday Life*, xvii.
[109] Ibid.

a response to Augé's *Non-Places,* and is a defense of globalization as an inevitable return to modernism in architecture and a cultural inevitability in an era – presumably one not ending any time soon – of global communications and globalized finance, industry, and trade. In the early 2000s, supermodernism emerged in architecture with an aesthetic that was meant to be as seamless as possible, creating spaces that were "sensitive to the neutral," and identifying the neutral with the privilege of being free of reference. Ibelings writes:

> After the explicitly defined spatiality of Postmodernism and deconstructivism, it looks as if the – decades old – ideal of boundless and undefined space is set to become the main *Leitbild* for architects. This boundless space is no dangerous wilderness or frightening emptiness, but rather a controlled vacuum, for if there is one thing that characterizes this age it is total control. The undefined space is not an emptiness but a safe container, a flexible shelf.[110]

Ibelings attributes the ideal of the controlled vacuum to globalization:

> Inevitably, increased mobility and telecommunications and the rise of new media, all of which have been ascribed a major role in the globalization process, also affect architecture and urban planning in that they alter our experience of time and – especially relevant in this context – space. . . . international interrelatedness and the emergence of worldwide networks in an ephemeral cyberspace have undoubtedly changed our perception of the world. As a consequence, the world, especially for the inhabitants of the affluent northern hemisphere, has become both smaller and larger. Smaller, because everything is, if not in reality then certainly electronically, closer; larger, because thanks to telecommunications, the rising tide of information and ever-increasing mobility, a larger portion of

---

[110] Hans Ibelings, *Supermodernism: Architecture in the Age of Globalization* (Rotterdam: NAi, 2002) 62.

the world is one way or another familiar, seems familiar, or is assumed to be familiar. It is easy to predict that mobility will continue to increase worldwide as long as prosperity continues to rise. Increasing prosperity is the most important factor in growing mobility.[111]

The global stage is organized into two types of actors within a supermodernist spatiality. One type is a class of increasingly mobile individuals to whom the convenient non-places of transit are merely a blur on the way to the familiar non-places of the hotel room, restaurant, mall, office building and chain store. The other type is a class whose mobility is no less far-flung, although they travel for survival rather than for business, shopping, or holidays. This other class consists of those who travel across Asia, the Middle East, and the Americas to build the non-places used by the wealthier consumer, or to work at low-paying service jobs that the homogenized global culture creates, jobs that a local workforce may not appreciate. Migrant workers are heavily policed, their mobility is sometimes restricted to being at the workplace, the guest worker camp, and designated shopping areas. Their status as guest workers can be characterized as another type of controlled vacuum.

The second type of globalization that emerges in Ibelings' discussion is based on telecommunications, which makes the whole world a familiar place, or makes it *seem* familiar. Familiarity is the signifier of global communications and the neutrality of non-places, rather than of the local, or of friends and relatives and home. Homogenization produces a sense of familiarity since every place is designed to incorporate the same non-regional characteristics. Prosperity and mobility in a familiar global environment do indeed make the world a larger space for the privileged, but at the same time they necessitate placing restrictions on those in the support systems, restrictions that are like a mirror image in reverse of the privileges of the ruling class, like an unintentional Rorschach test: very limited

---

[111] Ibid., 64.

mobility, a calculated poverty, and a concentration of the local, albeit one that is out of place – the migrants bring their traditions with them. The non-places that alienate Augé and inspire Ibelings are physical places where architecture speaks the language of economic advantage, and where 'vacuum" is a term for a type of space that sucks the life out of everything around it in the exposition of neutrality. Neutrality may be a euphemism for environmental disregard, the homogenization of values, an erasure of the regional, the proliferation of the borderless corporation, and the concentration of capital.

While Ibelings is caught up in a vision of globalization as progress through prosperity, Augé acknowledges that the concept of progress is changing. He attributes the change to the speed with which information is catching up to the present.

> Whatever the level at which anthropological research is applied, its object is to interpret the interpretation others make of the category of other . . . The second observation is not about anthropology but about the world in which it finds its objects, and more especially the contemporary world. It is not that anthropology has become bored with foreign fields and turned to more familiar terrain, thus risking . . . loss of its continuity; it is that the contemporary world itself, with its accelerated transformations, is attracting anthropological scrutiny: in other words, a renewed methodical reflection on the category of otherness. [112]

For Augé, supermodernity is signaled by three "transformations" in the anthropological landscape. "The first is concerned with time, our perception of time, but also the use we make of it, the way we dispose of it."[113] The measure of time in terms of progress is no longer useful in interpreting the situation of the present as it relates to history. Grand narratives that attempt to totalize a particular society provide only a reflection of the ideas of the anthropologist himself. The failure of "the great systems

---

[112] Augé, *Non-Places: An Introduction to Supermodernity*, 24.
[113] Ibid.

of interpretation that aspired to map the evolution of the whole
of humanity, but did not succeed"[114] cast doubt on the whole
project of mapping history itself. Augé contends that themes of
history are becoming more intimate, more anthropological,
concerning the family, daily life, and places that have personal
significance. The indication is that we are looking at the details
of the past in order to decipher what we have become.

> The theme is inexhaustible, but the question of time can be
> looked at from another point of view, starting with
> something very commonplace with which we are confronted
> every day: the acceleration of history. We barely have time
> to reach maturity before our past has become history, our
> individual histories belong to the history writ large. . . .
> Nowadays the recent past – 'the sixties', 'the seventies'.
> now 'the eighties' – becomes history as soon as it is lived.[115]

Ready information about events in the recent past, including
events in the areas of design, entertainment, technology, travel
and space travel, global politics, and finance, provides details
that enable the contemporary moment to be historicized. Traces
of the past carry over into the space of the present. Objects,
images, and design innovations that characterize a specific
period, nostalgia for that period, and the admixture of
generations of popular culture, locate the past in the present. The
historicized moment is part of the stream of continuous
information dissemination and is individualized as information
reaches its destination in the consumer, whose interpretation is
based on her own specificity.

The second indicator of supermodernity is the transformation of
space, an excess of space and a change of the scale of the world.
The space of the world is both smaller and larger, a conclusion
that Ibelings comes to as well. For Augé, the "excess of space is
correlative with the shrinking of the planet. . . . In a sense, our
first steps in outer space reduce our own space to an

---

[114] Ibid.
[115] Ibid., 26.

infinitesimal point, of which satellite photographs appropriately give us the exact measure."[116] We are in contact with satellites on a daily basis, literally expanding our reach into outer space, and providing glimpses of every point on the planet through free downloadable geographical mapping software.[117] Rapid transport closes distances across town and across the continent, and telecommunications transmits images, text and video from around the world that, once again, may not provide a thorough knowledge of events elsewhere, but which enable our awareness of people, locations, daily activities, and modes of visual and sound representation in a vast unofficial and often un-moderated common sphere. The world culture effect creates a familiar homogenizing view. The view is familiar because it is always available and the same things can be found everywhere, and it is homogenizing because it expands the space in which we make sense of the world without having to acknowledge or even notice difference, except in the most superficial, consumer-driven representations of difference. The space of global telecommunications is a supermodern space.

Ibelings imagines a class of international travelers for business and pleasure who are able to take advantage of the new speeds of information and transport, expressing optimism in tacit support of the wide social and economic gap that fulfillment of this fantasy requires. At the time Ibelings was publishing *Supermodernity,* the United Arab Emirates was becoming a region of super-building. Star architects such as Rem Koolhaas, Zaha Hadid, Frank Gehry, David Fisher and Jean Nouvel were given carte blanche to create buildings that are anything but non-signifying and neutral, yet conform to the idea of individuation, a design ethos of total abstraction – the importance of communicating the architecture rather than creating a message

---

[116] Ibid., 31.
[117] At the time Augé published *Non-Places* in 1995, global mapping software was not yet available, but his point about the shrinking planet is prescient. In 2004, Google acquired a CIA-funded company called Keyhole, Inc., which had developed a global mapping program called EarthViewer 3D. In 2005, Google released the updated Earth Viewer program as Google Earth. "Google Earth," Wikipedia, http://en.wikipedia.org/wiki/Google_Earth (accessed June 9, 2012).

via aspects of design or materials – and disregard for the culture or ecology of their surroundings (what Ibelings refers to as an "autonomous relationship with the city"[118]) that are signifiers of the supermodern age. For Ibelings, individuation in architecture is reflected in the idea of independence from the surrounding conditions:

> Probably the most important motive behind this independence from specific conditions, was the idea that modern architecture was by definition a new beginning and a break with the past. This explains why modern architects were so attracted to the concept of the *tabula rasa* defined only by length and breadth. The idea that the site can be seen as an immaculate, empty expanse may have been branded reprehensible by the postmodernists, but from a modernist point of view it is eminently sensible.[119]

For Augé, supermodernism is the other side of the coin of postmodernism. For Ibelings, however architecture's return to a globalized modernism is a theme he emphasizes repeatedly in defense of "reprehensible" architectural practices. The narratives of speed, travel, excess, and luxury, presented as exemplars of an unfettered architectural and cultural imagination, are supported by parallel narratives of inspired design genius – an individuation that places the application of new architectural technologies outside the consideration of social responsibility. Building sites are not only the *tabula rasa* for unbounded architectural practice, they are also employment sites, often sites of major environmental destruction, and frequently sites of human rights violations. The building site creates a design ecology within which the values of the remarkable new architecture are meant to flourish. However, architectural practice divorced from its milieu is anything but "sensible."

Canadian theorist Mark Kingwell discusses the relationship of supermodernist architecture to the public sphere in terms of the

---

[118] Ibelings, *Supermodernism: Architecture in the Age of Globalization*, 45.
[119] Ibid.

promotion of individual genius, and design concept as a supermodernist model for architectural practice in terms of public accountability:

> The question then becomes: are the monumental-conceptual works living up to the responsibility of public money and public attention, or are they large-scale con games feeding the self-indulgence of a new breed of installation artists, the architect as seer? To answer that question we must not only examine current architectural practice but appreciate marked slippages in the notion of public space. Though much of the rhetoric of late-modern debate was and is condemnatory regarding current urban experience . . . it is far from obvious that calls for returns to public space, or enlarged versions thereof, are valid, or anyway, are free of lingering vestiges of a utopianism we might regard as bogus or unsupported. Nor, for that matter, is it immediately clear that a more implaced or situated architecture is the answer to alleged losses in democratic accountability or individual connection to the built environment. Here, indeed, modernist narratives of emancipation and participation linger far past their dismantling in other quarters.[120]

In thinking about architecture as a language, and the language of architecture as part of a dialogue about service to the common good, Kingwell asks two basic questions: "Does it make thought more or less likely? And 2. Does it exclude for the sake of exclusion?"[121] In a New York Times article about the building boom in the Emirates, journalist Hassan Fattah interviews Frank Gehry on his vision for the controversial new Guggenheim Museum design and inadvertently answers these questions:

---

[120] Mark Kingwell, "Meganarratives Of Supermodernism: The Spectre Of The Public Sphere," Phaenex: Journal of Existential and Phenomenological Theory and Culture,
http://www.phaenex.uwindsor.ca/ojs/leddy/index.php/phaenex/.../109, (accessed February 20, 2012).
[121] Ibid.

"The daring designs [in the United Arab Emirates], some teeming with life and color, others more starkly formal, have one aspect in common: it probably would be hard to build them all in one district anywhere else. It's like a clean slate in a country full of resources," said Mr. Gehry, who appeared at the exhibition to show off his model for the Guggenheim Abu Dhabi. "It's an opportunity for the world of art and culture that is not available anywhere else because you're building a desert enclave without the contextual constraints of a city," said Mr. Gehry.[122]

The third transformative aspect of supermodernity is marked by the return of the individual. In the field of anthropology, which Augé places within a supermodernist context, the individual is emerging in the character of the anthropologist or ethnologist himself, a reflection back from the earlier practice of trying to locate the most representative person, the "average man" who could be the total representative of his society, who carries all the basic traits, who is somehow a sum of all present. It is not hard to think of the last existing member of a society in this case, rather than the first, as the individual who must come to represent the culmination of his society. Ishi, "the last Yahi," was from an area known as Wa ganu p'a, in the foothills of Mt. Lassen, sixty-five miles north of Sacramento, California. He was studied extensively by University of California anthropologists as the last remaining member of his nation, and eventually became their living subject, beginning a "'benign' five-year imprisonment at the U.C. Berkeley Museum of Anthropology"[123] between 1911, the year of his "discovery," and 1916, the year of his death. Ishi was not actually the last of his people. The Noso, who are a band of the Pit River Tribe, are his descendents, currently living in the same area Ishi had first

---

[122] Hassan Fattah, "Celebrity Architects Reveal a Daring Cultural Xanadu for the Arab World," New York Times, February 1, 2007, http://www.nytimes.com/2007/02/01/arts/design/01isla.html?pagewanted=all (accessed February 21, 2012).
[123] Lucy R. Lippard, On the Beaten Track: Tourism, Art and Place (New York: The New Press, 1999), 40.

described as his home. In 1999, the Smithsonian Institution returned Ishi's remains to the Pit River Tribe. In 2000, Ishi's brain was returned as well and he is now buried in an undisclosed location, free at last.

The history of Ishi and his relationship to the anthropologists at U.C. Berkeley is a story about the history of anthropology. The practice of gaining knowledge through the spoils of genocide, and the careless methods of the individuals who first took possession of Ishi and studied him, no longer represent the science of anthropology, but the science itself is still a subjective one. Data must be interpreted through the subject of the scientist. Augé's references to contemporary field practice are more about the practice that is created specifically around the anthropologist, what he describes as "field to text, text to author,"[124] in which analysis is contained in descriptive texts that express the author/anthropologist rather than the subject. Collective history and collective identification are not the methods by which the world tends to be organized and become interpretable to the individual anthropologist. "In Western societies, at least, the individual wants to be a world in himself; he intends to interpret the information delivered to him by himself and for himself."[125] The amodern, undifferentiated individual can act in physical space to claim it back from the organizing strategies of all of the narratives of politics, religion, genius, neutrality, individuation, and privilege. Perec's model for the amodernist in physical space is one that all can follow from wherever they are situated and with whatever materials are at hand. "Question your tea spoons."

Representational Space

What kind of space should be designated as having representational value when all places seem likely to represent

---

[124] Augé, *Non-Places: An Introduction to Supermodernity*, 37.
[125] Ibid.

something in addition to the meaning embedded in their basic physical aspects, the placement of objects within them, and their relationship to whatever is in the vicinity? Many ordinary places seem tied to representational systems that guide the visitor through them, tell a story, or signify history, including the space of nature. In the most literal terms, representational space must be said to include representation itself – images, text, symbols, numbers, speech – and more complex cultural adaptations – art, poetry, music, stories, advertising, legislation – and ideas – religious, ideological, philosophical, mythological, scientific – and creatures that inhabit representations – gods and saints, archetypes, economies, political systems, popular culture, classifications of all kinds – and something to put everything in – temples, brothels, kitchens, computer operating systems, zoos, universities, suburbia.

"Spatial practice" is the term used by Lefebvre to indicate the creation of space out of place: "Spatial practice thus simultaneously defines: places – the relationship of local to global; the representation of that relationship; actions and signs; the trivialized space of everyday life; and opposition to these last, spaces made special by symbolic means as desirable or undesirable."[126] What, then, is the practice of representational space, the practice that makes the space real? Tuan provides an example of the perceptual shift that occurs when a place becomes representational space:

> What is a place? What gives a place its identity, its aura? These questions occurred to the physicists Niels Bohr and Werner Heisenberg when they visited Kronberg Castle in Denmark. Bohr said to Heisenberg: "Isn't it strange how this castle changes as soon as one imagines that Hamlet lived here? As scientists we believe that a castle consists only of stones, and admire the way the architect put them together. The stones, the green roof with its patina, the wood carvings in the church, constitute the whole castle.

---

[126] Lefebvre, *The Production of Space,* 288.

None of this should be changed by the fact that Hamlet lived here, and yet it is changed completely. Suddenly the walls and the ramparts speak a quite different language."[127]

Inventories and locations alone, which already carry entire fields of association, cannot provide a measure of the capacity of the visitor to perceive an "aura" that is the representational milieu for the space. During a visit to Copenhagen in 1941, Heisenberg and Bohr had a discussion about research being done in the development of atomic weapons. The discussion was a very dangerous one for Bohr, a Jew in occupied Denmark, and he "therefore carefully noted every word uttered in our conversation, during which, constantly threatened as we were by the surveillance of the German police, I had to assume a very cautious position."[128] According to Bohr's letters, Heisenberg stated that he believed Germany would win the war, and he himself was researching the development of nuclear weapons for Germany towards this end. In 1943, Bohr and his family left Denmark for Britain and, later, for America, to escape arrest by the German police. That year Bohr joined the Manhattan Project and worked on the production of the first atomic bomb. The conversation at Kronberg Castle took place in 1924,[129] but Bohr and Heisenberg, who were players in the development of the bomb, were already setting the events in the fields of physics, which culminated in the 1945 bombings of Hiroshima and Nagasaki, in place. The space of the castle and the imaginative aura surrounding it expands across time to include the war, military occupation, genocidal persecution, and atomic bombs. But perhaps changes in the representational landscape in this story are those brought on not by the associations of Bohr, Heisenberg, and a meeting in 1941, but by Tuan's inclusion of

---

[127] Tuan, *Space and Place: The Perspective of Experience*, 4. Also quoted within this quote: Werner Heisenberg, *Physics and Beyond: Encounters and Conversations* (New York: Harper Torchbook, 1972), 51.

[128] Niels Bohr Archive, "Release of documents relating to 1941 Bohr-Heisenberg meeting," Niels Bohr Archive, http://nba.nbi.dk/papers/docs/d10tra.htm (accessed June 2, 2012).

[129] Interleaves, "Uncertainty at Kronborg," Interleaves, http://interleaves.wordpress.com/2011/09/05/kronborg/ (accessed June 2, 2012).

this ostensibly charming story of two scientists and a castle in 1924 as part of his own apolitical treatise on space and place. Relocating ground zero of the representational landscape from the story in Tuan's book to the book itself provides new instructions about how to read his text, where things are really not as simple as they seem and where stories within stories hint at much larger systems of representation, including that of pedagogy (Bohr was Heisenberg's mentor at the time of the Kronberg castle walk) and certainly that of settings, both real and fictional.

In *Postmodern Geographies: The Reassertion of Space in Critical Social Theories*, Edward W. Soja discusses human spatial sense as the sense of being separate from what is around us, causing a sense of alienation to arise. Soja quotes Martin Buber from "Distance and Relation," who writes, "It is the peculiarity of human life that here and here alone a being has arisen from the whole endowed and entitled to detach the whole from himself as a world and to make it opposite to himself."[130] Soja understands the detached human spatial sense that Buber describes as a necessary beginning to human differentiation of self from object, and an "essential act, this original spatialization, [where] human consciousness is born."[131] He continues: "Nothingness is thus nothing less than primal distance, the first created space, the vital separation which provides the ontological basis for distinguishing subject and object."[132] The primal differentiation of the human subject from the remainder of "the whole" allows for the creation of meaning and a further differentiation from the objects that make up the whole, in the creation of a representational space. Soja discusses a primal humanizing alienation in terms of the problem of the origination of subjectivity in the effort to overcome meaninglessness:

---

[130] Martin Buber, "Distance and Relation," *Psychiatry 20* (1957), 97 – 104, quoted in Edward J. Soja, *Postmodern Geographies: The Reassertion of Space in Critical Social Theories* (London and New York: Verso, 1989), 132.
[131] Soja, 132 – 133.
[132] Ibid., 133.

Thus, as Buber argues, human consciousness arises form the interplay – dare I add unity and opposition? – of distancing and relation. Entering into relations, being-in-the-world, Heidegger's *Dasein*, Sartre's *L'Etre pour-soi* or *être-là* ('being-there') is not possible without distancing, without the ability which allows us to assume a point of view of the world. But in this ability is also a will to relate, a necessary impulsion to overcome detachment, as the only means whereby we can confirm our existence in the world, can overcome meaninglessness and establish identity. . . . Entering into relations with the world, the creative connection between the human subject and the objects of his/her concern, is a search to overcome alienation, yet this too threatens to be alienating when it reduces the subjective self, when the subject is objectified through relations with the world. Thus existential alienation is a state of separation both from oneself and from the objective world – from the very means and meaning of existence.[133]

But we exist already in relation to the world, regardless of alienation. The connection is not creative, or does not have to be creative, unless we have broken it by distancing ourselves as a conscious act, or as an act of consciousness, not in order to attain subjectivity, but in order to manage a coherent organization of space and time. Alienation is not a primal phenomenon, but occurs as we make sense of things in terms of difference, categories, and individuation. Soja discusses the idea of a dialectic between subjectivity, on the one hand, and an experience of the self as part of the whole on the other, as being rooted in time, "in the temporality of *becoming*, and consequently in 'biography formation' and the making of history."[134] History, narrative, and the discernment of an "us" and a "them" are the record of an intentional re-attachment of human consciousness to the things around us in the process of making sense of place, and positioning the self and others in the

---

[133] Ibid.
[134] Ibid.

world, creating dualities as we do so. Cartesian logic first posits
a self, an I, and then relates the I to the world. Heidegger
discusses the essential state of being as inseparable from being-
in-the-world, and to be in the world is to belong to the everyday.
Heidegger, however, rejects the I as fundamental, and states that
being is a condition of sharing, of relationship. The everyday is
possibility not yet fulfilled. We exist in space, a measurable
entity, but we also exist spatially, which gives our existence an
intentional relationship to the space of the world. Possibility
(becoming), being in space (spatio-temporality), and having
intention (direction) are the elements of human spatiality. What
is the process, then, of the further differentiation that prevents a
subject, a person, from being there?

Feminist theorist and activist Monique Wittig considers human
alienation and the objectification of the world to be neither
primal nor essential, but claims that these states represent the re-
discovery of the beginning of the argument itself of domination
and exploitation as a way for humanity to be in the world.
Human society rearticulates the argument and affirms it through
the pretense of exposing a base layer – not in time, but in all
time – of the relationship of humanity to the rest of creation, a
base layer on which is built a power structure. In her 1980 essay,
"The Straight Mind," Wittig writes:

> The entire world is only a great register where the most
> diverse languages come to have themselves recorded, such
> as the language of the Unconscious, the language of fashion,
> the language of the exchange of women where human
> beings are literally the signs which are used to
> communicate. These languages, or rather these discourses,
> fit into one another, interpenetrate one another, support one
> another, reinforce one another, auto-engender, and engender
> one another. . . . The ensemble of these discourses produces
> a confusing static for the oppressed, which makes them lose
> sight of the material cause of their oppression and plunges

them into a kind of ahistoric vacuum.[135]

By this argument, hierarchies engender oppression. For Wittig, the ahistoric vacuum of oppression is the mark of patriarchal domination. "Lesbians, feminists, and gay men"[136] attempt to remove this mark with politically significant personal histories, using testimony as a historicizing discourse against the presumptions and "totalizing interpretations" of institutionalized heterosexuality. Wittig collapses time between the formation of social hierarchies and the immediacy of the limitations she experiences in her own time period. Sexuality and the representation of sexuality are significant players in constructing representational space, specifically within patriarchy. Wittig's discussion of heterosexuality as a symbol of authority rather than as sexual expression leads her to an analysis of pornography as a signifier of and an instrument for the domination of women as a class. She discusses pornography as both representation and as situation, having a specific function in the lives of women, and directed at women as an active agent of domination. Wittig writes:

> Semioticians can interpret the system of this discourse [of pornography], describe its disposition. . . . But for us this discourse is not divorced from the real as it is for semioticians. Not only does it maintain very close relations with the social reality which is our oppression (economically and politically), but also it is in itself real since it is one of the aspects of oppression, since it exerts a precise power over us. The pornographic discourse is one of the strategies of violence which are exercised upon us. . . it orders us to stay in line.[137]

In her discussion of the power of pornography, Wittig considers representational space overall as being a political space. One prevailing representational space is the space of male

---

[135] Monique Wittig, *The Straight Mind* (Boston: Beacon Press, 1992), 23.
[136] Ibid., 24.
[137] Ibid., 25 – 26.

domination. In the case of pornography, as well as in other pop cultural representations of gendered bodies, the space occupied by the female body is a male space. The lesbian is the subject who has broken off "the heterosexual contract," created a place for herself outside the problem of women's oppression, "for 'woman' has meaning only in heterosexual systems of thought and heterosexual economic systems. Lesbians are not women."[138] After having successfully arrived at a state of alienation in the process of becoming a subject in a world of objects and objectifications, naming, defining, and having power re-establish a relationship to the whole. The lesbian woman does exist, but the term as a category defines the woman chiefly by her sexual partners and suggests a totality of identity. It also suggests a network of affinities, however, and in this way is useful, politically and socially. Wittig's lesbian has not yet renamed herself "woman." Wittig writes from a place of urgency and the ideas in that place change rapidly as they affect the situation they address. They are based on the initial subjective awareness of difference that results from questioning one's place, one's social environment and the interconnections that occur within it that determine difference. This is not a difference that marks any essential trait in the subject, but one that marks the conditions and structures of the socio-political arena. Awareness of difference is awareness of how difference occurs. Perhaps things have changed between 1980, the date of Wittig's writing, and the present time. Change, then, is under the guardianship of those who are different, who are drawn out of the status quo and who form affinities, building different associations between subject and world.

Ten years later, Re/Search editor and publisher Andrea Juno posed an hypothesis to Avital Ronell: "As Walter Benjamin said, 'He who claims to be without theory is simply in the grip of an older, unacknowledged theory.'"[139] Ronell's response is to question the fiction of genius, identifying the concept of genius

---

[138] Wittig, *The Straight Mind*, 32.
[139] Avital Ronell, interview by Andrea Juno, in *Angry Women*, Andrea Juno and V. Vale eds. (San Francisco: Re/Search, 1991), 130.

as a locator of male superiority:

> I was at an international conference on feminism in Tokyo. Now I believe in making trouble – if women have any *duty* at all, essentially, it's to be a pain in the ass. So I said: "Women have never invented anything." This shocked a lot of people. Then I said: "Women will never invent anything." Then I said, "Nor will there ever be a woman genius." . . . *What* was speaking here – what kind of outrage was being committed? Then I said, "This is *good news!"* Because this isn't something women should aspire to – concepts such as "genius" and "invention" always have a single male signatory.

> Historically, genius has signified a privileged relation to "nature" involving male subjects. Yet genius also tends to bear marks of Otherness. . .Woman is *already* considered kind of monstrous – but not in this privileged, sheltered and sanctioned way that male genius has always been regarded. In a genuine feminist intervention what has to happen is a Will to Rupture – a Will to Break with these phantasms and divinizations. Women don't need a secondary and pious rapport to the possibility or goal of being recognized as a genius.[140]

Genius is a term for the quality of male intellectual power that separates the human from the rest of nature. In the narrative of genius and its relationship to nature, nature is feminine. The I-Thou and I-It relationship to everything maps the rational over the real and fosters a perception that humans are innately separated from things in the world because of human capacity for thought. Assigning intellectual curiosity and power to one gender only rationalizes the fiction of a duality in the human relationship to the world, and inside that alienation, there exists a dual human nature as well: rational male plus irrational female equals one rather bifurcated psyche in search of reconnecting to

---

[140] Ibid.

a world that it cannot escape at any rate. The dialogue
engendered through representations of, and by, multi-gendered
bodies is not resolved in settling accounts between men and
women, nor is it resolvable. The body takes up space, exists in
space, and is always on the move through the space of the
present. Women, however, move through an additional
representational space constructed around fictions about nature,
rational thought, and the embedded pornography of "woman."

In *Between East and West*, Luce Irigaray discusses the idea of a
"human becoming" as a way of finding balance within societies,
without swinging too freely between the problem of patriarchy
and the solution of matriarchy in order to find the place of the
female:

> Another sign: seduction or violence toward the woman,
> toward the feminine body, always appears as a social fact, a
> customary right, as it were, on the subject of which the State
> and the Churches generally remain silent. Woman still
> seems a private or collective good over which the father, the
> husband, the citizen have rights without the interested party
> having her say. And, according to certain penal codes, it is
> supposedly only toward his conscience, or toward God, that
> the man would be guilty if he sexually assaulted a woman,
> but not toward her. How could she herself be offended? She
> does not exist as civil person. She is body-nature that is
> available to masculine sexual instinct, to the desire or need
> for a child, etc.[141]

The discussion of gendered space is always a discussion of the
female body. It is a discussion of possession as either violence or
the withholding of violence, that places woman in a dangerous
space, even when she is in the same place as others. Her location
is the same, but the space she occupies is different. Hers is the
space of a nested self, one that has been denied an original
subjectivity; she acquires subjectivity, by which she can form an

---

[141] Luce Irigaray, *Between East and West: From Singularity to Community* (New
York: Columbia University Press, 2002), 112.

identity, in relation to the male. The male does not have to be an actual person, although the representative space of the female body influences individuals to take on social roles. The male, as representative object, occupies the representational space of woman, colonizing her subjectivity. In response to interviewer Juno's question, "What's more abstract than saying what a 'black' person or a 'woman' really is?" Ronell responds with a description of the predicament of living in a differentiated political space:

> All of these distinctions are based on Western metaphysics – therefore derived from so-called "abstract" systems of thought. So, a housewife who feels particularly depressed and wonders what is wrong with her is facing the question of *theorizing her predicament.* Precisely because we haven't found the answer and are only barely beginning to pose the question, we can't ignore the fact that this must have been institutionalized in very rigorous, systematic types of *discursive oppression.*[142]

The discourse of female oppression examines the representative space wherein the question of reclaiming female subjectivity – or even examining it to determine authenticity in gendered space – is possible. But feminism as reform, if we are to apply Vaneigem's idea that reform is no different from the system it attempts to correct and that it prolongs the system by making it bearable, becomes simply another, more bearable, aspect of patriarchy. A just society is not a part of the lineage of an unjust society. And as Rancière observes, "Unequal society does not carry any equal society in its womb."[143] A just society comes from a place outside injustice and is a separate society, not simply a better version of an unjust society. Irigaray is saying that women as subjects have no place within a patriarchal structure except as representation, and as such, women are an aspect of maleness. Irigaray sees male and female as separate

---

[142] Avital Ronell, *Angry Women,* 138.
[143] Jacques Rancière, *Hatred of Democracy,* trans. Steve Corcoran (London and New York: Verso, 2006), 96.

beings spiritually, and suggests that this difference deserves investigation. She, who is different, brings to a common space that which she alone possesses. But to do this freely, and to contribute her difference to a situation that requires it, she must be in possession of her own representational space. For Irigaray, difference is not a product of differentiation, but is a quality of being. If it is he, rather than she, who is different, then the exchange works equally as well.

In delineating a radical difference between female and male, whether spiritual, physical, emotional, or intellectual, it becomes impossible to pinpoint anywhere along the spectrum from male to female where one's biology determines how much of either gender one inhabits. It is more sensible, in terms of bodies (knowledge from the body) and common sense (acting on that knowledge), to speak of individuals, subjects and communities in terms of their humanity. What women know is knowledge from history, the experience of being different, and the event by which they become other. What men know may be less than that, since they fail to learn what women know. Women, too, have a "double-consciousness," a term W. E. B. Du Bois uses in writing about the discursive predicament of African-Americans, who inhabit a consciousness of "twoness" – looking at oneself through the eyes of the oppressor, and through one's own eyes – which is a curse as well as a blessing. If women have no real power in the formation of the present in terms of the social realm, women's influence on the creation of the future must be exerted from a position of further marginalization.

Irigaray continues: "In order to attain the status of civil person, woman must pass from natural identity, especially an imposed natural identity, to civil identity. Her most radical and indispensable (r)evolution is situated there."[144] The devaluing of women's contributions to societies is extreme, and women's oppression is evident in open as well as closed societies, so that these contributions take on great significance. Ronell suggests

---

[144] Irigaray, *Between East and West: From Singularity to Community*, 112.

"what is important now is to mobilize *hysteria* as a quasi-revolutionary force." Citing Hélène Cixous, she continues, "[Hysteria] is an inherently revolutionary power: it intervenes, breaks up continuities, produces gaps and creates horror – refusing conformity with *what is.* . . . . Hysteria as a response to what is unacceptable and intolerable in life . . . as a response to *emergency.*" [145]

The feminine as a principle, whether in fact or fiction, is considered necessary in some traditions to guard society against emergencies, disruptions and collective discontinuity. Anthropologist Michael Taussig suggests that in societies where gender is a marker of significant difference, where laws applied to women, for example, are restrictive or very specific to a point where women represent that law itself rather than representing aspects of their individual subjectivities, women are responsible for keeping the traditions of a society relevant and operational. In this case, women have a vital role in the preservation of a society's culture and history. "Female" has a ritual status and the female is the signifier of survival. Taussig bases his observations on field studies of the Kuna Indians of San Blas, Panama in regard to the requirements around traditional dress. Women in this matrilineal society have the responsibility to carry tradition from one generation to the next. They do this by making and wearing their own traditional clothing, which is required of them, while men tend to wear the shirts and pants typical of an American style of dress. The Kuna have been able to remain unassimilated to the end of the twentieth century against the odds brought on by "what is seen as the inevitable path of cultural destruction on account of Western religions and moralities, land-grabbing, Western diseases, Western language, Western clothes, Western junk food, Western alcohol, Western haircuts."[146]

The Kuna are well known for their molas, intricately appliquéd

---

[145] Ronell, *Angry Women*, 131.
[146] Michael Taussig, *Mimesis and Alterity: A Particular History of the Senses* (New York: Routledge, 1993), p. 129.

panels, blouses, and head coverings made by the women. Molas are often representations of others, not of Kuna society and customs, but of the concerns of visiting Westerners including agribusiness, the military, and the entertainment industry. A mola may typically include an image of a helicopter, heavy equipment, or an elephant or lion - animals not native to Panama - or a particularly poisonous type of local snake. The objects and animals depicted are meant to function as a place to put these intruders, a spirit world, so that they cannot infiltrate the culture. Taussig quotes "some thoughtful students of the mola" who come to the conclusion that "the single most important connection between the San Blas Indians and the outside world is the woman's mola blouse."[147] Molas made for tourists rather than for themselves, on the other hand, depict the birds, animals and flora of the area. The tourist may have access to the object but not to its sacred function. In this way, the culture survives, having incorporated machines, the military, elephants, colonizers, and the desires of foreigners. The representational space of the mola, which is made and worn by women only, is the space of refusal to assimilate, of keeping out foreign influences, and of the continuous enactment of myth. Change is inevitable, but as we see in the example of the Kuna, a culture can be preserved in a complete enactment of the present moment as a moment of keeping tradition.

In urban America, concepts of race and racial "characteristics," have created a representational space of race similar to the space prepared for women. People of color are signified demographically, where a neighborhood may be described first by its dominant racial or ethnic makeup, by its history of migrations, and by decline and subsequent gentrification that represent a timeline of sorts and the beginning point of a new demographic. The question of safety is usually a question of racializing the space – can one walk down a particular street without fear? The specifics of ethnic influence on the physical space of a community are experienced as the general feel of a

---

[147] Ibid., 183.

neighborhood: the tone, aesthetic and mood set by its inhabitants, as well as the dominant architecture, public amenities such as playgrounds and gardens, police presence, food stores, barber shops and other local enterprises. The basic question, as in the question of gender, is whether race is a factor in determining a spectrum of humanity, or whether race is a fiction that has no purpose beyond its uses politically and economically. Does racial designation and identity primarily serve as a means of controlling large segments of the population? When a specific population is targeted by the state for extra control, extra policing, or stricter control of access to public resources, for example, control is seen as characteristic belonging to the population rather than to the state – as though one particular group requires more policing than another due to innate qualities.

Du Bois writes about the relationship of Southern African-American communities to policing in *The Souls of Black Folks,* first published in 1903:

> Moreover, the political status of the Negro in the South is closely connected with the question of Negro crime. There can be no doubt that crime among Negroes has sensibly increased in the last thirty years, and that there has appeared in the slums of great cities a distinct criminal class among the blacks. In explaining this unfortunate development, we must note two things: (1) that the inevitable result of Emancipation was to increase crime and criminals, and (2) that the police system of the South was primarily designed to control slaves. As to the first point, we must not forget that under a strict slave system there can scarcely be such a thing as crime. But when these variously constituted human particles are suddenly thrown broadcast on the sea of life, some swim, some sink, and some hang suspended, to be forced up or down by the chance currents of a busy hurrying world. So great an economic and social revolution as swept the South in '63 meant a weeding out among the Negroes of the incompetents and vicious, the beginning of a differentiation of social grades. Now a rising group of

people are not lifted bodily from the ground like an inert solid mass, but rather stretch upward like a living plant with its roots still clinging in the mould. The appearance, therefore, of the Negro criminal was a phenomenon to be awaited; and while it causes anxiety, it should not occasion surprise.[148]

It could be said that the phenomenon was not only to be awaited, but was created. An African-American criminal demographic became established in the nineteenth century, crime rates having increased by what Du Bois suggests is one hundred percent, up from the zero percent of crime under the strict controls of the system of slavery. The stricter policing of African-American populations in all parts of the country today may be a remnant from the days of slavery, but it is constantly renewed and reinforced daily as a police practice in response to contemporary social problems. The fault is made to lie in the behaviors of members of African-American communities, even those behaviors that are far from criminal. Suspicion and intention is applied to every action and gesture. Du Bois speaks about the role of time in the relationship of the African-American communities to the past and the future, contained within the codex of the law, rather within an open space of possibility.

Again the hope for the future depended peculiarly on careful and delicate dealing with these criminals. Their offences at first were those of laziness, carelessness, and impulse, rather than of malignity or ungoverned viciousness. . . . For such dealing with criminals, white or black, the South had no machinery, no adequate jails or reformatories; its police system was arranged to deal with blacks alone, and tacitly assumed that every white man was *ipso facto* a member of that police. Thus grew up a double system of justice, which erred on the white side by undue leniency and the practical immunity of red-handed criminals, and erred on the black side by undue severity, injustice, and lack of discrimination.

---

[148] W. E. B. Du Bois, *The Souls of Black Folk*, 200.

For, as I have said, the police system of the South was originally designed to keep track of all Negroes, not simply of criminals; and when the Negroes were freed and the whole South was convinced of the impossibility of free Negro labor, the first and almost universal device was to use the courts as a means of reenslaving the blacks. It was not then a question of crime, but rather one of color, that settled a man's conviction on almost any charge. Thus Negroes came to look upon courts as instruments of injustice and oppression, and upon those convicted in them as martyrs and victims.[149]

Differentiation in skin tone still guides standard policing practices in America. The policing standards used in the American South became the system in use throughout the country. The term racial profiling is lodged at law enforcement regularly in defense of communities of color. If racial profiling is not practiced, individual members of law enforcement must try to judge fairly, or with common sense, across color lines in targeting criminals and in preventing crime. This is practically impossible within a system set specifically to police people of color. The task of erasing color barriers falls to people of color, who can do this most effectively by becoming white. Other options include a just system of police protection, fuller racial integration of neighborhoods with respect for difference, and an egalitarian distribution of the public wealth. A belief persists, however, that the people whose forced labor built the wealth of America and their descendants are lazy by nature, and are unwilling to work for economic power. The government must take care of them as though they are unable to care for themselves. Whether or not this myth becomes internalized is beside the point. Why a history of enforced labor should lead to a tradition of laziness is uncertain, and why this perceived laziness borders on criminal behavior makes little real sense, but perhaps the mirror comes into play: one sees oneself in the behavior of the other and makes a fitting accusation.

---

[149] Ibid.

A community may utilize being over-policed to its advantage by enacting a type of neighborhood self-policing, which appears informally as neighbors who spend time on the street, socialize on their own doorsteps, establishing a rapport with neighbors, and who take into account everyone coming and going through the neighborhood. This becomes a service in that it creates a human bond based on familiarity, routine, and an expectation of watchfulness. Community is the confluence of factors in a situation that is always evolving, which allows a neighborhood to create and retain its own essence. In representational space, segregation engenders community, whether it is based on perceptions of gender, race, or origin. The struggle against predatory policing in this type of space encodes personal and historical narratives, some of which are based on fear and mythology, and some of which are built out of necessity by the inhabitants so they can manipulate the representational space created by the power structure and create a new representational and physical space through their own actions. The double-consciousness comes into play.

In "Species of Spaces," Perec writes, "I would like there to exist places that are stable, unmoving, intangible, untouched and almost untouchable, unchanging, deep-rooted; places that might be points of reference, of departure, or origin . "[150] He continues to describe a brief fantasy about a place where he might have been born, a tree his father might have planted and which he would have seen grow, and an attic filled with "intact memories." The utter pathos of these lines belies the fact that they are true rather than sentimental, and they suggest that the point of origin of representation is located in the mutability and fluctuation of physical space. Neither physical nor representational space is stable. What is represented is not objects but subjects, and while moments may change, the nature of a moment and the power of the present do not. At the beginning of the section quoted above, subtitled "Space

---

[150] Perec, "Species of Spaces," in *Species of Spaces and Other Pieces,* 91.

(Continuation and End)," Perec writes about the relationship of narrative to space in specific terms: "This is how space begins, with words only, signs traced on the blank page. . . . Is the aleph, that place in Borges from which the entire world is visible simultaneously, anything other than an alphabet?"[151] And at the end, he writes, "To write: to try meticulously to retain something, to cause something to survive, to wrest a few precise scraps from the void as it grows, to leave somewhere a furrow, a trace, a mark or a few signs."[152] For Perec, writing is about space rather than representation. Narrative is called into being by the blank page.

Compare Perec's statement about writing as the beginning of space to the creative power of narratives described by Taussig under the heading "Miming the Real Into Being,"[153] where he discusses the tradition of shamanic medical chants of the Kuna. The shaman's song, in which he or she describes the medicinal plant to be used in the cure, the location where it was found, and the actions of harvesting the plant, is performed over the person to be cured as well as over the curative plant. The cure is brought about by the magic that the song not only describes but also actually brings into being via the description itself. In the unpublished Ph.D. dissertation of Norman Macpherson Chapin (1983), the shaman's song is described as, "telling the spirits of the plants how the Great Father placed them on the earth, how they grow, what their properties are, how they will be gathered and taken back to the community, and how they are expected to function as medicines to aid the patient.[154]

In contrast to this short description, here is an excerpt of the actual story described above as told by the shaman and as written by Chapin in the same dissertation:

---

[151] Ibid., 13.
[152] Ibid., 92
[153] Taussig, *Mimesis and Alterity: A Particular History of the Senses,* 105.
[154] Norman Macpherson Chapin, "Curing Among the San Blas Kuna," diss. (Tucson: University of Arizona, 1983), 75, as quoted in Taussig, 107.

Long ago, Great Father stood your trunks upright, they all had good appearance, he did not leave any of the valleys empty.

The medicine man begins to counsel your silver bark, your silver bark's *purpa* [spirit] is coming to life; medicines you are being changed, you are becoming medicines . . .

Long ago Great Father counselled your *purpa* for you, long ago Great Father brought your *purpa* to life for you, he stood your trunks in the bottoms of the valleys . . .

The medicine man, on the side (of the tree) where the day rises (east), is gathering your silver bark...on the far side of the day (west) . . . out to sea (north) . . . to the side opposite the sea (south) . . . he begins to cut your silver bark, he is cutting your silver bark, he is gathering your silver bark . . .

In the small basket he is placing your silver bark, all in pairs, all in pairs . . .

In this way it is hoped that your *purpa* will follow me; with you (the medicine man) turns around to go toward his home, with you toward the house, (his) legs are opening and closing, one leg goes before the other, toward the house. . . .
155

Taussig's interpretation of the story excerpted here is that it not only explains the plant's properties and the intentions of the healer, but it also creates the healing power of the plant. Telling the plant what its properties are instills those properties in the plant. "For the chant is not so much instructing the spirits as, through the mimetic faculty, bringing them into being."[156] The words of the chant describe the acts in detail, displaying the shaman's "intimate knowledge" of the magic of the cure, as well as his control of the cure. Taussig makes two connections:

---

[155] Chapin, 247 – 248, in Taussig, 107.
[156] Taussig, 108.

The simulacrum here is created with words, not objects! In fact two mimetic movements are involved. One is the duplication in song of the spirits, detail by slow-moving detail, in songs that can last up to several hours. The other mimetic movement depends upon this invocation of the spirits because, since they duplicate the physical world, to bring them forth by means of song is to mimetically gain control over the mirror-image of the physical reality that they represent.[157]

Taussig discovers a correlation between the Kuna shaman's performance of the cure and the narrative tradition in written literature wherein entire peopled worlds, fictional yet no less effective in having a presence in the reader and in the society itself, are created, adhered to, believed and acted upon. The simulacra created by literature are, like the shaman's song, a means of bringing forth an image of the physical space of the reader within the narrative. Space is created in the writing/chanting and exists as a mirror to the space of the action, the song, the writing, or the reading. Mimetic activity, representation and reproduction through the enactment of rituals of magic, in the sense described by Benjamin as well,[158] are the means by which we become other. If this is true of Kuna society as studied by Taussig, then it could possibly be true of Westerners, consumers of vast amounts of images and words, our social hierarchies beginning now to be built on hierarchies of image, mime, modeling, posing, positioning, and spinning words. Writing about the magic of another brings that magic to life. Narrative description instills words with the power to bring other worlds to life in the mind of the reader in page after page of vivid mental imagery – an entry into other worlds as they are explained in detail.

---

[157] Ibid.
[158] Walter Benjamin, *One-Way Street and Other Writings* (London and New York: Penguin Classics, 2009). First published in 1928.

Non-Places

The richness and complexity of representational space seems to empty out in the consideration of a third type of space, the non-place, a term coined by Marc Augé in *Non-Places: Introduction to an Anthropology of Supermodernity*, which refer to architecture and technology designed for transient use rather than interaction – places designed to be without historical significance and which contain few points of regional reference. But the non-place, like other spaces, is a contested space. Non-places are designed spaces, rather than spaces that form over time, based on regional history. Neither the architecture nor technologies of non-places need relate to their local situations in order to fulfill their design mission. Since they are designed for temporary occupation, spaces for travelers may have little relationship to the culture of a place a traveler may be passing through, for example. Within non-places, one practices the etiquette of strangers. Augé writes, "If a place can be defined as relational, historical and concerned with identity, then a space which cannot be defined as relational, or historical, or concerned with identity will be a non-place."[159] Augé's list of non-places includes airports, freeways, hotel chains, and supermarkets, as well as the Internet, software applications, and the human-machine networks that automate consumer and official transactions – ATMs and the networks of the national identity card and the driver's license. Uniformity and conformity are markers of the non-place. While identity is an activity of lived space, identification is an activity of the non-place. The non-place is measured in time rather than area, and specific points along the journey through non-places are numbered: flight number, ticket number, seat number, mileage, quantity, distance. Classification makes practical sense here: first class, five-star, VIP, staff only, Gate 28. The non-place has no facilities for untidy personal histories, and personal identity is situated very close to the body. Specificity is in the form of fingerprints.

---

[159] Augé, *Non-Places: An Introduction to Supermodernity*, 77 – 78.

The symbolic value of lived space gives it historical significance as a place that exists in space and time. For Hans Ibelings, the requirement of identification and its resulting anonymity in the environment of the non-place represents the uncluttered convenience of an ideally functioning supermodern environment. Like architecture that has an autonomous relationship to its city, the person transiting through a non-place has an autonomous/anonymous relationship to place and does not get caught up in the specifics of a cultural narrative, bypassing the anthropology of the event. Anthropology is a formal study of the other that locates the other very specifically in a different space and time, even if that time is the present. The journeys through anthropological space, in contrast to journeys through non-places, carry traces of the people who journey through them. Anthropological space is a space for settling. One condition of the contemporary, however, is that societies are mobile and the past is catching up to the present very quickly. As history speeds up, the significance of the grand narrative gives way to the vitality of the more social and intimate experience of daily life – family, home, activity, neighborhood.

The experience of a non-place can be one of solitude, less a shared experience than a repeated one in which a multitude of users have the same experience within a temporarily collective space. Non-places have their own protocol. All experiences of the users of a non-place are equivalent as long as the user follows protocol, the settings of which enable efficient access to goods, processes and services. The content of each visitor's experience has no specific value in terms of how non-places are designed to function. Non-places are not semiotic voids, however; the negative that they communicate is a negation of the local, a refusal of meaning and a re-signification of the present as blocks of timelessness. The symbolic value of non-places as objects in the landscape or mediascape is the replacement of the knowledge of the local with the protocol of the global. However much non-places are designed to function the same in all instances, history begins to attach itself, and in time, the proliferation of non-places engenders procedures of cultural homogenization, creating an intervention of the global as world culture. Homogenization is a coercive function of capitalism that replaces local culture with world culture. As a strategy of intervention into the authentic, homogenization and a negation of the significance of place, along with the accompanying enforcement of uniformity and conformity, is also a significant pattern in totalitarian societies, which use these as means of streamlining control of populations through the homogenization of daily life and the minimizing of difference. In non-places, where personal history has no significance and the continual creation of identity is interrupted, the ahistorical aspect functions to create distance from self and community, as well as from spontaneous creative activity. Conformity of architecture, action, behavior, and event is the singular option, whether one is in the non-space of the Doubletree Hilton Hotel in Shenyang, China, or the non-space of an immigrant detention and deportation center in the American Southwest.

From the late 1980s to the mid-1990s, government and educational web servers enabled a growing number of people to connect remotely, and in 1994, the first commercial search engine, WebCrawler, was launched. In 1995, the Internet became fully commercialized. This was a time of enormous speculation about the significance of the Internet as a virtual environment inside the environment of the flesh and blood world, and users and theorists were working within the framework of the new mass medium to come to terms with virtuality and mass connectivity. In a 2009 lecture about the feasibility of forming a reliable critique of the Internet, post-academic Internet theorist Geert Lovink, posited a "question of the day": how do we study emerging Internet cultures when the problem of critiquing the Internet is one of creating a critical position towards a phenomenon that changes in real time? As he remarks, "The object changes all the time."[160] The first step would be to stop trying to catch up to the ever-changing environment and, like artists who challenge the visual, temporal and sound environments of the contemporary by working through them in the contemporary moment, Internet theorists

---

[160] Geert Lovink, lecture at the European Graduate School, June 2009.

can only understand their medium by engaging in an immersive dialogue about the present state of the net world as it happens. A reliable critical theory of the Internet has not yet been written because it is always being rewritten by users in a multiple, random and collective conversation.

Although Augé does not discuss life online in depth, his description of the present era as one in which history is accelerated is apt. The Internet is an example of history catching up to itself, where all approaches to theory are untimely. According to Lovink, the organic approach would be to "develop research questions that operate from the inside."[161] For Augé, non-places are not only specific types of environment, they act as a force that directly corresponds to the idea of the value of the individual in a way typified by the Internet. Online identities are not so much in constant formation as they are in a constant state of change. In 1995, the year Augé's *Non-Places* was published, sociologist and psychologist Sherry Turkle published *Life on the Screen: Identity in the Age of the Internet*, a text detailing then-current dialogues about the Internet. Turkle describes the change in what is considered a healthy social presence based on what she had observed online at the time:

> Not so long ago, stability was socially valued and culturally reinforced. Rigid gender roles, repetitive labor, the expectation of being in one kind of job or remaining in one town over a lifetime, all of these made consistency central to definitions of health. But these stable social worlds have broken down. In our time, health is described in terms of fluidity rather than stability. What matters most now is the ability to adapt and change – to new jobs, new career directions, new gender roles, new technologies.[162]

Turkle recognized the emergence of identity, individualization, collectivity, and multiplicity as issues of keen interest among

---

[161] Ibid.
[162] Sherry Turkle, *Life on the Screen: Identity in the Age of the Internet* (New York: Touchstone, 1997), 255.

users of the popular Multi-User Dimensions (MUDs) and object-oriented MUDs (MOOs) or the 1990s. MUDs and MOOs are online text-based games in which a player's unstable identity represents one of the key strengths of the game, and where mutable identities move the action along in directions based on momentary interactions. Identification and naming are part of the game as the user is free to create any type of alternate online presence. Categorizing and stereotyping become objects of the game as well, as the user plays her heightened persona off the personas of other players. The embedded self loses its center and in these virtual environments.

Individual users and gamers are not the only actors with flexible online identities, obviously. As Turkle observed early in the age of mass Internet culture, "The new metaphors of health as flexibility apply not only to mental and physical spheres, but also to the bodies of corporations, governments, and businesses. These institutions function in rapidly changing circumstances; they too are coming to view their fitness in terms of their flexibility."[163] In the early 1990s, the art-activist group Critical Art Ensemble (CAE) noted that global concentrations of power, both governmental and corporate, were becoming as decentralized as online presences, and warned that political analyses based in nineteenth century narratives and centrally-organized opposition to economic and political oppression were no longer relevant in the current techno-political landscape. CAE were concerned about the possibilities for online resistance-based political activism in an environment where the opponent's power base is decentralized, and the opponent is nomadic. CAE use Herodotus' stories of the ancient Scythians as a metaphor for what resistance to the phenomena of decentralized global power structures may be up against. They write:

> With no fixed cities or territories, this "wandering horde" could never really be located. Consequently, they could never be put on the defensive and conquered. They

---

[163] Ibid.

maintained their autonomy through movement . . . A floating border was maintained in their homeland, but power was not a matter of spatial occupation for the Scythians. They wandered, taking territory and tribute as needed, in whatever area they found themselves.[164]

The corporation as a wondering horde is fitting in terms of global economics, industry, and trade, where corporate activity seems to involve crossing borders, invading regions for resources (oil, diamonds, minerals, timber, croplands, grazing land etc.), most often with the blessings of the government of the regions whose precious resources are being occupied or carted off, and taking the goods through massive pipelines, both actual and metaphorical. Cargill, Monsanto, Union Carbide, Coca Cola, and all of the major oil and gas companies, for example, have mastered the decentered style of operation. Corporations have had a history of colonialist exploitation since the first days of European expansion to the Americas and the East by the state-backed traders for precious metals, human beings, fur, tea, tobacco, dyes and spices. For CAE, the new ingredient is the Internet, a prime location for decentralized, cross-border resistance as well. Invisibility, anonymity, variety, diffusion of leadership, autonomy through movement – the Scythians, once again, suggest a process for advancing on the opponent. CAE declare that "Nomadic power must be resisted in cyberspace rather than in physical space," and continue with a few suggestions:

A small but coordinated group of hackers could introduce electronic viruses, worms, and bombs into the data banks, programs, and networks of authority, possibly bringing the destructive force of inertia into the nomadic realm. Prolonged inertia equals the collapse of nomadic authority on a global level. Such a strategy does not require a unified

---

[164] Critical Art Ensemble, "Nomadic Power and Cultural Resistance," in *The New Media Reader*, Noah Wardrip-Fruin and Nick Montfort, ed. (Cambridge: The MIT Press, 2003), 784.

class action, nor does it require simultaneous action in numerous geographic areas.[165]

Consider the infamous "Hacker Manifesto," a document that seems inherently political, written in 1986 by a youthful computer culture theorist, Loyd Blankenship, who called himself "++The Mentor++."[166] An excerpt describes not only his adolescent awakening to the expectation of a stifling conformity that awaits him in adulthood, but also the thrill of finding within computing culture an anonymous and autonomous affinity group:

> And then it happened... a door opened to a world... rushing through the phone line like heroin through an addict's veins, an electronic pulse is sent out, a refuge from the day-to-day incompetencies [sic] is sought... a [bulletin] board is found.
>
> "This is it... this is where I belong..."
>
> I know everyone here... even if I've never met them, never talked to them, may never hear from them again... I know you all...
>
> Damn kid. Tying up the phone line again. They're all alike...
>
> You bet your ass we're all alike... we've been spoon-fed baby food at school when we hungered for steak... the bits of meat that you did let slip through were pre-chewed and tasteless. We've been dominated by sadists, or ignored by the apathetic. The few that had something to teach found us

---

[165] Critical Art Ensemble, "Nomadic Power and Cultural Resistance," in *The New Media Reader*, 788.

[166] ++The Mentor++ is the handle of Loyd Blankenship, who was arrested for computer hacking in 1986, and after his arrest wrote a short essay called "The Conscience of a Hacker," which became known as "The Hacker Manifesto." "The Hacker Manifesto," Wikipedia, http://en.wikipedia.org/wiki/Hacker_Manifesto (accessed June 11, 2012).

willing pupils, but those few are like drops of water in the desert.

This is our world now... the world of the electron and the switch, the beauty of the baud. We make use of a service already existing without paying for what could be dirt-cheap if it wasn't run by profiteering gluttons, and you call us criminals. We explore... and you call us criminals. We seek after knowledge... and you call us criminals. We exist without skin color, without nationality, without religious bias... and you call us criminals. You build atomic bombs, you wage wars, you murder, cheat, and lie to us and try to make us believe it's for our own good, yet we're the criminals.

Yes, I am a criminal. My crime is that of curiosity. My crime is that of judging people by what they say and think, not what they look like. My crime is that of outsmarting you, something that you will never forgive me for.

I am a hacker, and this is my manifesto. You may stop this individual, but you can't stop us all... after all, we're all alike.[167]

But hacker politics are not a call to political activism, nor do they refer to random or coordinated acts of cyber vandalism against government agencies to disrupt services and bring attention to any specific injustice, which CAE recommends. The consciousness of the hacker evolved from the human-computer interaction itself. Blankenship's opposition to governments and corporations, school systems, and war address the policing of the Internet and attempts to centralize control over a decentralizing medium. His complaint is an ethical one: the criminal is the telecommunications industry that monopolizes technology and sells access to a system that he believes should belong to the people who use it. The political discourse is the discourse of the medium itself, which according to Blankenship, is a great

---

[167] Ibid.

equalizing force. Personal opinions, beliefs, biases or knowledge are incidental to the practice itself of collective interactivity. This is the non-issue based, contentless, nature of relational resistance, and although the Hacker Manifesto was written in 1986, it describes the contemporary ethos of the Internet as developed by its users. The battle against censorship and control from governments continues. But neither CAE nor ++The Mentor++ predicted the intrusive advertising and pop-news items directed at the user, based on the tracking of websites visited, social network postings, and the very text of personal email messages in a form of legal hacking referred to as marketing. Inside the physical spaces created to accommodate the Internet – the corners of the bedrooms, the arrangement of desks, the wired coffee shops, classrooms, cubicles and Internet café's – these places become both places and non-places, coming together in the interstices of contemporary computer practice, at an intersection of continuums of the present.

Augé's perspective in defining the supermodernist phenomenon of the non-place is a fusion of anthropological and theoretical discourses. His analysis of supermodernity is a demarcation of the limits of cultural anthropology and ethnography, wherein the anthropologist reveals his own methodological priorities, which become the actual function of anthropology. According to Augé, "anthropological space" is a place that responds to human activity and is malleable, social, and carries markers of change. "The inhabitant of anthropological space does not make history; he lives in it."[168] Supermodernity, on the other hand, "makes the old (history) into spectacle, as it does with all exoticism and all local particularity."[169] It turns history into advertising, so that history plays "the same role in [the spectacle of supermodernity] as 'quotations' in a written text,"[170] providing an even less authentic experience of place than tourism, for example. In Tourism, the imagination conjures a place that makes the reality of being there redundant. Augé uses the example of a game

---

[168] Augé, *Non-Places: An Introduction to Supermodernity*, 55.
[169] Ibid., 110.
[170] Ibid.

show in which the audience finds pleasure in imagining the winnings of the contestants: a cruise, a trip to a sunny vacation spot, an island holiday that the audience need not experience to enjoy in the space of their imaginations.[171]

Consumerism is a representational non-place full of pop songs, running shoes, hamburgers, sentimentalism, and other influences placed in front of the individual who gestures towards making a choice or identifying an emotion. Items are created and catalogued in taxonomies of the consumer moment, which the consumer is free to personalize as playlists and favorites, perusing branded space to find suitable presentations of the self within the delimited territory of inauthentic choice. In the non-place of consumer culture, it is the goods that are transient, the goods that visit the consumer. The space of daily life is a waiting room for consumer goods and a departure lounge for mass culture. Augé refers to this as "the cosmology of the consumer," wherein the consumer develops an identification with brands, and when actually traveling, recognizes familiar logos and products "from home." He finds home inside this recognition, reassurance from a very inauthentic ideal of the local. "For him, an oil company logo is a reassuring landmark; among the supermarket shelves he falls with relief on sanitary, household or food products validated by multinational brand names."[172] The alienation seems complete, as global consumerism brings the relief of the familiar to a stranger in a strange land.

Naomi Klein looks at the phenomena of world cultural homogenization through a lens that politicizes not only corporate strategies in building a trans-national consumer base, but also the psychological re-shuffling that occurs within the world citizen as consumer. She brings into focus a consideration of the transference of attachments based on memory and personal, familial, and community identity to attachments based on product branding, the expectations of pre-mapped experiences, and the impact of global consumption of the identical mass

---

[171] Ibid., 95.
[172] Ibid., 106.

media. Regarding the birth of the age of branding, as production moved overseas to more profitable climes, Klein reports:

> The astronomical growth in wealth and cultural influence of multinational corporations over the last fifteen years can arguably be traced back to a single, seemingly innocuous idea developed by management theorists in the mid-1980s: that successful corporations must primarily produce brands, as opposed to products. . . . At around the same time a new kind of corporation began to rival the traditional all-American manufacturers for market share; these were the Nikes and Microsofts, and later, the Tommy Hilfigers and Intels. These pioneers made the bold claim that producing goods was only an incidental part of their operations. What these companies produced primarily were not things, they said, but images of their brands. . . . Whoever produces the most powerful images, as opposed to products, wins the race.[173]

An important change that occurs in the shift from production to branding is the location of the narrator. In life the family, community, and personal memory locate the narrator in the individual regardless of subjectivity. In other words, branding is effective regardless of how the consumer puts the narrative together – regardless of what their perspective may be on any of the details of the narrative carried by the brand.

Within the representational space of global consumerism, the narrator is equivalent to the TV announcer and the subject is the audience. The pleasure of Augé's game-show audience over imaginary winnings is an instance of supermodernist narrative at work. The audience is alienated from anthropological place and from history while in the non-place of the spectacle. The supermodernist narrative is an active replacement of the markers of genuine culture with the desires of an imagined one. Denial of complicity is easy when the space of complicity is a simulacrum. Within that space is a complete forgetting of the communal

---

[173] Klein, *No Space, No Choice, No Jobs: No Logo*, 4.

offering and specificity of the local, written over by a homogenizing illusion created on a scale that is impossible to personalize, a task that falls to the consumer herself, who fails without realizing it. The spectacle is the language of colonialism and everyone is indeed marginalized. Debord discusses this in terms of the autonomy of places under corporate capitalism:

> Capitalist production has unified space, which is no longer bounded by external societies. This unification is at the same time an extensive and intensive process of *banalization*. The accumulation of commodities produced in mass for the abstract space of the market, which had to break down all regional and legal barriers and all the corporative restrictions of the Middle Ages that preserved the *quality* of craft production, also had to destroy the autonomy and quality of places. This power of homogenization is the heavy artillery which brought down all Chinese walls.[174]

Narrative plays a distinct role in denying anthropological place. The mutual pleasure of the audience members may show an aspect of human collectivity that seeks common ground, and in Augé's example, they find it in the fantasy scenario of the narrative. The narrative, however, writes tourism – whether one visits a new place or simply witnesses a suggestion of a visit on television – as an arm of colonialism.

In contrast, within a decentralized narrative, or within non-narrative connectivity, the subject and the central point are always on the move, becoming multiple and networked. This is the contemporary model as situated in the Internet, but also as situated in relational real-place networks of association and affinity. Electronic connectivity provides a space for dialogue across cultures in real time, changing the nature of the everyday and opening up the territory of multi-centered communities as decentralized networks. There is not only a usefulness to these non-narrative networks, there is also urgency, violent struggle

---

[174] Debord, *Society of the Spectacle*, Chapter VII, 165.

for basic rights, and even Utopianism, which the world can witness as it happens: Tunisia, Egypt, Iran, Libya, Bahrain, London, Aleppo. As in Augé's definition of anthropological space, a record is left, an online trail of news reports, video, images, and commentary – stratified and un-stratified, official, unregulated, informed, misinformed, and subjective.

The anthropologist studies himself through his study of the other, but a bit of ethnographic *détournement* is required if the anthropologist is to replace a study of the other with a study of himself, not merely using writing about the other to create a text of himself, but moving into the field of representation of the other to examine the ethnographic evidence he presents to the world. In the 1970 film, *Petit à Petit,*[175] the French ethnographer Jean Rouch creates a semi-fictional narrative in which the anthropologist-subject relationship is reversed. In the film, three young businessmen from Niger come to Paris, ostensibly to study the architecture and placement of multi-story office buildings. The Nigeriens begin their investigation with a study, instead, of the bodies of Parisians, measuring the heads and counting the teeth of people on the street. They improvise commentary on clothing styles (not attractive), body types (too thin), and public displays of affection, as well as architecture and its uses. The film is a parody of ethnographic practice, and as obvious as the parody may seem, *Petit à Petit* presents more than a simple turning of tables; the film deconstructs ethnography as well as documentary filmmaking as processes in the creation of the narrative of the other, foregrounding the filmmaker/ethnographer himself as the main subject. The ethnographer is replaced, and the subjective eye of documentary genre is rightfully put to full use, free of the expectations of objectivity and scientism. The resulting film is a blend of multiple perspectives from which a singular resolution is never derived. The issue is not one of the subject (traditional ethnographic practice) or the objects of study (colonialism), but filmmaking itself. Rouch's work, in handing over the tools of

---

[175] Jean Rouch, *Petit à Petit,* DVD (Panthéon Distribution: Paris, 1994).

documentation to the supposed subject, is an invitation to engage a visual culture of identity politics, and to use the camera as a tool of resistance against the all-encompassing homogenization of colonialism, on the one hand, and the extremes of differentiation on the other.

By 1970, civil rights, gay liberation, and women's liberation were coherent movements with a mutable many-voiced ethos of control of representation: of the group, of the self, and of the self as a figuration of the group. Much of the representation (image, sound, text) from within these movements, and much of the dialogue between them, was contradictory; agreement or resolution was fleeting, and as polemical or totalizing as some of the philosophies that emerged from these movements may have seemed, the movements were vital actors in the formation of a new and unfixed consciousness about the self and about the other. New terminology was formed through authentic living. Communities inventing the new bits of language came together, changed, and moved in many directions at once. The terminology of resistance and respect for otherness continues to inform our perceptions and interpretations of the global uprisings that we access every day via video uploads to social networking sites. Lest this observation become swept up in a time-traveling Utopian sentimentalism, Sherry Turkle comes to the rescue with a different conclusion about ubiquitous connectivity. In an April 2012, New York Times article, she writes:

> I've learned that the little devices most of us carry around are so powerful that they change not only what we do, but also who we are. We've become accustomed to a new way of being "alone together." Technology-enabled, we are able to be with one another, and also elsewhere, connected to wherever we want to be. We want to customize our lives. We want to move in and out of where we are because the thing we value most is control over where we focus our

attention. We have gotten used to the idea of being in a tribe
of one, loyal to our own party.[176]

Our connection to others may be instantaneous, but it requires a
shorthand of text messaging, which may keep our contacts at
bay more than they bring them closer to us. The scene of
friends' texting, checking emails, checking weather forecasts
and restaurant reviews rather than talking to one another is
familiar to many of us. Turkle suggests that the technology is not
responsible for our alienation, but that we have made choices
that create the habitual attention to the screens of the smart
phone and other devices rather than to the environment, to
people around us, and to people directly in front of us. What she
does not mention, however, is the most significant element in the
phenomenon of the public space of private messaging, which is
that consumerism has entered the interstices between public and
private interaction and has created a nodal point between the
person and the object of her communication, one that must be
accessed and paid for, like a toll, before she can speak. The
loyalty is to the smart phone contract and the bill it produces at
the end of each month, not to a "tribe of one."

Interstitial Space

A fourth type of space is created in time rather than in place,
and exists in and through both place and non-place. It may be
thought of as interstitial space, what anarchist writer Hakim Bey
calls the Temporary Autonomous Zone (TAZ).[177] This is a place

---

[176] Sherry Turkle, "The Flight From Conversation," The New York Times
Sunday Review, http://www.nytimes.com/2012/04/22/opinion/sunday/the-flight-
from-conversation.html?pagewanted=all (accessed June 11, 2012).
[177] Hakim Bey is a pseudonym used by Peter Lamborn Wilson. In a conversation
with Wilson at Bard College in the early 2000s, he mentioned that he was no
longer using a pseudonym and now writes under his given name. He is still
widely known as Hakim Bey in relation to his 1991 publication, T.A.Z. The
Temporary Autonomous Zone, Ontological Anarchy, Poetic Terrorism.
(Brooklyn: Autonomedia, 2003).

that is always there, yet not always initiated, a place that is accessed by activity rather than signified by objects, landmarks or amenities. Bey identifies the TAZ as a region of chaos where neither order nor dissolution has currency, and where communication has no relationship to regulation. Undefined spaces of public and private discourse are included in this type of zone – temporary because they are based on use rather than on spatial characteristics, and autonomous because the use is deregulated; the inhabitant of interstitial space is no longer in a zone of commerce or law. Time is the main element – *times* of rebellion, of unrestrained pursuits of pleasure, of intellectual stimulation, and of freedom. Autonomous zones exists inside, beside, and mapped over other kinds of space and include the dinner party, the poetry reading, the space of making art, and the space of the rave, the orgy. The TAZ is chaos, a spiraling fractal, outer space, a borderless void, an "island in the net,"[178] lacking definition and directionless, yet active and willed into being. Bey did not invent the TAZ, he simply named it. Hackers, for example, have always existed in the interstices created by the structures of regulated computing.[179]

In his 1985 manifesto, *The Temporary Autonomous Zone*, under the heading "The Psychotopology of Everyday Life," Bey cites two "generating forces" behind the concept:

> The concept of the TAZ arises first out of a critique of Revolution, and an appreciation of the Insurrection. The former labels the latter a failure; but for us *uprising* represents a far more interesting possibility, from the standard of a psychology of liberation, than all the "successful" revolutions of bourgeoisie, communists, fascists, etc.
>
> The second generating force behind the TAZ springs from the historical development I call "the closure of the map."

---

[178] Ibid., 96. *Islands in the Net* is a 1989 book by Bruce Sterling, referenced here by Bey.
[179] Galloway, *Protocol: How Control Exists After Decentralization*, 161.

The last bit of Earth unclaimed by any nation-state was eaten up in 1899. Ours is the first century without *terra incognita*, without a frontier. Nationality is the highest principle of world governance – not one speck of rock in the South Seas can be left *open*, not one remote valley, not even the Moon and planets.[180]

Revolution is a process, which, if successful, results in a closure to the question of social organization. Insurrections and uprisings, on the other hand, are immediate and urgent, opening up the question of social organization and enacting reorganizations as needed. The map of the Earth reveals a topology of claimed territories, including sky, outer space and ocean floor, which are parceled based on their nearness to a particular state. A particular state's claim to a portion of the sky or the sea recedes as the distance grows greater and an international border law takes over. For Bey, the map of the world is a "political abstract grid, a gigantic *con*"[181] made singular, without alternative, and presented to us as final and complete, so that we believe the abstraction to be the reality. "Within the fractal complexities of actual geography the map can see only dimensional grids. Hidden enfolded immensities escape the measuring rod." The map of the world, like a revolution, is closed. He continues: "Only psychotopography can draw 1:1 maps of reality because only the human mind provides sufficient complexity to model the real." Like psychogeography, it is a suggestion, "in a sense, *gesture towards*, certain features," spaces that are not only physical, but are communal as well.

Bey evokes Benoit Mandelbrot's formula as poetry and as a model for fractal chaos:

> In the Mandelbrot Set and its computer-graphic realization we watch – in a fractal universe – maps which are

---

[180] Bey, *T.A.Z. The Temporary Autonomous Zone, Ontological Anarchy, Poetic Terrorism*, 100-101.
[181] All the following short quotes on this page are from Bey, 101.

embedded and in fact hidden within maps within maps etc., to the limits of computational power.

If we were to imagine an *information map* – a cartographic projection of the Net in its entirely – we would have to include in it the features of chaos, which have already begun to appear, for example, in the operations of complex parallel processing, telecommunications, transfers of electronic "money," viruses, guerilla hacking and so on.

Each of these "areas" of chaos could be represented by topographs similar to the Mandelbrot Set, such that the "peninsulas" are embedded or hidden within the map – such that they seem to "disappear."…In other words, the M Set, or something like it, might prove to be useful in "plotting" (in all senses of the word) the emergence of the counter-Net as a chaotic process, a "creative evolution," …a "mapping" of the TAZ's interface with the Net as a *disappearance of information.*[182]

Writing in 1985, Bey imagines an Internet with an infinite number of hidden spaces, suggesting that the Internet is uncontrollable by its nature, and cannot be completely regulated. Once the user creates or locates an online autonomous zone, referred to as a darknet or deep web, information may vanish before the eyes of the state, the regulators, and from the spiders of commerce. Mandelbrot himself has written on the M Set as applied to the Internet:

At first the experts thought they could use an old theory that had been developed in the 1920s for telephone networks. But as the Internet expanded, it was found that this model won't work. . . . Then they tried multi fractals, a mathematical construction that I had introduced in the late 1960s and into the 1970s. . . . To test new Internet equipment one examines its performance under multi fractal

---

[182] Ibid., 110.

variability. This is even a fairly big business, from what I understand.

How could it be that the same technique applies to the Internet, the weather and the stock market? Why, without particularly trying, am I touching so many different aspects of many different things?[183]

According to Mandelbrot, the Internet follows the general theory of roughness – a theory that applies to the stock market, as he mentions, as well as to the probable construction of coastlines, clouds, rainforests and everything that is not, basically, in the shape of a smooth curve. The Internet has no central control, for example, but has a self-replicating structure. It organizes itself. The borders of the TAZ are rough as well, not designed around a central organizing principle. In the preface to the 2003 edition of his book, Bey expresses a deep disappointment in the way users developed the Internet into a place where communication may be frequent but is completely drained of substance, and where "a few thousand 'hits' pass for political action."[184] He denounces it as a useful space for insurrection. The retrofitted TAZ must exist in regions where smell, taste, and tactility are possible, and communication is done in person. For Bey, the Internet is a sensual void and the TAZ exists where the fine mixing of the senses allows a full experience of others in the moment.

It is hard to resist the communicative power of the Internet, however, and regardless of Bey's disappointment over what it has become, it still seems like a good place to build autonomous networks of affinities. More urgent questions regarding the Internet and autonomy persist, the most obvious being the hierarchical nature of Internet protocol. All online access and all traffic to and from a particular computer are dependent on the DNS, the Domain Name System. Galloway explains the role of

---

[183] Benoit Mandelbrot, "A Theory of Roughness," n.d., Edge, http://www.edge.org/3rd_culture/mandelbrot04/mandelbrot04_index.html (accessed February 25, 2012). This article is from a talk by Mandelbrot before the Reality Club in New York, at an unspecified date in the 1980s.
[184] Bey, xi.

the DNS in Internet hierarchy: "All DNS information is controlled in a hierarchical, inverted-tree structure. Ironically, then, nearly all Web traffic must submit to a hierarchical structure (DNS) to gain access to the anarchic and radically horizontal structure of the Internet."[185] Secondly, there is the question of how, and for how long, users will be able to maintain enough freedom from regulation, government censorship and surveillance, aggressive marketing, and the aggregation of personal information by commercial and other interests, to continue to regard the Internet as a relatively open and borderless space. The most unregulated sector of the Internet is the commercial sector, and anonymity rather than identification is something the user must strive to achieve, since identification is already a requirement of being wired. The server must know the point of connection, i.e., where the user's computer is, in order to do its job of sending and receiving data.

While Bey has discarded the Internet as an autonomous zone, connectivity is still the means by which the TAZ is created. According to Bey, the basic unit the TAZ is the band, a "Paleolithic model [that] is at once more primal and more radical"[186] than the nuclear family unit. The band is part of a horizontal pattern, a network of groups, individuals, cohorts, friends, and lovers, but the band is nomadic as well. "The TAZ is a guerilla operation which liberates an area (of land, of time, of imagination) and then dissolves itself to re-form elsewhere/elsewhen."[187] Remnants of band networks are still to be found in lesbian and gay culture within the lingering suspicions about the promise of a societal stamp of psychiatric, legal, moral, and marital equity. An expectation of social acceptance is what got many people into trouble in the first place, and in the case of "gays," it seems to have opened a door to military service and suppressed a radical critique of the ideal family. The new queer family looks a lot like every other family,

---

[185] Galloway, 9.
[186] Bey, *T.A.Z. The Temporary Autonomous Zone, Ontological Anarchy, Poetic Terrorism,* 102.
[187] Ibid., 101.

with two parents and one or two children, living separately and privately, no longer based in a community that is locatable outside of representational space. The non-hierarchical band model allows for temporal continuity and spatial mobility, whether the tradition is Paleolithic, as Bey asserts, or simply part of a continually developing resistance to norms. In pre-legal gay communities, for example, the band was a model for survival and included a generous ethos of accepting almost anyone who stepped forward into the circle of community. Bey is not discussing mere survival, however, but suggests that we move well into zones of pleasure by participating in a "festal culture."[188] What he means, is the basic right to party: "The essence of the party: a group of humans synergize their efforts to realize mutual desires, whether for good food and cheer, dance, conversation, the arts of life; perhaps even for erotic pleasure, or to create a communal artwork, or to attain the very transport of bliss – in short, 'a union of egoists' . . . in its simplest form."[189] Mutual desires bring on the pleasure of the party, the happening, and the collaboration – generous moments rather than the mean moments of competition. These are durational events, located in "intercalary intervals"[190] of unlegislated time.

Bey's Temporary Autonomous Zones does seem like a rough place, or at least a place where men might fare better than women, and it would seem likely that even though rules of social hierarchy are not part of the concept, those who inhabit the zone would have brought remnants of privilege and power with them, if only in the form of processes. It is not a question of chaos versus order; if chaos is what guides the universe, then women as well as men are native to its regions. Nor is it a question of future concerns, but more a question of the experience of the author, Bey, himself, as a man in the world. In a 2002 essay, "My Summer Vacation in Afghanistan," writing under his given name, Peter Lamborn Wilson, he states:

---

[188] Bey, 102.
[189] Ibid., 104.
[190] Ibid., 103.

One thing I learned by talking to [Afghan] men however was that many of them could not afford to marry, since Afghan custom requires the groom's family to pay a bride price . . . The burqa therefore cannot be seen simply as a symbol of oppression of women (though it is that) but also as a symbol of the *value of daughters.*

Also, the notion that Moslems "hate women" because they veil them must be weighed against the conscious beliefs of most Moslem men: i.e., that they value women *far more* than – say – Hollywood America, where women are used to sell products through fleshly exposure. Given sexual relations in Afghanistan, the burqa can be seen as a form of freedom from harassment and exploitation. I'm not saying this is my opinion. I'm just trying to explain the attitude of the average Afghan.[191]

In a later lecture at Bard College, Wilson/Bey did put this view forth as his opinion, saying that covering up women completely shows more respect than allowing women to wear what they wish.[192] The question of Islamic law or religious dress codes is not relevant to Bey's view of women as either protected or exposed. Either judgment precludes a woman's ability to have a function in society not based on her own victimization – she either avoids its direct results (bodily or psychological harm), or she falls prey to sexual exploitation. Either way, she has never had a subjectivity of her own. Bey's assumption that both custom and culture are fundamentally male domains, and that including woman as an element that must be reconciled rather than as a primary element, and seeing woman as a point of contestation between East and West, clearly places her within the enclosed space of maleness, not beside him, or together with

---

[191] Peter Lamborn Wilson, "My Summer Vacation in Afghanistan," The Fifth Estate, Summer 2002, 15.

[192] I was present at this lecture, where Wilson/Bey was a visiting artist in the Film/Video Department where I taught. I cannot recall the date of the lecture, but it was close to the time that the article quoted above was printed, since we were given this article to read prior to his lecture. The lecture was most likely in the summer of 2002 or 2003.

him, but as a part of his own consciousness. It may be necessary to feminize the TAZ, therefore, or to broaden its scope to include representational space as well as the interstitial spaces of the everyday. The inclusion of representational space, where the power of gender is determined, is required if ethical egoism ("a union of egoists") is to be a part of what enables the creation of the autonomous zone. In other words, gender, as well as other representations of difference within mainstream culture, must be especially considered if the party, the orgy, or the happening are to exorcise the old order, so that these considerations can lose their excess significance. And in face-to-face encounters, which is the recommendation of the TAZ, the space of the mind is especially important if the poetry of the mixture of the senses is to be interpretable, to have syntax.

In *A Field Guide to Getting Lost,* Rebecca Solnit recalls the Passover tradition of leaving a door open for the prophet Elijah, and through this tradition, as she remembers it from childhood, she found a door to discovery. She writes, "Leave the door open for the unknown, the door into the dark. That's where the most important things come from, where you yourself came from, and you will go."[193] She connects the open door to not only allowing the unknown to come in, but also to going out into the unknown, something that is familiar to artists whose process involves finding the material, the form, or the story rather than merely representing something already known. The opposite method would be one of calculation and control, illustration rather than discovery, expectation rather than uncertainty. The unknown is an autonomous region, one more primal, perhaps than zones of resistance. The desire to return to a place that no longer exists, or to come upon a mysterious place, is similar to the impulse to create art. The space of art making, of losing yourself to the unknown or the darkness, is created and visited continuously, and has not yet been fully mapped. Even if the world is completely mapped, or affinities and links are mapped in cyberspace, there are still many mysterious, overlooked, lost, and hidden spaces. Maps of the world have designations that are

---

[193] Rebecca Solnit, *A Field Guide to Getting Lost* (New York: Viking, 2005), 4.

only temporarily relevant, in fact, and it is possible that at some point in the future, the designated names and claims may become passé, and the land will be *terra incognita* once again.

In a chapter entitled "Abandon," Solnit describes the decommissioned urban landscapes of the early1980s that became the natural landscape of punk.

> Coming of age in the heyday of punk, it was clear we were living at the end of something – of modernism, of the American dream, of the industrial economy, of a certain kind of urbanism. Urban ruins were the emblematic places for this era, the places that gave punk part of its aesthetic, and like most aesthetics this one contained an ethic, a worldview with a mandate on how to act, how to live.

> What is a ruin, after all? It is a human construction abandoned to nature, and one of the allures of ruins in the city is that of wilderness: a place full of the promise of the unknown with all its epiphanies and dangers.[194]

An urban ruin is open to vandalism, chaos, and unsupervised behavior; a space free of the tamping down of the imagination, the mark of adulthood. It is transformed, not under close scrutiny, and outside the immediate concerns of commerce. Solnit describes her punk years as being in a social wilderness of transgressive behavior, intoxication and eroticism. She recalls, "I was fifteen, and when I picture myself then, I see flames shooting up, see myself falling off the edge of the world, and am amazed I survived not the outside world but the inside one."[195] The wilderness "has a time, too," she writes, "the time of youth, and of night."[196] A crucial function of interstitial space is to provide a place for youth to dive into the world of turmoil within and explore the self before becoming captive to the complex socio-economic system that eventually normalizes everything.

---

[194] Ibid., 88 – 89.
[195] Ibid., 90.
[196] Ibid., 91.

A young person on the verge of breaking into adulthood begins to have a longer focus, to look further into the horizon, which is the imagined destination. Urban ruins are where the past of the abandoned building collides with the anticipated future of the urban explorer. The drive for autonomy that directs the eye to focus on the ruined buildings up ahead is fueled by a still-childish imagination, but it is mixed with adolescent rage and a strong desire to escape from home, parents, school, boredom, and the assault of hormones. Children at play perhaps know more about the value of interstitial spaces than any adult, even the most playful adult, and are not troubled, like adolescents, by an incipient knowledge of the struggles ahead. A child finds a new world in following ants along a trail, or in the scent of a pile of autumn leaves – just as she has taken a flying leap into it – as well as in the first realizations of how letters work to form mental sounds, which form words, which create not only images but also stories and ideas.

The Illustrated Dictionary of Architecture defines "Interstices" as "Spaces or intervals between parts of a structure or between components,"[197] and accompanying the definition is a drawing of beams and rafters in what appears to signify a space between two floors of a building. The dictionary defines "Interstitial" as "forming a narrow or small space between parts of other elements."[198] The architectural meanings are apt in terms of how interstitial space can be structured over time, or are found inside spaces that have other designations. The Situationists found the spaces between buildings and the space where two buildings are joined to be events in themselves. Is the event merely another suggestion to look deeper into the space of the everyday, or is something actually happening in the space between buildings? Certainly architecture is happening, and the history of one element in comparison with the other is brought into focus

---

[197] Ernest Burden, *The Illustrated Dictionary of Architecture* (New York: McGraw-Hill, 2002), 178.
[198] Ibid.

based, perhaps, on architectural styles or the dates of construction, for example. The spaces between buildings provide information about the timeline of the neighborhood and are the places that mark the point where decisions became realized in the space, in the creation of place.

In interstitial space, time can seem to stand still or to run at a different pace from ordinary time. The official space of tradition, law, and commerce becomes tangential to interstitial space, or is mapped over it, or becomes a container for it; these spaces can be symbiotic or in conflict, simultaneous or re-purposed. Taking time to seek spiritual community or epicurean delight, experience sensory pleasure, find inspiration, figure things out, make love, become intoxicated, have unregulated dialogue, and create art is the way into the interstitial space. The studio, the workshop, the writer's room, the gourmand's kitchen, the unmade bed – these places and their recombinant nature represent retreat as well as entrenchment and possibility, and are the places where cultural assumptions and habits lose their currency. Avital Ronell describes the process in this paragraph on writing, from *Stupidity*:

> Writing has been different things for me, and I shall never really know how to name it, except by pet names and metonymy, by different experiences of nausea and mania. . . If anything, writing is a non-place for me, where one can abandon oneself to abandonment – I, the infinitely abandoned (one of my "issues"). I am always on writing, especially when I am crashing, and stalled in the time of suspensive nothingness, the hiatus, the interruption, where nothing happens, and it is a hollow time, a time of recovery without recuperation.[199]

---

[199] Avital Ronell, *Stupidity* (Urbana: University of Illinois Press, 2003), 31.

Part 3: Authenticity

The Actor-Network and Irreducible Subjectivity

The non-places of supermodernity are important indicators of the global nature of human relationships through commerce and government and, as areas of transit and temporary occupation, they measure the specifics of regional culture, human diversity, and political systems. Non-places can be set up under any form of government, as colonialism and global corporatism begin to result in similar policies towards the reorganization of space and the role of the surrounding community. Rather than an imperialist subjugation of a population to the new laws of a colonial government, corporate colonialism need only to involve making deals with the existing government, although police and military support is commonly provided to transnational companies, especially those in agriculture, mining and other industries where the corporate intervention involves extensive land use, environmental pollution, or a disruption of local culture. But in corporate colonialist systems, governments may be unstable, so the corporation must establish its own economy and its own governmental structure, one that is able to abide whatever changes take place in regional power struggles. On the level of local influence, cultural homogenization through consumerism is the most successful means of asserting a global measure of uniform contemporaneity across societies that have different ecologies, technologies, forms of government, systems of religious control, and immanent social needs. Homogenization, which has been identified as a function of capitalism, is a measure of difference and of the control of difference.

In *Supermodernism,* Ibelings describes a supermodernist architectural ethos that reflects the function of homogenization as well as of a subsequent setting up of a social hierarchy of non-place:

> It cannot be denied that a great many designs and buildings have seen the light of day since the 1990s that are characterized by a coolness, smoothness and abstraction that frustrates any attempt to invest them with meaning and that have no particular relationship with their surroundings. And this applies just as much to the architecture of the thoughtful few as it does to the products of the unreflective majority.[200]

Unlike postmodernist architecture, characterized by statements made about space, architectural practice or location, which often result in stylistic collisions, supermodernism deflects a reading of social involvement or commentary through a pretense to neutrality. The semiotic vacuum that remains is a fitting metaphor for the space of this architecture. The style is not as devoid of messages as Ibelings wishes it could be.[201] Through formal abstraction and lack of regional considerations, the buildings, many designed by star architects, directed at "the thoughtful few" and ostensibly marveled at by "the unreflective majority," are sometimes complete non-sequiturs in the environment, out of place and dominating the natural landscape and regional townscape, effectively disrupting organic processes of community-building, and uprooting an entire work force.[202]

---

[200] Ibelings, *Supermodernism: Architecture in the Age of Globalization,* 143.

[201] In the preference for an architecture without meaning, there may be a suggestion that the "thoughtful few" have risen to power because of their disregard for regionalism, a disregard displayed as large supermodernist structures in the environments of both the thoughtful few and those who have built them, who clean them, and who work at the front desks. Analyzing design, construction, or motive might tip the balance away from abstraction and towards realism, or practicality.

[202] A concentration of supermodernist architecture can be found in the fantasias of Dubai, Abu Dhabi, and Beijing contracted between 2000 and 2005. To their

As mentioned earlier, human rights enter the picture even at the planning stages. Many large building projects in the Emirates, for example, whose signifier is globalization, cannot be carried out in a period of global economic crisis without the use of foreign migrant construction crews, whose conditions of employment often mean forfeiting their claim to basic human rights.[203] Attention to human rights is not only about worker abuse, it is also about erasing details of the existing social structure, whose traditions are funneled into quick transitions by corporate development, and whose familiar spaces of daily life are wiped off the map. There is a loss of public agency when business and government are conducted away from the people. There is no coolness present, only an oppressive heaviness that infuses the architecture with the questionable ethics of its construction, and which becomes a fitting symbol for the supermodernist social condition, that of enforcement. The non-places of supermodernism exist closer to home as well, if Dubai or Beijing does not happen to be one's home. The homeless shelter, the unemployment office, the social services office, and the precinct station bring into the clean architectural scene of supermodernism a jury-rigged sensibility. The post-post-

---

credit, some of the architects are using the liberal, or in some cases, absent building codes to test new technologies of sustainable and low-impact architectural environments. But as Ibelings notes in the remainder of the passage quoted above, "there is growing evidence of a tendency to employ innovative technology for the purpose of conjuring up novel sensations," bringing the intentions back away from social consciousness and towards social disregard. The sustainability aspect is explored for the fun of it, because it is technically sweet, that is, difficult to resist.

[203] Human Rights Watch, "'The Island of Happiness': Exploitation of Migrant Workers on Saadiyat Island, Abu Dhabi," May 19, 2009, http://www.hrw.org/reports/2009/05/18/island-happiness (accessed March 4, 2012). As of March 2012, conditions for workers have improved, due largely to the efforts of human rights advocates who have successfully lobbied New York University, the Guggenheim Museum, and the Louvre, all of which are constructing compounds at this site, to demand independent monitoring of workers rights.

modernist functional box that arises on the landscape is made of cardboard, or else it has an illegibly tagged New York City Housing Authority sign bolted near the entrance.

Either way, the situation comes back to the body that feels it first-hand. A global sort of subjectivity and relation to body and identity emerges that is in conversation with still-present local, regional and personal framings of subjective reality. Lefebvre's dissection of spatial experience lays out the categories of physical space (nature, the cosmos), mental space (logic, formal abstraction) and social space (social practice and "sensible phenomena," including the imaginary, projects and projections, symbols, and Utopias).[204] The body moves through space, and a place is mapped over the body in terms of culture, custom, representation, and exercises of the mind. The Bauhaus legacy, according to Lefebvre, means that: "[Social] space opened up to perception, to conceptualization, just as it did to practical action. And the artist passed from objects in space to the concept of space itself."[205] The "three moments of social space" are "the perceived-conceived-lived triad (in spatial terms: spatial practice, representations of space, representational spaces)."[206] By means of a rigorous application of form to function in everything from teapots to educational complexes, the Bauhaus ethos made clear the necessity of all that it was not. The designs of the Bauhaus, which came from a recognition of totality – the total work of art as the design of living, the total system of integrated object, material, body, navigational route – described a precise space for living. The Bauhaus made clear with its

---

[204] Lefebvre lays out the logic of his differentiations of space throughout *The Production of Space,* but the clearest guide to these ideas can be found in the first chapter, "Plan of the Present Work," 1 – 67.
[205] Lefebvre, 125.
[206] Ibid., 40.

objects and, eventually, with its architecture, the interactive relationship of all the elements within a space.

It is fitting that Walter Gropius declared the Bauhaus to be an apolitical school, however much it grew from the zeitgeist of Weimar Germany, within a social environment that valued free thinking as part of a determined push into an uncensored future. Similarly, it would seem that Latour's Actor-Network Theory is not a political theory. However, like the Bauhaus ethos, when applied to a political situation, or to politicized space (for example, where the citizens and the state are in conflict, or where systems of inequality are set in place and then challenged) ANT reveals its political function. Like its relational function, ANT's political function is based on the connecting points of the interaction of its elements. When political power structures such as the state-corporate complex are re-coded as a system of networks, the "generative paths" linking the elements/actors who have consolidated political and economic power become apparent. Everyone else's connections to the same systems can be mapped as well, and a network of inequalities can no longer be taken as a reflection of naturally occurring hierarchies. While many know that they live under the authority of a large and largely unresponsive (except in regard to use of violence to maintain order) state-corporate conglomerate – and that they may be near the bottom rung, as it were, the apolitical ANT reveals that there is no bottom and there is no top, only an active and always-forming matrix of the present moment. The Bauhaus sought to create an organized city based on categories of use and need, and designed complexes that were meant to be small villages, but which disregarded the value of the existing social connections. They wanted to start over, and disregarded the particular spatial and cultural history that an implementation of their designs for a new city would destroy.

Like autonomy, authenticity is a catalyst, an influence that creates links between subjectivities, concepts, objects, and environments. Authenticity is neither an object nor a goal, nor is it like a kernel of truth embedded at the core of identity, location, or exchange. It causes a reaction in collective experience. The claim of authenticity never has to be made. It is not a value or quality, but is a pathway along routes of continual negotiation and change. What is changed, or exchanged, includes elements of the human psyche, and of nonhuman consciousness as well. It includes connections between the interior and the exterior, and like its opposite, the consumerist spectacle, it can embrace whatever is amenable, whatever makes itself available for experience. This includes constructs of consumerist culture that are everywhere: advertising, fashion, the organization of life into a system of routines and habits, tourist economies, homogenization of desire, mass consciousness, destruction of regionalism, environmental exploitation, and the corporate-military-state complex. Authenticity within these constructs requires possession of the present through the conscious interrogation of the moments of daily life, questioning how mundane activity is organized, as well as questioning the truly extraordinary.

Authenticity can be compared to Internet protocol, an algorithm to be applied to problems simply stated, constructing events without morality and without making value judgments – an algorithm that can create new links and avenues out of a seemingly closed hierarchical system into a decentralized system of continual give and take. A protocol for authenticity would include that which is voluntary, ungovernable, and potentially immeasurable. Unlike protocol, it requires dedication and commitment from ethical actors whose individual connectivity may be either long or short term, but who can stimulate change when acting collectively. Change, in real terms, may mean the overthrow of dictators, for example, as we continue to witness in

Arab states. Or it may manifest as holding corporations accountable for their employment practices, which occurred recently when Apple customers demanded that Apple, Inc. make improvements in the conditions of the Chinese workers who assemble iPhones and iPads. The citizen and the consumer are hooked into the market and are fully embedded in the space of the corporation-state, but they are also able to respond proactively to situations of injustice and become effective constituents in a previously closed process. Action opens the network. Each individual or group, each link formed, may have a different idea of the content of their actions, but the end result, as in the end result of a new line of code added to a program, is a rupture in the system that enables pathways to form away from the structure of hierarchies and new functions to be enacted.

Authentic culture does not emerge from consumerist culture. Oppressive realities do not contain possibilities for change, openness, democracy, justice or environmental health. The harmful schemes that have emerged from excessive capitalism and corporatism have resulted in an enforced homogenization of many aspects of individual and collective living, including the homogenization of language. The earth itself is being stripped of the diversity of species as the rate of animal and plant extinction increases, and as desertification occurs in former rain forests. Because the hierarchical models for understanding space, place, and relationship have functioned for millennia, we use them to understand the world. Hierarchies concentrate power but are not designed primarily for social stability. They allow the violence of war, poverty, theocracy, dictatorship and oligarchy, genocide, and environmental devastation to become the ordinary backdrop for life on earth. First contact is complete. Homogenization and stratification are the tools of the corporate-state-military complex. Networks, ecologies and autonomous agents are the tools of change, already in place. Locating the authentic in situations of global crisis is critical to the survival of the planet.

A rhizomatic model of culture, where identity refreshes itself
without the burden of identification, allows a critique of the
everyday to be constructed. The authentic can be located, even
within the extremes of global consumerism, allowing for a
discovery of various and simultaneous starting points for
political resistance. An application of ANT to the seemingly
automatic processes whereby most are trapped in a work-
consume-survive triad, places the individual in an active role.
Individual identity remains the irreducible element, the one that
is always in relation to the other elements as part of what
becomes experience, and the one that changes in these
relationships. The experience of the self and of others is a
conversation, the occurrence of which, when taking place within
a hierarchical power structure whose ordering system is based
on current political and economic inclusions/exclusions,
prevents interaction and mutability, and it is here that identities
become fixed. Latour writes:

> Instead of constantly predicting how an actor should
> behave, and which associations are allowed a priori, AT
> [Actor-Network Theory] makes no assumption at all, and in
> order to remain uncommitted needs to set its instrument by
> insisting on infinite pliability and absolute freedom. In itself
> AT is not a theory of action, no more than cartography is a
> theory on the shape of coast lines and deep sea ridges; it just
> qualifies what the observer should suppose in order for the
> coast lines to be recorded in their fine fractal patterns. Any
> shape is possible provided it is obsessively coded as
> longitude and latitude. Similarly any association is possible
> provided it is obsessively coded as heterogeneous
> associations through translations. It is more an
> infralanguage than a metalanguage. It is even less than a

descriptive vocabulary; it simply opens, against all a-priori reductions, the possibility of describing irreductions.[207]

By the logic of the actor-network, "infinite pliability and absolute freedom" are outside the sphere of political authority, however much these qualities are suspended or denied either partially or absolutely by most governments. An infralanguage, a connection that is not necessarily language-based, develops outside the space of power struggles and polemics. The question emerges regarding whether an open society is possible at all, however, and perhaps the pyramidal model of government, economics and population control is a necessary fiction.

The "mental space" of Lefebvre's spatial triad is the space of categories of experience. It is where the power of ideology, which is the practice of valuating experience, affects the physical space. In an ideological clash that may occur in physical space, sticks, stones, bones and words can all be recognized as tools. The creation of ideologies and the categorization of experience form a foundation for the hierarchy of experiences, ideas, and circumstances. The establishment of a social hierarchy permits a rational denial of the influence of systems for power in the observation of direct experience. The experience of the quotidian is seen as singular, even if it is a communal experience, and singular experience becomes the foundation for a non-aligned and socially isolated sense of identity. While the formation of individual identity may represent the irreducible experience, the experience is not one of isolation or alienation. Irreducible identity has a temporal aspect that allows for the recognition of one's relationship to histories, which are necessary in the formation of personal identity. This also opens up pathways for migration into human interaction as

---

[207] Latour, "The Trouble With Actor-Network-Theory."

one finds allies and forms affinities. Connectivity occurs in the interrelationships of human and nonhuman bodies, machine bodies, ideas, ecologies, and technologies based on the assertion of personal identity from within the experience of community. The individual need not live inside a fantasy of individualism in order to attain a satisfying measure of personal freedom and make a claim for human rights as a birthright. The individual's constructed identity has the identical value as his or her true or possible other identities. The point is not to authenticate the individual, but to authenticate the construction and the experience of that constructed self.

Subjectivity and Collectivity: Félix Guattari's *The Three Ecologies*

> How do we change mentalities, how do we reinvent social practices that would give back to humanity - if it ever had it - a sense of responsibility, not only for its own survival, but equally for the future of all life on the planet, for animal and vegetable species, likewise for incorporeal species such as music, the arts, cinema, the relation with time, love and compassion for others, the feeling of fusion at the heart of the Cosmos?
>
> Félix Guattari, *The Three Ecologies*[208]

Guattari's *The Three Ecologies* is a call to action on individual, collective, mental, emotional, and levels of

---

[208] Félix Guattari, "The Ecosophic Object," *Chaosmosis* (1995), quoted in translator's notes, Guattari, *The Three Ecologies,* trans. Ian Pindar and Paul Sutton (London and New York: Continuum, 2008), 82.

interrelationship. Guattari contends that we are caught in a current of global capitalism that pulls us, stupefied, into the ecological disaster that is rendering the earth unlivable. The doomsday call is not a warning from Guattari so much as it is an exposé of the invitation from the forces of global capitalism to participate in our own destruction, a rather forceful and hard-to-resist summons from a powerful authority. We all hear it. Guattari answers the invitation with the formation of an ecological philosophy, what he terms an "ecosophy," an approach to solving the contemporary crisis by laying out a foundation of resistance on three levels: the individual, the collective, and the environmental. Guattari refers to each as part of an ecology, and together they comprise a means of resistance. Included in the ecologies are human and nonhuman elements, technologies and processes, natural environments, plants and other animals, built environments, communications systems, ideas, empathy, artwork, economies and interactions between and among these elements. The elements are built and created in their own continuous interactive stream in the creation of a singularity. "Singularity" is not synonymous with "individual," but refers to a condition that the individual can access. Guattari's three ecologies are mental ecology, social ecology and environmental ecology. These interactive ecologies are not Guattari's invention, nor are they systems that we must build; he is identifying networks that already exist. His description of the three ecologies differentiates specific aspects of a system of connectivity that, as a whole, functions as an undifferentiated network of multiple and non-hierarchical points of exchange. For the system to be effective in restoring equilibrium in the individual, collective, and environmental realms however, it must be activated as a network of opposition.

Guattari's term ecosophy, a combination of ecology and philosophy, has embedded in it an idea of a consciously renewed ecology that speaks of many more agents and influences than the concept of survival of the fittest, the model that has been in place since the nineteenth century, can accommodate. Ecosophy is the process of recreating a just world. The term singularity, for example, which is the object of mental ecology, places the individual in a milieu of influences and actions, human and nonhuman, and erases suggestions of isolation within an individual essential self, a self that is ostensibly engaged in a fight for survival, space, and generation. In discussing the first of the three ecologies, Guattari writes, "For its part, mental ecosophy will lead us to reinvent the relation of the subject to the body, to phantasm, to the passage of time, to the 'mysteries' of life and death. It will lead us to search for antidotes to mass-media and telematic standardization, the conformism of fashion, the manipulation of opinion by advertising, surveys, etc."[209]

Mental ecology is a quality of subjective presence that is integral to collective human and nonhuman systems. It requires a conscious resistance to manipulation and control by consumerism, which is the mental and physical space of the everyday within the global culture of capitalism. A balanced mental ecology resists enforced conformism and cultural stagnation by making connections across disciplines and species that can operate outside the space of consumerism to reconfigure the space/ecology/mentality of the self. Consumerism creates a capitalist subjectivity,[210] which permeates individual subjectivity as well as creating a mass subjectivity. It alienates, isolates, and minimizes authentic subjectivity by offering limited and conformist frames of reference for possible ideas, ideologies, and actions within the specifics of the everyday. Capitalist subjectivity is the ideology of capitalism. Mental ecology "organizes micropolitical and microsocial practices . . .

---

[209] Guattari, *The Three Ecologies*, 24.
[210] Ibid., 34.

regarding the formation of the unconscious,"[211] in order to create or locate the event that allows the consciousness to break free. An individual consciousness of resistance to consumer culture forms in the moments of the everyday in an ethical and aware practice of daily life, as well as in the creation of an aesthetic that projects alternate states of consciousness or suggests new systems of interpretation and interrelatedness.

Guattari's event may be the smallest element or occurrence, an element that could easily go unnoticed, but if noticed and employed as an element of resistance to the mind-meld of capitalist subjectivity, may be the cause of a singular transitioning into creative and re-creative experiences of the present. As in Badiou's concept of the event, the real is created from within the simulacrum. Badiou's formula for the re-creative experience, for the precipitation of the event, is repetition in the creation of a passage from finite to infinite (1 + 1 + 1), along with the operation of the cut, an interruption or rupture inside the process of repetition, creating a dialectical result of universality and singularity. The event is the interruption, the event causes change, and the event is always political.[212] If one applies Badiou's formula to his own insistence that English is not a language of philosophy, and that Greek, French and German are languages of philosophy, one could easily see that working from within the limited framework of the English language, as an American with no American language other than a borrowed English, for example, one is still able to locate the elements of the real or reach the point of the event using these philosophically-impoverished words.

---

[211] Ibid.
[212] Notes based on Alain Badiou in lecture, European Graduate School, August 2010.

A concise description of everyday life as consisting of "Kinship networks . . . reduced to a bare minimum," and "domestic life . . . . poisoned by the gangrene of mass consumption,"[213] identifies the devaluation of the space and time of everyday life as a signifier of the present crisis that can be read in the most mundane and non-scientistic way. In bringing everyday life and the intimate experiences of the individual and the family immediately to the forefront of his argument, Guattari lays the foundation for the necessity of action at the level of daily life in every moment of our routine. Vaneigem describes the everyday as a miserable workaday reality of being suspended in a medium of mere survival under the corporate rule of the terms of our labor. For Vaneigem, all objects and ideas are designated as product; entertainment is culture and consumerism itself is cultural engagement. Guattari begins his analysis at this point and opens it up to the reality of a complete and ever-present non-corporate space, one that already exists and is always in flux. The struggle against consumer culture carries within it a struggle against governments that have no responsibility to the governed, and policing entities that are in place chiefly to patrol and control a civilian population. The challenge is to perceive and recognize the authentic matrix of daily life and to dislodge from within that matrix the manifestations of false culture and extremes of power imbalance, so that what stays afloat is an authentic culture.

The space of Guattari's three ecologies is a networked space. The distinctions between the environmental, social and mental ecologies by which Guattari differentiates the arenas of human experience enable a specific focus that neither creates hierarchies of rights (personal, civil, state, corporate) nor prioritizes one element of the society over another. Recognizing

---

[213] Guattari, *The Three Ecologies*, 19.

difference and permitting difference to operate in its full capacity stimulates ecological equilibrium. Badiou describes the function of difference as much more than a nodal point of resistance against enforced conformity. For Badiou, difference is produced "by means of repetition of the identical."[214] The question of difference carries within it the question of identity as an oppositional process. These questions are not ideologically based, but are questions about the nature of subjectivity and of creating non-opposing and always-in-process individual and collective singularities. Heterogeneity is an actant as well as a product of the ecosophical network, as the contributions from diverse sources to the world ecology are integrated into the stream of the present. Interdependence is a guide to creative action where diversity is a catalyst; multiple points of entry and exit in a dialogue of irresolution provide insight to multiple living histories and guide action into a possible future. This is the process of mental ecology (subjectivity) and social ecology (collectivity) working together.

Haraway examines the human-nonhuman network in terms of bodies and flesh as well as ecologies, and suggests that the network is one in which biological evolution and co-mingling of species, in the writing and re-writing of the codes of DNA, for example, enact primal knowledge. Organisms and environments interact in a relationship of continuous exchange of information. In her essay, *The Companion Species Manifesto: Dogs, People, and Significant Others,*[215] Haraway describes nature and culture as neither totalities nor ordered composites of human and

---

[214] Badiou, lecture, European Graduate School, August 2010.
[215] Donna Haraway, *The Companion Species Manifesto: Dogs, People, and Significant Others* (Chicago: Prickly Paradigm Press, 2003), 8 - 9. Haraway has borrowed the term "partial connections" from the writings of British feminist anthropologist Marilyn Strathern. The additional Haraway quotes in this paragraph are from the same passage.

nonhuman creation of experience. Nor are they dialectically opposed elements in a struggle for synthesis, but rather are "relations of significant otherness," the terms of which are the creation of "'partial connections;' i.e., patterns within which the players are neither wholes nor parts." She suggests a different context for thinking of the relations between nature and culture, what she terms "naturecultures," as a kinship network where biologies and technologies are "co-travelers," and whose exchanges are "written into their genomes [as] a record of couplings and infectious exchanges." A re-ordering of the image of total ecology into a kinship network is merely a description, however. The network is not only wide, it is also deep and, as in Badiou's system of repetition and rupture, there is no resolution:

> There cannot be just one companion species; there have to be at least two to make one. It is in the syntax; it is in the flesh. Dogs are about the inescapable, contradictory story of relationships – co-constitutive relationships in which none of the partners pre-exist the relating, and the relating is never done once and for all. Historical specificity and contingent mutability rule all the way down, into nature and culture, into naturecultures. There is no foundation; there are only elephants supporting elephants all the way down.[216]

Haraway is discussing much more than a strategy for understanding ecological relationships. Like Guattari, she speaks the language of the relationships, which is neither the language of beings nor the language of nothingness, but is the language of metamorphosis, recognizing beings and nothingness as representations of process. Haraway writes, "Species is about biological kind. . . . Post-cyborg, what counts as biological kind troubles previous categories of organism. The machinic and the

---

[216] Ibid., 12.

textual are internal to the organic and vice versa in irreversible ways."[217] Categorization, including that which delineates states of being, creates points of stoppage rather than points of connection, or partial connection, along a network of affinities.

The sense of responsibility that Guattari hopes to find within the humanist elements of the three ecologies attaches motive (survival) to ethical action (doing the right thing). But the content of survival is found chiefly in the networked space of the ecologies and not in a particular sense that humans may have of their own responsibility to preserve the planet. Ecological problems within the mental, social and environmental spheres remain intact regardless of the form of government under which a population is collected. The global order has been built on complexes of interrelationships that are designed to bypass social responsibility in favor of profiteering, as well as on strict control of populations. The Creative Art Ensemble's description of a decentered globalized capitalism correctly identifies the challenges this presents to effective resistance – the enemy cannot be targeted as one large superpower, but is comprised of multiple sources of power; it is leaderless, transnational, and creates economic contracts across all types of governments. Political borders denote corporate zones and the new economic boundaries become visible when an ecological or moral catastrophe occurs: British Petroleum's pollution of the Gulf of Mexico, De Beers' trading in blood diamonds, Bechtel's demands that indigenous people in Bolivia pay for rights to use rainwater, Monsanto's patenting of the food chain in India – and Indiana, Cargill's illegal destruction of primate habitats in Madagascar to produce palm oil, and persistent state-corporate refusal to develop already known ecologically sound technologies that may slow the processes of global warming.

---

[217] Ibid., 15.

Manifest destiny, permission granted by divine right to New World settlers to overtake and claim stewardship of the American continent, is still a guiding principle of American foreign policy, spreading regime change and consumer culture as well as opening vast foreign territories to a borderless style of corporate exploitation. The list of state-corporate partnerships that benefit from divine edict is a long one. Taking responsibility seems too weak a threat to corporate greed and corporate control of populations. But Guattari's ecosophical system represents a complex and potentially endless kinship network that creates ruptures in these systems of control.

Since authority and population control operate on a global scale, it is on this scale that we must respond, even in the process of reclaiming our individual power to act. Guattari calls for nothing short of global revolution as the only means of survival:

> The only true response to the ecological crisis is on a global scale, provided that it brings about an authentic political, social and cultural revolution, reshaping the objectives of the production of both material and immaterial assets. Therefore this revolution must not be exclusively concerned with visible relations of force on a grand scale, but will also take into account molecular domains of sensibility, intelligence and desire.[218]

In *A Grammar of the Multitude,* under the heading "The Principle of Individuation," Paulo Virno describes the multitude as signifying "plurality – literally; being-many – as a lasting form of social and political existence, as opposed to the cohesive

---

[218] Guattari, *The Three Ecologies*, 20.

unity of the people."[219] The cohesive unity – "We The People" – is the goal of the Enlightenment ideal of individual rights and freedom within egalitarianism, along with the designation of the duties of the citizen in relation to the state. Citizenship creates the individual and binds her to the state. In the Americas, the economic system of human slavery, the legacy of which has long tentacles reaching into all aspects of contemporary American society, had disenfranchised large segments of the population, representing, in some parts of the New World, the majority of inhabitants. Different, but not difference, is all that individualism allows, at the same time giving those who are different fewer resources within its system of rights and duties.[220] A consensus by a patriarchal tradition that depends on the outright ownership of not only the labor of another but also the body of another had been reached determining who "all" is before individual rights were granted to all. People who had no

---

[219] Paulo Virno, *A Grammar of the Multitude For an Analysis of Contemporary Forms of Life,* trans. Isabella Bertoletti, James Cascaito and Andrea Casson (New York: Semiotext(e), 2004), 76.

[220] During a critique I was leading at the Kansas City Art Institute in the early 1990s, one Native American student prefaced the viewing of his video work with the reminder that Native Americans, as a category, have the highest number of laws applied to them of any group in the United States, and suggested that a group's favor with the state was inversely proportional to the amount of legislation that applies to the group. It is difficult to find information about the exact number of laws that apply to a specific type of citizen, but a clue to Native American legal status can be found at a site by Lindsay G. Robertson, dated June 2001, "Native Americans and the Law: Native Americans Under Current United States Law," University of Oklahoma Law Center, http://thorpe.ou.edu/guide/robertson.html (accessed May 4, 2012), which provides a sampling of treaties, laws and agreements between indigenous nations and the United States government. Through an excess of legislation, indigenous Americans become illegal aliens, and it requires additional specific legislation to make their presence on ancestral land legal again.

power under the tradition of patriarchy were unable to participate in the founding of a new democratic era and an unjust system was created in the name of egalitarianism, within a vast forward-looking program of colonial expansion, genocide and environmental destruction.

If we translate "we the people" into Virno's multitude, where "the many are a singularity,"[221] the question of individual rights becomes a question of differentiation. Communities of resistance arise where injustice creates a distance between the individual and the collective, as in women's rights organizations or the Black Panther Party, for example. The experiential knowledge that marginalized groups have amassed, and which they embody, makes them valuable within a collective process of building culture. The gay community, as well, is one of resistance, although it is gradually being assimilated. Difference, or minority status, is authentic with regard to the gay community but only if one denies the continuum of human sexuality and categorizes populations who love or have sex differently as innately or permanently outside the status quo. Marriage equality and the rush of a sympathetic "heterosexual community" to support marriage equality, when there was no prior rush to simply support the decriminalization of homosexuality or same-sex love, or even a rush to halt the systematic street violence against perceived homosexuals, signifies that same-sex relationships are palatable if they can be made to fit into the social structures that are already in place. Relationships that, by their essence, question the foundation of the isolated family as *the* foundation of human relationships can be assimilated into a corner of that structure, whereby the inherently threatening nature of their challenge is severely compromised.

---

[221] Virno, 76.

Squeezed into a corner of the coveted norm, one must also wear blinders to the complete history of women's oppression, the historical institution of marriage, and the need by the state to re-situate the individual, his or her body, desire (in theory), and sexuality (in practice) so that it, too, conforms. Gay history, women's history, African-American history and all other separated histories as addendums to History, reinforce the marginalization they ostensibly challenge. The measure of equality is not to be found in permission to participate in the status quo. The system cannot be reformed from within, as Rancière reminds us. The cooperative democracy that is required for the planet's survival is not a thing, nor is it a gift from those in power, but is an active and ongoing process of participation. Within scenarios of progress, the specific subjectivity of African-Americans or of sexual minorities, for example, is sacrificed to the status quo. Holding on to the subjective self, however mutable it must be, and living within a collective history are tools for "troubling the previous categories of organism,"[222] for grassroots connectivity and exchanges of the DNA of knowledge and process.

In his 1997 lecture at Goldsmiths College in London, entitled "Race, The Floating Signifier,"[223] Stuart Hall describes a process by which humans become classified by race and are placed in categories that seem not only correct and obvious, but also undeniable. Racial difference is clearly visible to the eye, and systems of control use "obvious" difference to sustain climates of fear of difference where mundane forms of discrimination

---

[222] Donna Haraway, *The Companion Species Manifesto: Dogs, People, and Significant Others*, 15.
[223] Stuart Hall, "Race, the Floating Signifier," lecture at Goldsmiths College, University of London, 1997. The lecture was recorded and produced as a videotape of the same title directed by Sut Jhally for the Media Education Foundation. Jhally's video can be found online at http://video.google.com/videoplay?docid=-8471383580282907865 (accessed May 9, 2012).

may seem to make sense. Hall argues that visible difference is the condition underlying discussions of race, but is not the condition underlying racism. Unlike the immediate process of making correct or incorrect suppositions about people in the common arena of the everyday, the inevitability of being fixed within a racial identity has roots in European expansion to the Americas and the first exposure of Europeans to large populations of those who are authentically different. Hall argues that a guarantee of physical difference is necessary if predictions about behavior, intelligence, physical talent, proclivities, and disposition – things that influence social status and access to power – are to have credibility. Personal traits and racial characteristics are made equivalent, and as such, are the things by which we determine how persons of any particular classification are to be treated within a society, even on a global scale.

DNA testing becomes the scientific tool that produces a guarantee of racial difference, one that may finally do the job after the failures of religion to guide us in questions of who is equal in God's sight, and of anthropology to provide data of measurable physical difference. DNA testing, however, cannot provide an adequate means of classifying humanity, and according to Hall, "until you can classify, you can't generate any meaning at all." [224] When science fails, we fall back on common sense knowledge of physical and cultural distinctions – those qualities that we can see with our own eyes – as evidence that race is a fixed quality. One group is valued over another, or devalued, granted more or fewer rights, given more agency and access to privilege or less, based on evidence of race and ethnicity. Racial stereotyping maintains order by promoting violence to individuals, and by granting permission to certain groups to be violent in the name of social stability and the common good. Hall argues that to debate the obvious, that people are different and *appear* to be different, is to ignore and enable the function of racism that creates a language of race

[224] The quotes in this paragraph are from Stuart Hall, "Race, the Floating Signifier," in lecture at Goldsmiths College, 1997.

itself. Another perspective is that race is a language-based construction, "autonomous of any system of reference," not able to be tested against our actual experience of human diversity, but only within "the play of language." This view tends to ignore difference and in doing so, ignore histories and collective experience. Rather than fixing racial identities, it denies them entirely. Hall describes race as a discursive language in full acknowledgment of difference:

> There are probably differences of all sorts in the world. Difference is a kind of anomalous existence out there, a kind of random series – all sorts of things in what you call the world. There's no reason to deny this reality or this diversity. It's only when these differences have been organized within language, within discourse, within systems of meaning, that the differences can be said to acquire meaning and become a factor in human culture and regulate conduct. That is the nature of what I'm calling 'the discursive concept of race.' Not that nothing exists of differences, but that what matters are the systems we use to make sense, to make human societies intelligible. The systems we bring to those differences, how we organize those differences into systems of meaning within which we can find the world intelligible. And this has nothing to do with denying the "audience test" – if you look around, you'd find we do, after all, look somewhat different from one another.[225]

The position for the anti-racist is not so much "we are all the same," as it is "we must discover the value of diversity." At the center of the question of diversity is the formation of subjectivity within collectivity. Race is not a fixed signifier, it is a floating signifier, one that morphs and mutates with situations, locations, time periods, and in relation to political and social climates. Hall describes race in terms of how it functions within a society: "Race works like a language, and signifiers refer to the systems and concepts of the classification of a culture to its making

---

[225] Ibid.

meaning practices. And those things gain their meaning not because of what they contain in their essence, but in the shifting relations of difference, which they establish with other concepts and ideas in a signifying field."[226]

Science has failed to guarantee that there are essential biological human differences or that race carries within its genes the markers of fixed identity, fixed social placement, or a fixed range of possibilities for relating to the world. Because the weight of racial difference is relational within the discourse of any place or culture, the floating signifier of race carries meaning through history. Racial subjectivity can be read and acquires meaning especially when examined or experienced in terms of authority, privilege, marginalization, social position and agency.

Guattari speaks of *"components of subjectification"* rather than of "subjects" in discussing how subjectivity, racial and otherwise, is formed, making a distinction between the individual and subjectivity. Are components replaceable or interchangeable, or do they come from somewhere outside the body and history of the subject? He states, "Vectors of subjectification do not necessarily pass through the individual, which in reality appears to be something like a 'terminal' for processes that involve human groups, socio-economic ensembles, data-processing machines, etc."[227] Vectors are not objects, or subjects, but are agents that animate a process. Vectors have properties of direction, magnitude, and positioning relative to "socio-economic ensembles." Subjectivity, as in racial identity, is not fixed in time, space or even in history. Race and other human properties and signifiers of identity are real and may remain fixed, or may be temporary, but either way subjectivity is always in relation to the contemporary moment and to the history of identity. It is always in relation to communal history and the writing of history in the present. History is not the only factor. Other factors are innumerable and

---

[226] Ibid.

[227] Guattari, *The Three Ecologies*, 25.

allow for a continuous re-positioning of subjectivity, however modest or radical, always in relation to the subjectivity of others. Relationality is the constant. Guattari's components of subjectification are autonomous influences working in relation to one another to reveal interiority.[228]

Guattari's subject is less a product or creation of an overarching social-cultural-political system than it is a moving part in a network of continuously renewed systems of the present. The diversity we seek, that is meant to replace the constant judgment of difference, therefore, results from fluid individual subjectivities – persons – occupying space in the eventual creation of many communities that are distinct and intertwined within cities, regions, nation-states, and spanning/ignoring/in spite of borders. The influences on each of these elements are potentially endless and include all possibilities of social chaos, violence, and oppression as well as liberation and balanced ecologies. Networks of connectivity are not diagrams for building a better world, but rather describe objective reality in relational terms, which can be charted, and which is always in flux. Far from describing a system of relations wherein nothing is stable, a non-hierarchical organically formed network reveals the emergence of authentic subjectivities and co-responsive collectivities. This is a conversation that is always taking place. In speaking of racial identity, Stuart Hall describes the experience of a world in which there are no guarantees about identity: "Once you enter the politics of the end of the biological definition of race, you are plunged headlong into the only world we have, the maelstrom of a continuously contingent un-guaranteed political argument, debate and practice, a critical politics against racism, which is always a politics of criticism."[229] Guattari's question, quoted at the beginning of this section, asking how we change mentalities, giving back "to humanity . . . a sense of responsibility," is answered here: in plunging into the maelstrom of an un-guaranteed universe, our

---

[228] Ibid., 24 – 25.
[229] Stuart Hall, lecture, Goldsmiths College, London, 1997.

collective responsibility, which we can not see otherwise, becomes apparent.

The organization of law and of power is rendered transparent in the process of locating and creating an authentic self within all aspects of our mobile, mutable, transitioning subjectivities. The singularity is always in conversation with the collective. The problems facing the collective are on the scale of planetary survival. Global awareness is the same thing, at this point, as local awareness. Subjectivities must not strive to fix identity, and must refuse a "perfect mastery of consciousness."[230] We must resist the denial of the collapse of the global into the local; we must allow the interplay of individual and communal forces, of local and global together. If the process seems vague, Guattari suggests that it is like the process of making art: "As in painting and literature, the concrete performance of these [ecosophical] cartographies requires that they evolve and innovate, that they open up new futures, without their authors (*auteurs*) having prior recourse to assured theoretical principles or to the authority of a group, a school or an academy . . . Work in progress!"[231]

Lefebvre comes to a similar conclusion in writing about revolution. The old style of revolution no longer applies, even if the struggle is still between the workers and the ruling class. The division between the ruling class and workers crosses all lines, divides all areas of contemporary society including the sciences, arts, and knowledge itself. Lefebvre describes the contemporary field of resistance:

> Revolution was long defined either in terms of a political change at the level of the state or else in terms of the collective or state ownership of the means of production as such. . . . Today such limited definitions of revolution no longer suffice. The transformation of society presupposes a collective ownership and management of space founded on the permanent participation of the 'interested parties', with

---

[230] Guattari, *The Three Ecologies,* 27.
[231] Ibid.

their multiple, varied and even contradictory interests. . . .
On the horizon, then, at the furthest edge of the possible, it
is a matter of producing the space of the human species –
the collective (generic) work of the species – on the model
of what used to be called 'art'.[232]

Autonomy, Non-Governance. and the Irreducible I: The Films of Barbara Hammer and Charles Atlas

The "finest allegory of simulation"[233] is the very short story,
"*Del rigor en la ciencia*" ("On the Exactitude of Science"),
which Jorge Luis Borges co-wrote with his frequent collaborator
Adolfo Casares, and in which cartography outdoes itself – a map
is created that is as large as the territory it represents; it is
impossible to use.[234] Baudrillard uses the allegory of the map to
describe the process whereby the simulacrum "engenders" the
territory, or object, "the generation by models of the real."[235]
Theoretical writing, or describing the influences and processes
that result in the continuum of daily life – the space of
capitalism, the networks of oppression, the networks of
resistance, and interstitial spaces, ideas and actors – begins to
seem like a similarly unmanageable cartography. Hakim Bey
responds by simply moving aside, into an autonomously created
and named zone of temporary non-interference. Lefebvre's
revolution is one of orientation and Deleuze and Guattari open
up a real territory by providing a view through subjectivity to the
realization that "each of us [is] several."[236] Latour and Haraway
bring a multitude of human, nonhuman, machinic, social and
other presences to the discussion. The territory of the discussion

---

[232] Lefebvre, *The Production of Space*, 422.
[233] Baudrillard, *Simulations*, 1.
[234] See Appendix for the complete text of the story.
[235] Baudrillard, *Simulations*, 2.
[236] Deleuze and Guattari, *A Thousand Plateaus: Capitalism and Schizophrenia*, 3.

expands until it seems to be the size of the territory it is discussing, and the human subject that began the conversation millennia ago has become a tiny agent in an expanding system that attempts to explain our world and our place in it. Perec intervenes with his lonesome exercises in mapping just the present moment, revealing scenes that contain assurances without the fascism of scientistic certainty or the need for end points, insisting that the cartography does not define the territory, but vice-versa. Perec's maps are easy to follow.

The perspectives of these theorists and writers are interwoven, not only one with the other, but also through a shared time period that is neither modern nor post-modern, but is amodern and inclusive. Some theorists share the observation that we can learn to see the present moment and the larger context of our lives more clearly if we borrow from the art making process. Bey's artist is a "Poetic Terrorist," for example, who has the responsibility to wake up the audience from the mesmerizing effect of the commodity spectacle. In an essay, "Chaos," Bey writes:

> The audience reaction or aesthetic-shock produced by PT [Poetic Terrorism] ought to be at least as strong as the emotion of terror – powerful disgust, sexual arousal, superstitious awe, sudden intuitive breakthrough, dada-esque angst – no matter whether the PT is aimed at one person or many, no matter whether it is "signed" or anonymous, if it does not change someone's life (aside from the artist) it fails.[237]

In an essay from the same volume, "Murder – War – Famine – Greed," Bey spells out the role of the terrorist-artist, who "possesses . . . the total radicalization of language . . . which will strike not at living beings but at malign *ideas*, dead-weights on the coffin-lid of our desires. The architecture of suffocation and paralysis will be *blown up* only by our total celebration of

---

[237] Bey, "Chaos: The Broadsheets of Ontological Anarchism (Dedicated to Ustad Mahmud Ali Abd al-Khabir)," in *T.A.Z. The Temporary Autonomous Zone*, 5.

everything – even darkness."[238] The artist's product may show careful attention to perspective, may be realist, may contain tricks and illusions to fool the eye, but it is inside the artist's process rather than in the product of the artwork that the break occurs, where the prior inability to breathe or to move or to know our desires is "blown up."

Bey's terrorist-artist is aiming for significant impact, but Schirmacher has a much cooler view of the radical potential in creative processes. He writes, "It seems obvious that the media is a body-machine that no longer belongs to a modern framework of the grand narratives of emancipation and progress but, rather, to the trivial postmodern tales of 'everybody is an artist' and 'anything goes.'"[239] Hot or cold, the relevance of art is in its performance and relationship to audience. Schirmacher continues, "Postmodern communication technology provides opportunity for mass participation and blurs the distinction between creator and audience."[240] His homo generator is the artist who generates statements that disrupt the effects of commodity culture as a mechanism for control in actual and virtual realities alike, creating another human reality through technology; she is a "radical technologist."[241] Homo generator runs on ambiguity rather than certainty, and not only lives comfortably inside technologies, she creates new aspects of humanness with them. Her discussion about the creative process begins with a discussion of DNA, the construction of the human and of the animal, both "artifacts by nature."[242] Homo generator's revolutionary process is devolution; she is neither singular nor collective, but is sign, symptom, and species.

---

[238] Bey, "Intellectual S/M is the Fascism of the Eighties – The Avant-Garde Eats Shit and Likes It," in *T.A.Z. The Temporary Autonomous Zone,* 42.

[239] Schirmacher, "Homo Generator: Media and Postmodern Technology," in *Culture on the Brink,* 69.

[240] Ibid.

[241] Ibid., 70.

[242] Schirmacher, "Homo Generator: Media and Postmodern Technology," in *Culture on the Brink,* 71.

Lefebvre discusses art processes in terms of requiring a revolutionary model that includes more than "the rational organization of production and the equally rationalized management of society as a whole."[243] For Lefebvre, revolution must be a permanent collective process, without a finished product. In the last pages of *The Production of Space,* he writes: "On the horizon, then, at the furthest edge of the possible, it is a matter of producing the space of the human species – the collective (generic) work of the species – on the model of what used to be called 'art'; indeed, it is still so called, but art no longer has any meaning at the level of an 'object' isolated by and for the individual."[244]

While Bey's artist mines the productive space of chaos and may be a lone figure providing a new language for creating autonomous spaces, and Lefebvre's autonomous actor is a collective, a "local power,"[245] each describes the creation of an alternative to universal commoditization that currently controls populations economically and socially. The process is the means, and especially in terms of Lefebvre, in order for it to work, it must not reach a point of completion. He is referring to the process as being at the "edge of the possible." The artist's authentic process is one of not only stirring up or shocking people to a new awareness, but more specifically of working at the edge of what is possible to articulate and push past that point, not to shock or stimulate, but to see what is there.

Gary Genosko's introduction to *The Three Ecologies* synthesizes Guattari's relationship to art processes:

> The best artists don't repeat themselves, they start over and over again from scratch, uncertain with each new attempt precisely where their next experiment will take them, but then suddenly, spontaneously and unaccountably, as the painter Francis Bacon has observed, 'there comes something

---

[243] Lefebvre, *The Production of Space,* 422.
[244] Ibid.
[245] Ibid., 382.

which your instinct seizes on as being for a moment the thing which you could begin to develop'. Life is a work in progress, with no goal in sight, only the tireless endeavour to explore new possibilities, to respond to the chance event - the singular point - that takes us off in a new direction. As Bacon once remarked, 'I always think of myself not so much as a painter but as a medium for accident and chance.'[246]

The process of starting over with each new work is an experimental process, regardless of medium or genre. Bacon's process not only allowed or welcomed "accident and chance," he expected these elements to speak through him and bring chaos into the performance of the artwork. As in the work of Bey's Poetic Terrorist, chaos restores order by breaking out of the fiction imposed by an enforced social stasis and, in the process, finds the truth that is already there.

Everything is not chaotic, however, and everyone is not an artist. We learn to make art in the process of becoming autonomous, which is not an end process, but which enables the creative invention of the contemporary and finds a space to move it into. In terms of Actor-Network Theory (ANT), the autonomous space is created by links, and there are no boundaries or bounding boxes, as other metaphors of the art process describe. Relationships created in the art process are temporary, depending on actions and the creation/direction of new links. ANT maps the process of the production of space and the production of actions and perspectives, which are autonomously created and communicated across a range of links with virtually infinite possibilities for direction and expansion in both space and time.

In writing about artistic "virtuosity," Virno refers to the artistic process as performance:

[246] Gary Genosko, Translator's Introduction, Guattari, *The Three Ecologies,* 8. The quotes from Francis Bacon within the text are from David Sylvester, *The Brutality of Fact: Interviews with Francis Bacon* (London: Thames and Hudson, 1987), 54 and 140.

Let us consider carefully what defines the activity of virtuosos, of performing artists. First of all, theirs is *an activity which finds its own fulfillment (that is, its own purpose) in itself,* without objectifying itself into an end product, without settling into a "finished product," or into an object which would survive the performance. Secondly, it is *an activity which requires the presence of others,* which exists only in the presence of an audience.

An activity without an end product: the performance of a pianist or of a dancer does not leave us with a defined object distinguishable from the performance itself, capable of continuing after the performance has ended.[247]

As with Bey's Poetic Terrorism, and with ANT's network, an audience is necessary. However, the creation of an audience is not equivalent to the creation of a work of art that does not produce a finished object, especially since the product is the performance itself of the work. Virno cites pianist Glenn Gould as a virtuoso performer who wanted to remove the audience from his performances, making the act of performance an act of labor rather than an act of art. The problem, then, is in defining the product of Gould's labor, a product that remains as work and never materializes into object. The process of painting most often produces an object, as do other art processes. In an authentic experimental process, the art object is not the location of the art, however – the object does not contain the art; the object is the residue and record of the process, the evidence of a performance. The art, as experiment and as autonomous activity, is located in the performance, although the object as the record of the performance continues to speak to the audience long after the process of making it is finished.

The audience is required, and is always present in both the performer and the performance in the processes of queer artists, whose work, in order for it to be queer, must be an

---

[247] Virno, *A Grammar of the Multitude For an Analysis of Contemporary Forms of Life,* 52.

announcement of presence itself. Queer used to mean "gay and lesbian," and it continues to be used as slang for "homosexual," but the term has evolved to include a spectrum of sexualities and bodies that find themselves out of alignment with the status quo. It has evolved into an unfinished discourse on all kinds of difference related to transformation – being and becoming, transiting through discourses of the body and identity (including the cyborg and nonhuman identities), as well as discourses on crossing into territories and physical places, especially territories that are used to delineate nationality, race and ethnicity. Queer is a virtuoso performance that is never finished. Queer has mixed everything up and has done so rather brilliantly, and stupidly, starting from the grassroots level. The stupidity of queer is its foolish forays into the unknown of social and personal identity, mixing things up without much thought for where legitimization might come from. The consequences are serious, dividing families, being alienated from the norm, risking poverty, violence, and psychological distress. Each of these is a Pandora's box, which intrepid queers open both knowingly and in complete ignorance. There is an element of hope in this story, as well, which seems to come from love. Queer theory has proponents and experts now, but before there was queer theory, there were simply queers: leaderless and lawless, forming affinities and inventing themselves in the process. The unacknowledged mother of queer theory, however, is the feminine – powerful, pliable, loathed, feared and desired.

Two filmmakers who work within an ethic/aesthetic of the queer I and the principle of the feminine are Barbara Hammer and Charles Atlas. Hammer's films from the 1970s instruct the viewer in how to speak in a language of eroticism and self-discovery that was being invented in the process of filmmaking; hers is mostly a performance-based language of the inseparable body-mind, spoken in the tense of the past-future. Hammer's early films are part narrative and part social process. She worked with performers and artists, but also with other women – anyone who could make herself available on the day of shooting.[248] The performers in the early films improvised within a set of instructions, and tried out – or tried on – any number of new assertions of self in a play to reclaim nothing less than their humanity. The performers were portraying an ideal as well: autonomous women in a collective experience of activism, sex, food, and communion with the natural world.

In her films from the 1970s, Hammer sets up a dialogue that is simultaneously interior and exterior, and that defines and then negates the essential speaking I as it migrates to other forms of speech: we, us, our, all. In films such as *Dyketactics, Superdyke,* and *Double Strength*, made between 1974 and 1978, Hammer isolates the feminine presence from its restrictive political and social framework, which was a place of weakness and degradation, and examines the feminine as a free body without references. Abstraction of image, an uncertain timeline, and the suggestion that the work has dipped into an ongoing narrative unify performer and audience. Images on the screen are meant to carry through to actions in other physical spaces, so that what is shown on the screen can be enacted in real life. There is no difference between the real life of the performances and the continuation of the performances without camera or film. Hammer treats the space beyond the threshold of social acceptance as another complete and expanding universe. She does not create that universe so much as point in its direction. She reveals that the feminine presence without references is a lesbian. The feminine presence in her films is one without an opposite, ungoverned and ungovernable. The body is where space begins, and in Hammer's work the body language spoken is a Creole of nature worship and physical erotic genius. She might not use the word feminine in reference to the project of her early films, but the misogyny that her work exorcises is

---

[248] As a young woman, I volunteered to be in Hammer's film *Superdyke*. It seems as though I fell easily into the project, along with a variety of friends, lovers, and women I knew from San Francisco's queer scene. Based on Hammer's directions, we painted some of the props in our living room – cardboard shields that read "Amazon."

certainly hatred of the feminine. Misogyny is deeply ingrained and conditioned into every aspect of the social realm, so much so as to seem natural; we are born into this hatred. While Hammer was making these films, gay men were being ridiculed, beaten up and arrested for their femininity (and they still are). Lesbians, however, were striving for some form of visibility – for the right to exist outside of the traditional male and female binary. Visibility may create a target, but invisibility causes a slow death. Artists like Hammer took on the challenge to fabricate the visible dyke.

Dyketactics (1974),[249] a film just under four minutes, which Hammer refers to as "the first lesbian-lovemaking film to be made by a lesbian,"[250] creates a subject – lesbian woman – that is both singular and iconic. The film opens onto a group of women walking barefoot through grass. They carry candles and a dildo. Are these for ceremony or for play? Is there a difference? Laughing, jumping, dancing in circles, lying on the ground, and then playing in a stream – these actions summon a fictitious primal woman, apolitical, and pre-historic. Hammer borrows freely from New Age feminist tropes of goddess and nature worship in a pantomime of Western pagan ritual, but the borrowing and miming is a foil for the real action, a ritual display of "lesbian-lovemaking" in scenes where non-sequential aspects of the editing present time and place as abstract elements. Intellectual frameworks are not articulated in this work; sensual love and sexual pleasure form the medium for women's knowledge. The performers work with a vague awareness (and obvious amusement) of an inauthentic but no less valid history – stories and lies that speak to the truth of being outside of history. A body-history of women is fabricated from a core of sexuality and the notion of the prison of women's biology is rejected, its construction toppled by the lush sensuality that the body brings forth. The community declares

---

[249] Barbara Hammer, *Dyketactics and Other Films from the 1970s.* DVD. Barbara Hammer, 2007.
[250] Hammer, *Hammer! Making Movies out of Sex and Life* (New York: The Feminist Press, 2010), 27.

itself in this ahistorical setting, with its false mythologies and inauthentic rituals. "I do. I speak. I am here." In *Dyketactics,* the sexual scene that follows scenes of communal ritual – the first lesbian sex scene created by a lesbian – must therefore be the first lesbian sex scene, period. Inherent in Hammer's filmmaking is the assumption that the lesbian cannot be defined by anyone else, and besides, the definition is not text-based. It is based in experience, the activity that "stupidity exposes while intelligence hides."[251] The rituals require no research. They are a blend of popular culture and the communal enactment of a highly nuanced performance of feminism, neither correct nor incorrect, neither tested nor historicized. This performance of feminism is an effective collective mash-up of sexual activity, the desire to be free of oppressive references, and permission to invent an unfinished product of the feminine.

Hammer's lesbian subjectivity is composed of familiar, sentimental and even kitschy poetic metaphors for naïve pleasure. Sensual and sexual love takes place surrounded by flowers and trees, fruit, sand and soil, curious rock formations, sun and shadow, bones and candles. Her process creates a new, yet familiar (flowers, circles and sunlight), visual language of direct sexuality and the open female body. The body is open in the sense that it no longer hides. It has become visible and has done so on its own terms – actual as well as idealized. Details of identity, or the expression of individual identity, seem less significant than the idea of pushing the newly fabricated self, the newly constructed subjectivity, into existence by collectively performing her. She has been removed from history and so creates a play space of the present in order to drive a wedge into the space of the future.

The lesbian body expresses power as breasts, vulva, clitoris, hands, buttocks, toes, eyes, mouth. Hammer's films reverse the process of pornography's creation of the female body as an obscene manifestation of male consciousness. The lesbian body is the woman without men. It opens up the space around it by

---

[251] Avital Ronell, *Stupidity,* 10.

using ordinary surroundings (sand, soil, water) in the ritual summoning of ungoverned and ungovernable woman. The camera must be a lesbian as well. It explores this body with a different eye; pleasure seems apparent both in front of and behind the lens. Questions arise about isolating the lesbian – as entity, behavior, and relationship – from a broader context, but Hammer's films decenter the broader context and suggest that all subjectivities share a politicized social space, without margin and without center. In her films, there seems to be little question that lesbianism produces a politics of opposition, and the images of daily life as well as of an imagined Utopia (as filmed in public parks) are part of a political language. She writes, "The 70s were a heady time for newly self-identified feminist women. Many of us were attracted to each other and didn't hesitate to act on those passions. We were in and out of bed between protests, demonstrations, and art making."[252]

Where *Dyketactics* conceives of the primary feminine subject, *Superdyke* (1975) represents the lesbian multitude. The "Superdykes" of the film are urban *guerillieres,* who rove the streets of San Francisco in bands, marching to City Hall to announce their presence in the world, and infiltrating corporate spaces with their lesbian desire. One Superdyke brings vibrators into Macy's Department Store and uses them (while fully clothed) at the sales counters, in the aisles and on the escalators, surrounded by curious and amused shoppers. The revolution is full of slapstick humor, combined with a casual pastiche of non-specific and loosely constructed references to origin stories. The film closes on a scene "in the country": a ritual is performed inside a teepee where naked women and girls sway arm in arm, and then examine and pass along a series of dried bones; they cleanse one another with sand, and then leave the teepee to perform a circle dance. Native kitsch, indeed. But is this in any sense a space of collective memory, a space of a matriarchal past? Are the performers going backwards in time, or are they moving into the future? The humor, the jury-rigged mythology, the performance of rituals that have no history outside of this

---

[252] Hammer, *Hammer! Making Movies out of Sex and Life,* 26.

film, become an invitation to participate. There are no elitists here. Theoretical or mythological exactitude is not part of the program. The atemporal aspect of the narrative, as it seems to move between past and future, addresses the writing of history as past and future together, a perspective that being left omitted from the record provides. The space-time of these films brings to mind Hakim Bey's "intercalary intervals"[253] of unlegislated time, and space (sun, stream, field, bed) as place within a subjective timeframe. One does not have to be an anthropologist to understand the language of a circle of women, the countryside, sunlight, and an open and naked multitude of dancers.

Haraway rejects the feminist imagery that Hammer embraces, although Hammer only discusses one part of the binary opposition she has set up; she does not name the other (male, patriarchal, socially conditioned). Haraway writes:

> Identities seem contradictory, partial, and strategic. With the hard-won recognition of their social and historical constitution, gender, race, and class cannot provide the basis for belief in "essential' unity. There is nothing about being female that naturally binds women. There is not even such a state as "being" female, itself a highly complex category constructed in contested sexual scientific discourses and other social practices. Gender, race, or class-consciousness is an achievement forced on us by the terrible historical experience of the contradictory social realities of patriarchy, colonialism, and capitalism.[254]

If Haraway is correct, if being female is a construction of patriarchal capitalism, then what in the world is a lesbian? Haraway seems to contradict everything that Hammer's films express, except that Hammer's perspective has always been that of the performer rather than the intellectual, and her discoveries, conclusions, and the I that she is naming, are figurations of

---

[253] Bey, *T.A.Z. The Temporary Autonomous Zone,* 103.
[254] Haraway, "A Manifesto for Cyborgs," in *The Haraway Reader,* 13 – 14.

protest, glimpses of autonomy, and performances of otherness. She is not searching for the essential female – an end product. She is fully engaged in filmic experimentation and discovery, refusing to differentiate between audience and performer, during either the filming or the screening process. Regarding *Dyketactics,* Hammer writes, "Every frame in the film has an image of touching. Touch precedes sight in ontological human development and the connection of the two was an important aesthetic principal in my early films. The audience feels in their bodies what they see on the screen."[255]

While *Dyketactics* is a beautiful film, one of the most remarkable films of Hammer's early collection is *Double Strength* (1978), in which Hammer and movement artist Terry Sendgraff perform on a trapeze, while their voice-overs express passion, tenderness and joy at the beginning of their new love relationship. The movement on the trapeze is rigorous and graceful. The body's intelligence is juxtaposed with the mind's refusal to analyze. The first voice speaks:

> There's some way that I connect with you that is not intellectual, but is emotional, and body-wise, that is very satisfying to me. And when you were . . . had your head between my breasts this morning, and when you were sucking on my breast, I just . . . I was . . . it was just thrilling. I just had very deep rushings going through. And it was good because it was continual. It wasn't just one and then it was over. How are you feeling?

The second voice responds:

> This morning, especially when I had my head between your breasts, I felt like I was home. I felt like I was in pure contentment. It's like, the softness of your skin . . . I just . . . I don't know . . . I just can't . . . the words don't seem to really be able to say what it's like, because it just goes all the way inside of me. It touches everything inside of me.

---

[255] Hammer, 65.

> It's like I can feel it all the way in my blood, my bones, and even in my hair and my eyes, and it's almost like a feeling of . . . purity, in the sense, with me, purity meaning openness and perfection, and like the universe, like an eternity that goes on and on and on in a flowing that is right. It just feels right. It feels natural, in a sense of being part of nature, part of being altogether and whole.[256]

Nature, purity, sucking, soft skin, contentment and home: this list mixes place, quality, action, adjective, and emotion, which convey the promiscuity of Hammer's language. The movement artists move into an autonomous space through their love relationship. The film is a record of a conversation that becomes the voice-over, but it is also a record of the autonomous and ungovernable female body. The body speaks, not of activism and politics, but of physical "rushings" and "flowing." The body is naked because the performance is a process of reclamation, an acknowledgment of the irreducible I, free of references. The irreducible I is not a finished product. It is mutating, performing itself in blood, bones, breasts, eyes, hair – thrilling itself into view rather than searching for a dense core. In the context of the over-legislated female body, this out-of-context feminine presence and its non-intellectualized voice put body and mind back together in the world.

Charles Atlas, whose work belongs to an entirely different visual spectrum, speaks another language of performance within a similar realignment of space and time. His 2011 film, *Turning,* on which he collaborated with composer Antony, is a documentary about the 2006 European tour by the group Antony and the Johnsons. Each production along the tour includes a series of live performances by thirteen women who, each in turn, stand on the stage beside the band, posed on a revolving platform. Two cameras that are focused on the revolving performer send images, mostly in close-up, to a video mixer that Atlas uses to create a composite live image. The composite

---

[256]Barbara Hammer, *Double Strength,* on *Dyketactics and Other Films from the 1970s.*

image is projected behind Antony and the band during their performance. Each woman is simultaneously live on stage and live on video. Promotional text for the film appears on the *Turning* web site:

> *Turning*, based on a critically acclaimed tour of Europe by Antony and Charles Atlas, is a music documentary that explores the heart of that performance. Through its synthesis of Antony's songs and unfurling video portraiture of the 13 remarkable women who performed on stage, *Turning* creates an intimate and cinematic experience exploring themes of identity, transcendence and the revelation of essence.[257]

Footage of Antony's performances is crosscut with spontaneous and candid interviews of the performers backstage and on the road. Many of the performers are transgendered, and all of them talk about a turning point in their lives when gender became a decision rather than a confining category. While Hammer's subjects must strip down to a body without references in order to escape a narrow definition of woman and a suffocating feminine ideal, for Atlas's subjects, the feminine is an additive quality. Giving a great deal of attention to hair styles, makeup, gowns, breasts, pouting full red lips, coy posturing and stiletto heels, they emanate a hyper-realized feminine presence, an exaggeration of the ideal of the status quo to a point that effectively challenges it. The feminine appears through personifications of the Gorgon as well in the performances of Kembra Pfahler and Johanna Constantine. The personas created by Pfahler and Constantine symbolize fear of the feminine, fear of the female psyche, of her sexual power, and what Kathy Acker calls a "*hatred of gender* . . . a hatred of the expectation that I had to become my womb. My hatred of being defined by the fact that I had a cunt."[258] Pfahler and Constantine symbolize what is inside "the cunt," turning it inside out, using body paint

---

[257] Charles Atlas and Antony, "Turning," Turning, http://www.turningfilm.com/ (accessed July 4, 2012).
[258] Kathy Acker, interview by Andrea Juno, *Angry Women,* 177.

to cover as well as highlight the horror of the feminine. Pfahler, in full yellow, black and white body paint and a wig that is almost four feet across, explains, "I take a lot of rational thinking to get like this. There's nothing freakish about it." When asked by an off-camera voice about the theme of one particular evening's performance, Constantine, whose body is painted as a skeleton, dripping blood, replies, "Act natural." There is laughter off-screen, but she defends her position: "I'm acting natural. It's such a relief. Natural beauty, one's soulful inclination to be at one with the universe."[259] In *Turning*, nature is artifice, as in Hammer's films, where the rituals in nature are artifice as well.

Each of the posed performers, whom Atlas refers to in the film as "girls," seems to accumulate power and strength as she turns on the podium. His live video mix holds a mirror to each performer's persona, simultaneously revealing and concealing it in layers of electronic effects. Depth and surface communicate in an unresolved field, and self and other come to mean the same thing. The figure of the "girl" exists in popular culture, not as a female child, but as a woman distinct in her humanity – having a more diminutive humanity than that of a man – but no less willful. The girl is certainly on the same level as the boy, who is not the male child, but an unformed and forming youth who, like The Fool of the Tarot deck, is about to step off the plane of the known into the promise of the unknown. Antony's lyrics for "Today I Am A Bouy,"[260] a song performed in the film, address boy-ness and girl-ness:

---

[259] Kembra Pfahler and Johanna Constantine, interviewed by Antony in Charles Atlas and Antony, *Turning*, directed by Charles Atlas, produced by Vibeke Vogel and Lucy Sexton (Denmark: Turning Film, Bullitt Film and Beo Film, 2011).

[260] Antony has created his own spelling of the word "boy," as "bouy." In an email correspondence, Charles Atlas explains the spelling: "The way I interpret it is as a kind of alternative way of singing 'boy.' He has also spelled girl as 'guhrl.' It's kind of primitive or pidgin English and leaves a little room for imagination rather than the straightforward way of pronouncing it." Email correspondence between Cecilia Dougherty and Charles Atlas, June 21, 2012.

One day I'll grow up, I'll be a beautiful woman
One day I'll grow up, I'll be a beautiful girl
One day I'll grow up, I'll be a beautiful woman
One day I'll grow up, I'll be a beautiful girl

But for today I am a child, for today I am a bouy
For today I am a child, for today I am a bouy
For today I am a child, for today I am a bouy

One day I'll grow up, I'll feel the power in me
One day I'll grow up, of this I'm sure
One day I'll grow up, I'll know a womb within me
One day I'll grow up, feel it full and pure[261]

Is Antony's "bouy-hood" something that will keep him afloat until the fulfillment of androgyny that the lyrics promise? Boy (bouy), in this case, is the child version of both girl and woman. This feminine persona has no opposite, no dialectical counterpart, but grows from either gender into an infinitely mutating feminine presence.

Atlas' live video mix constructs a narrative of the performances of the band, on the one hand, and the women turning on the podium, on the other, capturing a drama that is both reality and performance. Atlas's live video mix interprets the performers presentations of the feminine as the realization of an ideal without counterpart, as she emerges into a hostile, gender-bifurcated society. In the film, one of the performers, Nomi Ruiz, a singer, describes a moment in her youth in the Bronx where her voice is mistaken for the voice of a girl:

I was a little naïve, I guess, to the whole gender thing that was going on when I was really young. I knew it was happening, but I just . . . I guess maybe I just thought I was crazy or something. I would play recordings for my friends,

---

[261] Antony, "Today I Am A Bouy," performed by Antony and the Johnsons, recorded at The Barbican Centre, London, 2006. This song appears on Antony and the Johnsons, *I Am a Bird Now* (New York: Rebis Music, SC105cd).

and I remember I did a song with this rapper from the neighborhood. It was kind of like a duet, and everyone was, like, 'oh, that's such as beautiful duet between a girl and a boy,' and I was just . . . that was the first time it really occurred to me that my voice was being interpreted as a woman's voice from people who were listening to it. And that was the first time . . . wow . . . That's possible, you know, to have that security in singing and being perceived as what I wanted to be perceived as."[262]

Once Ruiz had put gender into a perspective of choice, her life changed, but the question of visibility arises immediately. She states, "Every detail of your existence is out there for everyone to see. It just rips me open. I guess for me, turning represents freedom. Freedom from society, from art, from gender and everything that oppresses us."[263] The realization that she could make a choice, could "turn" from boy to girl, happened while she was performing a duet; performance is the vehicle that enables a presentation of self-determined gender.

Another performer, Joey Gabriel, speaks about having been homeless as a teenager in Boston:

Behind the bus station . . . there was this grate, behind a building, that in the winter blew up hot air, and we would all sleep in there in kind of a transgendered jigsaw puzzle. And I always had trouble sleeping, and I remember sitting there and looking down at all these people and just kind of hoping that I would remember them. In a way, you know – it's so strange – I never wanted to escape it. It doesn't deserve to be hidden, or in the darkness, you know? Because they matter, you know, and I wanted to matter, because I was so judged. One of the things I wanted the

---

[262] Nomi Ruiz, interviewed by Antony, in Atlas and Antony, *Turning.*
[263] Ibid.

most was never to be judged, and I wanted to be beautiful.[264]

The outcasts, sleeping together on a grate behind the bus station, are people who matter, people with something specific to contribute to the discussion of gender's mutability based on lived experience. There was no place in society, no actual place to go except to be huddled together on a grate behind a bus station. To be beautiful is a way back into society on more self-defined terms, and glamour is like body armor – acceptance with a vengeance.

The film defines gender as a highly regarded and thoroughly considered, yet ambiguous quality. Ambiguity is far from uncertainty, however. While Hammer's lesbian subjects create specific selves with a spontaneous and nebulous set of signifiers, and Atlas' subjects create true expressions of themselves by changing their bodies and their appearance, and performing an opposite gender, both do away with the idea of the male counterpart, that essential figure of social authority. To be human – male, female, transgendered, specified, unspecified, fixed or changeable – does not necessitate a power imbalance based on bifurcated gender roles. In Hammer's films, the body without references is a lesbian, and the lesbian without a history is writing her own chapters, inserting them into the larger story of human consciousness. In Atlas' film, the body that assumes a surplus of dramatic references is transgendered, excluded from the larger story of the social basis of sexuality. In both cases, the self-determined subjectivities of these narratives are engaged in a political struggle for the power to act on their own terms within the social realm.

The fight they are engaged in is real, but who started it? What possible threat are women without men, and men who have given up male privilege? Both filmmakers relocate their subjects into already existing histories by making them visible not simply as individuals, but as phenomena, forcing the old histories to

---

[264] Joey Gabriel, interviewed by Antony, *Turning.*

conform to a new shape and to make room. In doing so, the shape of history changes. New knowledge is added, and power is assumed. Each subject abandons the signifiers of gender that she inherited, and then takes on or invents new signifiers that rearrange the language of gender, making it much more user friendly. Each possesses an undeniable germ of authenticity that takes root in the collective psyche, and each has an "inclination to be at one with the universe."[265] Being, becoming and turning: the revealed subject is the unadorned and naked female body engaged in a collective fantasy of primal origins, and it is also the hyper-feminine body, in transit between genders, each manifesting the mutable, irreducible I.

Out of Place: The Amodernist Fiction of Kathy Acker and Laurie Weeks

Kathy Acker and Laurie Weeks are feminist writers a generation apart whose writing takes for granted a subjectivity that is diffracted, not a solid presence so much as a range of mutable identities within a spectrum of instability. Ambiguity is an active agent in the writing, and uncertainty is the milieu for actions and events in both their works. In Acker's novel, *Kathy Goes to Haiti* (1978),[266] and in Weeks' novel *Zipper Mouth* (2011),[267] the main character has two personas, one who speaks in the first person and seems to represent the writer herself, lending an autobiographical credibility to the story, and the other, a fictional character composed of elements of history, memory (the authors' own, hearsay, friends' stories, etc.), politics, and literary and pop cultural allusions. This initial ambiguity in both works throws references to the speaker into a field of multiplicities, changing the nature of narrative authority and literary authenticity. If the stories are true, the reader is a bit

---

[265] Johanna Constantine, interviewed by Antony, in Atlas and Antony, *Turning.*
[266] Kathy Acker, *Literal Madness: Kathy Goes to Haiti, My Death My Life by Pier Paolo Pasolini, and Florida* (New York: Grove Press, 1987).
[267] Laurie Weeks, *Zipper Mouth* (New York: Feminist Press, 2011).

of a voyeur, and the relationship between reader and writer is clearly a standard one. If the characters are not "real," and the stories are not true, the reader is in a symbolic or allegorical territory of tropes and figurations, another literary standard. But these works confound an easy either-or reading, and represent more accurately how identity, self, and subjectivity may be experienced as continual fluctuation and re-creation, taking the object-ness out of the construction of self and collapsing the distance between the writer, her characters, and the reader.

In her 1992 essay, "Ecce Homo, Ain't (Ar'n't) I A Woman, and Inappropriate/d Others: The Human in a Post-Humanist Landscape," Haraway writes about the figure of the female, or more specifically, feminist figuration:

> Figuration is about resetting the stage for possible pasts and futures. Figuration is the mode of theory when the more "normal" rhetorics of systematic critical analysis seem only to repeat and sustain our entrapment in the stories of the established disorders. Humanity is a modernist figure; and this humanity has a generic face, a universal shape. Humanity's face has been the face of a man. Feminist humanity must have another shape, other gestures; but, I believe, we must have feminist figures of humanity. They cannot be man or woman; they cannot be the human as historical narrative has staged that generic universal. Feminist figures cannot, finally, have a name; they cannot be native. Feminist humanity must, somehow, both resist representation, resist literal figuration, and still erupt in powerful new tropes, new figures of speech, new turns of historical possibility.[268]

In both *Kathy Goes to Haiti* and *Zipper Mouth*, the main character enters a space of subjectivity that is already filled with others. Acker and Weeks do not push aside any of the others

---

[268] Haraway, "Ecce Homo, Ain't (Ar'n't) I A Woman, and Inappropriate/d Others: The Human in a Post-Humanist Landscape," in *The Haraway Reader*, 47.

who already inhabit the narrator's space in the story, however; they write around and through them creating a subjectivity that shares time and space with the author's as well as the reader's own experiential contexts, and resist interpretation in terms of the generic universal. It is impossible to be taken into an already familiar fictional humanist landscape, or to be brought back into the tropes that situate "human as historical narrative," in this work. Acker and Weeks write into the crowded space of subjectivity in the representation of the interrelationships of non-generic humans, and they do so to bring the readers, whose daily lives come into regular contact with these figures, inside the work.

Acker's novel, *Kathy Goes to Haiti,* has been described as a sexual adventure, and Acker is spoken of as a "sex-positive feminist," [269] a phrase that in a few strokes excuses her feminism and suggests that she can be admired because, perhaps unlike other feminists, she enjoys sex. It is useless to describe Acker's novels only in terms of plot when the story, or the writing itself, confronts the reader's basic assumptions about the relationship of literature to the literary history in which it participates. In this novel, a white, twenty-nine year old American tourist named Kathy gets off an American Airlines plane at the airport in Port-Au-Prince and takes a taxi into the city. She receives propositions for sex and marriage proposals throughout the novel, including from the taxi driver on the way into town from the airport. In the novel, Kathy travels between Port-Au-Prince and Cap Haitian, a small city on the northern coast of Haiti, and has sexual encounters and affairs, chiefly with the character Roger, who is the son of a wealthy landowner and who is also a drug dealer.

---

[269] A brief description of *Kathy Goes to Haiti* from the Wikipedia page "Kathy Acker": "*Kathy Goes to Haiti* details a young woman's relationship and sexual exploits while on vacation." http://en.wikipedia.org/wiki/Kathy_Acker (accessed January 12, 2012). This quote provides a brief example of how unsuitable descriptions using familiar literary tropes can be in relation to Acker's work.

In the following passage from *Kathy Goes to Haiti*, the character Kathy has just met Roger's wife, Betty. She is trying to befriend Betty, an American, who spends most of her time in her bedroom, pining for a pet dog that has been left with her mother somewhere in the American Midwest. Kathy thinks that Betty can be happy in Haiti and tries to entice her away from the house.

"We were wondering where you were," Roger says to Kathy.

"I want to go soon. I want to get back to the pension for dinner."

"You can get a ride back with my father's engineer. He'll be leaving about now. I'll ride into town with you. I'll go see where he is." Roger goes back downstairs.

The two women follow him. "I loved being able to meet you," Kathy says to Betty. "Why don't you visit me at the pension and we can go swimming and sunbathing together?"

"Roger'll have to drive me there. I have no other way of getting there."

"Come visit me. I can give you the books I've finished reading so you'll have some new books to read."

"OK. I'll come tomorrow or the next day. You're getting a bad burn. Here's some good suntan oil and here are some Haitian matches."

"Oh, they're beautiful."

"The engineer's waiting," says Roger.

Roger's girlfriend climbs into a huge gray jeep.

"Aren't you going to come with me, Roger? I thought you were going into town with me.

"I'm not going tonight. I'll see you tomorrow night.

She wanted to fuck all day, and now she's not going to be able to. "Goodbye Roger."

Roger throws her a kiss.

[The chapter ends, and a new one begins.]

PASSIONS

Your past comes back and hooks you. Your insane search for affection because your mother didn't want you, disliked you, and she wouldn't tell you who your father was. You kept looking for a home. Your need gathers. Passion collects. You're in it now, baby . . . passions, just as they are . . .

You're going to bang your head against that wall again. No affection. You. Where are you going to find love?[270]

Acker colonizes rather than inhabits her characters – in control of them but seemingly not able to take care of their needs or desires, which seem to spring up independent of the story line. Her dialogue, which may appear stiff and awkward, is close to the way people actually speak, sometimes contradicting themselves, changing the subject, seeming distracted, but reaching an end point nonetheless. In the second to last line, Acker slips out of the character of Kathy and becomes Acker the author. At the end of the chapter, she anticipates the sex scenes of the next chapter. At the beginning of the next chapter, "Passions," she addresses the reader as well as herself (in mixed role of protagonist and author) in the second person, in a mental monologue that brings forth the theme of strong sexual desire and experiences of sexual abuse as two non-contradictory aspects of the female body in the world.

Both Acker and Weeks' stories contain action, events and narrative causality, but ultimately the stories are not building to a resolution, and cause and effect are absent from the overall structure. The autobiographical content is not necessarily centered in the character's thoughts and feelings, nor is it entirely contained in the events of the storyline. In the essay, "Kathy Acker," from *Lust for Life: On the Writings of Kathy Acker,* Peter Wollen describes possible routes through her work: "She once said she didn't expect anyone to read all the way through any of her books from beginning to end – 'even in *Empire of the Senseless,* which is the most narrative book, you

---

[270] Acker, 75 – 76.

could read pretty much anywhere,' or, in other words, you could make your own montage, you could appropriate and re-order."[271] The content is not to be found in the storyline, and therefore the story does not provide autobiographical insights, but rather the content is in the contexts of the writing, which includes the contexts of the reader as well.

Kathy Goes to Haiti is infinitely more than a sexual adventure. The novel has multiple settings: the politics of American tourism in impoverished countries; the selling of perfect Caribbean geography along with the imperfect, pre-modernist societies that inhabit them; and the meeting of two differently disempowered groups – Haitian men, and women. It requires a literal reading, the way children learn to read "Dick and Jane," line after line, a descriptive, repetitive reading of subject-verb/action-object; and it also requires an alternate simultaneous reading, inside the context of the history of militarism and colonialism as they are wrapped up in racial politics, poverty, and sexual domination. Illustrations for the novel by artist Robert Kushner, which accompany the original publication, but which have been excluded from the *Literal Madness* collection, are simply drawn images of boy and girl, in black and white, of sex and difference. Yet some of the drawings are descriptive of not only subject/action/object, but also clearly of the compression of racial and sexual politics that Acker uses to create floating signifiers of not only race and gender, but also militarism and colonialism. Acker writes tourism as colonialism very clearly. In these two ways of reading *Kathy Goes to Haiti* – as literal Dick and Jane story, or as anti-militarist text – the multi-dimensionality of the modernist-colonialist program of occupation and exploitation is disclosed. Complex politics are mapped over tense scenes of banal dialogue and inactivity. Politics and mundanity slip into and out of each other, enabling the interplay between tourism and the effects of long-term colonialism, poverty, and political disenfranchisement. Time is a

---

[271] Peter Wollen, "Kathy Acker," *Lust for Life: On the Writings of Kathy Acker,* Amy Scholder, Avital Ronell, and Carla Harryman, ed. (New York: Verso, 2006), 1.

factor as well. Tourism to non-industrialized nations, especially those with beautiful landscapes or miles of beach, is always pictured as a trip back in time to a simpler era. The character, Kathy, creates tension in the novel by having landed in an interstitial space, politically and sexually. She has power as a white middle class person, and she has little or no power as a woman. She remains in her own time zone, the time zone of modernism, as it were, and is only drawn into the amodernist time zone of the other, becoming the other, at the end of the book, in the last line. Throughout the novel, Kathy has the privilege to leave, but she cannot leave. Her privilege binds her and it keeps her there.

Acker constructed the novel by writing the beginning and the ending first, and then working her way towards the middle. The chapters are structured by alternating travel narratives of Haiti with sex scenes. The descriptions of sex present the bodies of the characters in an almost claustrophobic way – the reader is on top of and inside the bodies of the characters with no room for perspective, no way out of the uncomfortable triangle of Kathy, boyfriend, and reader. The bodies in the sex scenes are like biological entities, body parts with their own consciousness and reactions. There is almost never a sense of love building, but only of love being announced and denounced. Nor is there a sense of the kind of casual yet passionate, non-binding, sexual experience that is the holy grail of feminist eroticism. Instead, there is a sense of urgency, apprehension, danger, pure physical desire, and physical discomfort. The alternating chapters about travel and chapters about sex play with the reader, in a way, like the nineteenth century paper toys that have a drawing on each side of a disk that, when spun, merges the two pictures into one image – a bird and a cage, for example, becomes a bird in a cage. Travel scenes and sex scenes become sex tourism. In the essay, "Kathy Goes to Haiti: Sex, Race and Occupation in Kathy Acker's Voodoo Travel Narrative," that appears in the anthology on Acker's writing, *Kathy Acker and Transnationalism*, Shannon Rose Riley discusses the illustrations by Robert Kushner in her interpretation of how image, text, travel and sex are intertwined:

The alternating chapters that move back and forth from travel narrative to pornography and the relation of the images to the text suggest that pornography was already embedded in the voodoo travel narratives that emerged during the U.S. military occupation of Haiti.[272] The intermingling of travel narrative and interracial pornography also points to the pornographic desires of tourism, and disrupts the myth of the wholesome "American" tourist as mediated through the "goes to" genre. Moreover, the formal structure of the text short-circuits male desire as normally figured in the pornographic genre and as explicitly depicted in Kushner's illustrations. This results from the constant interruption of ejaculatory aims by the travel narrative and a general cluttering of too much emotional, political, cultural, and economic information.[273]

Emotional, political, cultural, economic – good terms to either preface or wrap up a discussion of harsh situations. The sense of place that Acker puts into the novel, and which the reader absorbs, is not located in these terms, however. The novel speaks just under these terms, or, rather, in the vernacular that these terms attempt to structure. The sense of place in the novel is located in the writing of the "I." Who is speaking, and in what sense of the present are they speaking? Peter Wollen discusses Acker's I as a signifier of appropriation. He writes:

> In her early writings, the problem facing the heroine and narrator is that of the first-person pronoun, the "I," the linguistic index of identity. Acker appropriated other people's texts, mainly things that had been told to her by friends, or, for a brief but crucial period, by fellow workers in go-go dancing joints, and mixed them in with aspects of

---

[272] The U.S. Marines were stationed in Haiti from 1915 to 1934.

[273] Shannon Rose Riley, "Kathy Goes to Haiti: Sex, Race, and Occupation in Kathy Acker's Voodoo Travel Narrative," in *Kathy Acker and Transnationalism*, ed. Polina Mackay and Kathryn Nicol (Newcastle upon Tyne: Cambridge Scholars Publishing, 2009), 32 – 33.

her own experience, all told in the first person, because, as she put it later, "I didn't want to be like a sociologist."[274]

Acker challenges the idea of singular subjectivities and removes the estrangement, but not the strangeness, between all of the actors involved in her literature. She is not a sociologist. Latour's examples of faulty sociology, practiced by what he calls "sociologists of the social," understand the social in terms of groups and categories. "For sociologists of the social, the rule is order while decay, change, or creation are exceptions," states Latour. [275] Acker's practice adheres to the "sociology of associations," giving precedence to instability, indeterminacy, change, interaction, affinity, conflict, and movement, however, over the fact of the object, in order to receive or transmit truly representative words and images of the place/situation under investigation.

In a 1989-90 interview conducted by Sylvère Lotringer, Acker discusses experimenting with using the first person in writing as a "model of schizophrenia"[276] early in her writing process:

> Acker: I wanted to explore the use of the word I, that's the only thing I wanted to do. So I placed very direct autobiographical, just diary material, right next to fake diary material. I tried to figure out who I wasn't . . . I was experimenting about identity in terms of language. That's how I started out.

> Lotringer: But the first person is just a free-for-all word, whoever grabs it becomes it.

> Acker: I also came to the decision that it was a false problem because it's a thing that's made. You create identity, you're not given identity per se . . .

---

[274] Wollen, in *Lust for Life: On the Writings of Kathy Acker,* 9.

[275] Latour, *Reassembling the Social,* 35.

[276] Kathy Acker, "Devoured by Myths: An Interview with Sylvère Lotringer," in *Hannibal Lecter, My Father* (New York: Semiotext(e), 1991), 8.

Lotringer: Dissociation as process . . .

Acker: Yeah. The idea that you don't need to have a central identity, that a split identity was a more viable way in the world. I was splitting the I into false and true I's and I just wanted to see if this false I was more or less real than the true I: what are the reality levels between false and true and how it worked.[277]

Acker's process seems to have less to do with schizophrenia or dissociation than it has to do with challenging the singular, authorial voice. The authorial voice is always the presence of the patriarchy. The true and false I's are an alternative to the trope of the soul-searching protagonist who is looking for a core self, something to hold onto, or a central identity that will provide him with not only a solid sense of himself, but also a solid time and place within which to place that self. This is the patriarchal model of the person out of place, looking for his assigned place, his category, within it. Acker's writing succeeds in de-stabilizing that model, and it destabilizes critiques of literature based on that model as well. For those who read this as a travel narrative, or as a pornographic novel, a description of the work might barely exceed one or two sentences about women, travel, and vacation sex; likewise, the critic who reads the text literally can merely write around the work, circling it but never diving into it.[278] Acker employs *détournement,* pornography, pastiche, plagiarism, and autobiography, among other amodernist devices discussed above. The last element, autobiography, is what binds the work together as a piece of true fiction.

Peter Wollen discusses the structure and process of this novel as well, in an article published by the London Review of Books a few months after her death in 1997:

---

[277] Ibid., 7.
[278] For a typical example of an ill-conceived critique, see James R. Frakes, "Ooh Ooh. And Then Again, Ah Ah," New York Times, January 17, 1988.
http://www.nytimes.com/1988/01/17/books/ooh-ooh-and-then-again-ah-ah.html (accessed June 16, 2012).

In another interview she explained that her book *Kathy Goes to Haiti* was "mathematically composed: every other chapter is a porn chapter; each chapter, except for the central one, mirrors the facing chapter."

Once again, the construction of a text through a pre-determined methodology – cut-up or a mathematical procedure or a set of guidelines. As she notoriously confessed, or exaggerated, in conversation with Lotringer, "I don't have any imagination . . . I've used memories, but I've never created stories by making things up."[279] The fantastic elements of her writing are generated textually, rather than by acts of creation – the author is divested of her authority, mediumistic in relationship to a text generated through impersonal methodologies. The narrator, the 'I', herhimself, becomes a construct of that text, rather than the other way round.[280]

Following Acker's narrative from the edges to the center is like following one of Mandelbrot's fractals in reverse – an implosion, a backwards movement in time. This is where the obscenity of the interdependence of wealth and power, poverty, submission, slavery, and colonialism occurs. It occurs in the reality outside the book that the narrative refers to, it occurs in the political space of America's relationship to Haiti and of the relationship of tourists, all of whom are sex tourists, to the place that is other than home. Tourism is inextricably linked to sex outside the place of the home and is the kind of territorial occupation that follows military occupation. The tourist can place him or herself inside this kind of pornography, which is something that happens in tourism because the tourist is outside of himself, i.e. not at home.

---

[279] The correct first sentence of the quote paraphrased above is, "I never thought I had imagination." From "Devoured by Myths: An Interview with Sylvère Lotringer," in *Hannibal Lecter, My Father*, 8.
[280] Peter Wollen, "Death (and Life) of the Author," London Review of Books 20.3 (1998): 8-10, http://www.lrb.co.uk/v20/n03/peter-wollen/death-and-life-of-the-author (accessed January 12, 2012).

In the case of sex tourism, the act of sex is a phenomenon of transference as well, but in *Kathy Goes to Haiti*, the process of transference is interrupted when the consciousness of the American tourist, Kathy, begins to be colonized by the consciousness of the native Haitian. Westerners see all societies that are not modern as being backwards, or situated back in time. The technology the people employ to survive colonization keeps them in the present, however. Theirs is the technology of the black hole, a technology given to them unwittingly by the colonizers. The irresistible gravity of the narrative of exploitation pulls everything into itself in one obscene tunneling to the center. Acker's story ends with the main character, Kathy, dazed and disoriented, drugged and bewitched after a religious ceremony, as she steps from the doctor's hut into a blinding white sunlight. She visits the center of the black hole, becoming the people, becoming the sand and dirt, the sun, and the Voodoo spell itself. From the last few paragraphs of the novel:

> The père motions Kathy to get up. He turns her around three times. He pushes her around the vevers [signs drawn on the ground with bits of grain] three times clockwise. He picks up the small plastic red-frame mirror and passes the mirror around her body. He shows Kathy to herself. . . .
>
> Chickens and goats run around. The ground's so dry, it's almost sand. This sand flies everywhere. Children squall and yell. Women sit on the sand-covered almost nonexistent doorsteps of huts and low wood chairs outside the huts. Women talk to each other. Women with baskets on their heads walk in the fine dust. Women carry huge amounts of wet clothes in their arms. There are a few men.
>
> "Goodbye," says the girl in the bright green skirt.
>
> Kathy turns around and walks outside into the sun. She's more dazed than before.[281]

The narrative structure as well as Acker's anti-colonialist critique is resolved in these lines. The critique of modernism and postmodernism is embedded in the amodernist perspective of the

---

[281] Acker, "Kathy Goes to Haiti," in *Literal Madness,* 170.

author/character of the novel's guide/protagonist, Kathy. In the realm of religious magic, a universal dimension of representation, the colonizer has met her match, and rather than a struggle for dominance, there is an immersion into universal consciousness. Subjectivity is universalized in its instability.

Acker must be read as a feminist theorist who visualizes identity, writing, and colonialism from within her moveable, mutable identity, and not as a "sex-positive feminist" and pornographer, although these may be true as well. Acker's feminism creates a universalized perspective from within a female life, which allies her with Haraway's feminist figuration of "human," a figure that is neither male nor female. Haraway describes the project, one that Acker's writing fully engages:

> I want here to set aside the Enlightenment figures of coherent and masterful subjectivity, the bearers of rights, holders of property in the self, legitimate sons with access to language and the power to represent, subjects endowed with inner coherence and rational clarity, the masters of theory, founders of states, and fathers of families, bombs, and scientific theories – in short, Man as we have come to know and love him in the death-of-the-subject critiques. . . . My focus is the figure of a broken and suffering humanity, signifying an unending series of mimetic and counterfeit events implicated in the great genocides and holocausts of ancient and modern history. . . . But, it is the very nonoriginality, mimesis, mockery, and brokenness that draw me to this figure and its mutants.[282]

How does a specific person ever find a language with which to speak as herself within this process of mutating genders, races, and all of the possible traits, actions, and elements that are to be reconfigured, post-Enlightenment? Where can she achieve an authentic presentation of herself, and find an active, functioning,

---

[282] Haraway, "Ecce Homo, Ain't (Ar'n't) I A Woman, and Inappropriate/d Others: The Human in a Post-Humanist Landscape," in *The Haraway Reader*, 48.

collective identity as well? The Enlightenment figure of man has been fully realized by the final mapping of the human genome, seeming to cement our fate and confirm the truth of the hierarchies of knowledge and power that he has developed for himself, and for nature as well. This figure creates interactions, but refuses to acknowledge any that he has not created. This figure can only see the whole as a sum of discreet and "original" parts, and strives to complete a final balance – chemical, biological, societal – between these parts. Haraway states that the only way out of this paradigm is to dismantle it and to use other routes to knowledge and power: "'We,' in these very particular discursive worlds, have no routes to connection and to noncosmic, nongeneric, nonoriginal wholeness than through the radical dismembering and displacing of our names and our bodies."[283]

Acker does all of this within a postmodernist frame of reference. However, her work follows a method more than a style. Her relationship to modernism is antagonistic, but the antagonism is only a backward glance, and postmodernist methodologies provided her with a set of wheels that convey her work into an amodernist literary perspective that strives to replace the figure of man with the figure of human. Her narratives provide authentic representations of self and other, space, place, and non-place, as mixing, cohabiting, morphing elements inside a non-linear space-time. She inhabits and abandons her text, becoming the characters and then denying them:

> Acker: I didn't really understand why I refused to use linear narrative; why my sexual genders kept changing; why basically I am the most disoriented novelist that ever existed. (Laughs). . . . I was like a [deaf]-dumb-and-blind person for years, I just did what I did but had no way of telling anyone about it, or talking about it.[284]

---

[283] Ibid., 49.
[284] Acker, "Devoured by Myths: An Interview with Sylvère Lotringer," *Hannibal Lecter, My Father*, 10.

Lotringer: One way of making your work legitimate, I guess, is to work it though your persona. If you are not the I, but the I becomes you, then you have to offer it as some kind of performance.

Acker: Yeah, I think that's very precise. So it's like an actress, I act through the novels . . . When I'm writing I become the characters in the novel, but the characters in the novel aren't me. People always think they're me, and it's a drag." [285]

Avital Ronell's text *Stupidity* comes into focus once again. Acker was an intellectual who wrote from her gut, a practice, which, in the quote above, she calls disoriented, and "[deaf]-dumb-and-blind." The character, Kathy, is stupid. Her speech is self-conscious, her decisions are careless, and she jumps thoughtlessly into every situation that she encounters. She has no power except the power to leave, which she loses at the end of the novel. Kathy's stupidity is a vehicle for Acker's set of observations on the mix of political influences that provide a setting for the novel. The stupidity of the protagonist does not refer to the particulars of Acker's own life, but to an unquestioning acceptance of history as written. The figure of the white woman alone in a Black foreign place is the multiplication of two negative marginal identities, Black (man) and foreign (woman), and opens up for inspection and repudiation the territory of an abject otherness necessitated by the Enlightenment figure of man. Ronell's *Stupidity* is a discussion not only of the values a society uses to measure its members, but a discussion of the organization of history, including the history of thought, and through a specific organization of history, the power to designate a direction into the future. Ronell writes,

"Stupidity" can be seen to have settled within the philosophical project. Defended against the rents in knowing, philosophers are those who dwell in the problem and live by enigmas; though their tone is often superior, it is

---

[285] Ibid., 20.

in their job descriptions to avow that they are confounded by the limits of the knowable, to begin their reflections, if they are true philosophers, in a mood of stupefaction."[286]

Laurie Weeks' 2011 novel *Zipper Mouth* is similar to *Kathy Goes to Haiti* in that the most insightful reading of the novel is through its structure rather than in the literal aspects of its stories. *Zipper Mouth* is a tale of drugs and love on New York's Lower East Side in the earliest days of gentrification, when developers were just beginning to exploit the economic growth potential of the lower avenues. The love story is broken up by other kinds of text, which could function as background material to the present time of the love story, but which do more to merge past and present than to provide a substantive history of the main character, who remains nameless throughout. Incidents of betrayal in childhood, teenage fixations with Vivien Leigh and Sylvia Plath, and adult fixations with drugs and love are laid out in disjunctive narrative segments that position the events of the novel like puzzle pieces that the protagonist is trying to fit together. Death is a presence that balances on the periphery of every scene, fluttering between threat and promise. The love object is called Jane, and the most consistent storyline is about the protagonist wanting but never having Jane's love. Flirtation drives the dialogue in one of their early conversations:

> One of the first times we hung out Jane said to me, "So what have you been doing?" The answer was, "Dope." Or "Staying hungover in bed, waiting for a check, contemplating suicide and TV." But I said, "Oh, you know. Hiding, mostly, avoiding phone calls from annoying people who want to be my friend." Jane laughed. She goes, "I guess I'm one of those annoying people who wants to be your friend." Insect wings fluttered in my chest. No. She was straight.[287]

---

[286] Ronell, *Stupidity*, 68.
[287] Weeks, *Zipper Mouth*, 23.

The protagonist and Jane become friends, and Jane continues to flirt with her. Eventually, the narrator makes a pass at Jane, but she is gently rejected. Their friendship gradually takes them in the direction of drug addiction. The narrator's love for Jane is only heightened by the humiliation of rejection, and by the emotional safety net of the drug high.

> After the first rushes of ecstatic conversation, Jane and I wandered from room to room, speaking occasionally in undertones. We were specters facing each other through soundproof glass, semaphoring unintelligibly. Languorously we'd drape ourselves across the bed, a chair. Puking occurred in slow motion. She may as well have kicked me in the teeth when she lay down with her feet on the pillow next to my face, her head way down there as far away from my mouth as she could get, and this cruelty made me crazy with love.[288]

At an early stage of writing the novel, its chapters could be arranged in several ways, and organizing them into an appropriately sequenced novel became a challenge for Weeks. Putting the sections together was like piecing together a puzzle based on the shapes of the text.[289] In an interview with reviewer Karen Schechner, Weeks discusses the puzzle aspect in a way that brings the literary form into the physical plane of the text: "I was writing other things all the time but this book was in boxes, thousands of pages, thousands of segments to put together like a puzzle . . . And again, I didn't know how the book was going to come out."[290] The novel's structure is tied to the process of putting the narrative together, finding how it "was going to come out," rather than plotting it. The puzzle, as a trope of the interconnectedness of human experience and the value of

---

[288] Ibid., 72.
[289] Based on my experience of working with Laurie Weeks over the period of a summer, in the 1990s, when she had asked me to help her edit the material.
[290] Laurie Weeks, "Laurie Weeks: Making Magic Out of the Real," interview by Karen Schechner, Lambda Literary,
http://www.lambdaliterary.org/features/11/20/laurie-weeks-making-magic-out-of-the-real/ (accessed January 21, 2012).

proximity, is an important element of Perec's 1978 novel, *Life, A User's Manual*, which is the story of a puzzle-maker and the Paris apartment complex in which he lives, including the interconnecting narratives of the people who have lived there over several generations. The story takes place in the moment after the puzzle-maker's death – a five hundred-page moment. In the Preamble, Perec explains "the art of jigsawing":

> To begin with, the art of jigsaw puzzles seems of little substance, easily exhausted, wholly dealt with by a basic introduction to Gestalt: The perceived object – we may be dealing with a perceptual act, the acquisition of a skill, a physiological system, or, as in the present case, a wooden jigsaw puzzle – is not a sum of elements to be distinguished from each other and analysed discretely, but a pattern, that is to say, a form, a structure: the element's existence does not precede the existence of the whole, it comes neither before nor after it, for the parts do not determine the pattern, but the pattern determines the parts: knowledge of the pattern and of its laws, of the set and its structure, could not possibly be derived from discrete knowledge of the elements that compose it.[291]

Knowledge of the pattern and its laws, set structure – mathematical, but nonetheless a good model and metaphor for finding the story by piecing it together. In *Zipper Mouth*, as in *Life, A User's Manual,* the puzzle is three-dimensional: time, space, and action form the many-sided, irregular shape of experience. In *Zipper Mouth,* the puzzle has not been completely assembled, however; while the network it traces is not yet fully connected, it is not broken. The pieces remain intact for the reader herself to pick up, explore, and connect, mirroring the author's initial process of assembling the chapters into a book.

Weeks' differentiated text segments include fan mail, email, lists, poems, and stories from the perspective of the narrator as a

---

[291] Georges Perec, *Life A User's Manual*, trans. David Bellos (Boston: David R. Godine, 1978), Preamble, n.p.

child. Together with a zigzagging story line, they formulate the history of the heroine's desire, tracing a network of connections through time and in a space that seems more chemical than physical or mental. *Zipper Mouth* is a lucid response to the closure of "access to language and the power to represent," that Haraway contends belongs to the "bearers of rights" to "a coherent and masterful subjectivity." Weeks provides alternatives to the old figurations and uses the narrator's voice to delineate a number of influences that are connected and at work in any ordinary moment:

> September light shattered against the cars. The usual buzzing in my head and sensation of skidding toward psychosis had begun. I didn't care. I am happy today, I reflected, flaming along, torched by the sun. Sunlight showered down onto hubcaps, bike rims, chain-link fencing, aluminum cans. How best to use the gleaming day? As always the first item on the agenda was to call in sick to work. People holding paper cups of coffee, heads teaming with five-year plans, strode by while store owners hosed down their little scraps of sidewalk, each illuminated by a medieval gold corona. How was it that I wasn't scrubbing down for neurosurgery as per my blueprints for the future back in sixth grade? How was it that I didn't care? The world ablaze around me, a gift. [292]

The agents of new figuration are Haraway's "mutants," who have failed to stay in place, who have abandoned official knowledge and official writing, and who have assumed the power to know and the power to represent. Mutants, like Weeks, use writing to move outside of – not in the margins of, but in disregard of – the old power structures of knowing and speaking. Her stories are not meant to be locked down. Her knowledge is fluid, continuing to send and receive information. Social scientist John Law suggests that in looking at the organization of power, we might think in terms limited to networks, so as not to hierarchize society into macro and micro, looking at how some

---

[292] Weeks, *Zipper Mouth*, 105.

networks succeed in "stabilising and reproducing themselves," gaining in size and power, and becoming macrosocial. The argument is that knowledge is a social product. He writes:

> I put "knowledge" in inverted commas because it always takes material forms. It comes as talk, or conference presentations. Or it appears in papers, preprints or patents. Or again, it appears in the form of skills embodied in scientists and technicians. "Knowledge", then, is embodied in a variety of material forms. But where does it come from? The actor-network answer is that it is the end product of a lot of hard work in which heterogeneous bits and pieces -- test tubes, reagents, organisms, skilled hands, scanning electron microscopes, radiation monitors, other scientists, articles, computer terminals, and all the rest – that would like to make off on their own are juxtaposed into a patterned network which overcomes their resistance. In short, it is a material matter but also a matter of organising and ordering those materials. [293]

While Acker and Weeks are not writing science or working with test tubes, they are producing material knowledge, organizing it into patterns of occurrences. The knowledge they produce has been tested (once again, the test) through experience, and has survived in the interstices of official history through an alternate means of patterning. The pattern of alternate means of creating knowledge is not the same one everywhere; women and members of non-modernist societies have different relationships to sovereign power, different patterns of information exchange, belief systems, economies, relationships to eco-systems, experiences of space-time, etc. There is no known limit to possible patterns or relationships that collectives construct, but these constructions are not permanent entities or objects; they

---

[293] The ideas of networks comprised of text as well as objects, and of macro and micro-social orders are discussed in the 1992 article, "Notes on the Theory of the Actor Network: Ordering, Strategy and Heterogeneity," by John Law, from which the subsequent quotation comes as well. The article is available from the Centre for Science Studies at http://www.lancs.ac.uk/fass/sociology/papers/law-notes-on-ant.pdf (accessed January 16, 2012).

are maps of experiential knowledge. Continuity and persistence are the vehicles for alternate means of gaining knowledge. Women's knowledge is illicit, sometimes associated with witchcraft or intuition, intellectual inferiority (stupidity and naivety), "over-emotionalism" (hysteria), or with the obscene (enslaved, submissive, receptive, beautiful, lustful, desirable) and over-legislated (capable of producing children/property and capable of inciting violence) female body, or all of the above. None of this is essential to being female, or in the case of others of any gender not in power, to being other, and all of it is learned. It never occurs to those who, failing to notice aporetic openings, misread texts like *Kathy Goes to Haiti* and *Zipper Mouth*. These texts represent a completely different context for knowledge and are not vying for a place within the context of old figuration. They are not trying to be intelligible in the old language of figuration, but are at home in the context they have uncovered with experiential data. The two contexts are linked; one finds the other unreadable, and the other finds the one transparent.

Within modern societies, women's knowledge can become intelligible if it is in the form of the novel, especially the first-person account, whether fictitious or autobiographical. The confessional narrative does not transfer women, or the writer as a woman, into the place of power within the same hierarchical system. It merely explains all of the above, in the first person. Acker and Weeks, however, appropriate the genre of women's confessional narrative and change the framework, or dispense with the framework, by dismissing fixed notions of time (past, present, future, simultaneity), place, occurrence, and voice, and by failing to resolve, or asking to be absolved for any of the actions or events that are confessed in the text. In her interview by Karen Schechner, Weeks states:

> I'm not interested in simple recitation of autobiographical occurrences that issue from a supposedly static reality because for me anyway that's not helpful, it almost blinds me. . . . my body, my entire being, is an unstable field of experiential data – faint scenes, the voices and words of everything I've seen or read . . . and I'm writing from within

that field to explore and contest the numbness, narrowing of vision, the mandated destruction of imagination that turns one into an abstraction to oneself. An obedient one. Simply, for example, by trying to pin you down to a single, fixed identity based on artificial categories of hierarchy and value that discipline and punish according to the needs of power."[294]

When considered from the perspective of the macrosocial, the knowledge Weeks carries in her "entire being" is a challenge to the social order. The phenomenon she describes is experienced subjectively but is not interpreted as personal, in the way that it applies to her person alone; it is something that everyone has the power to access. Access is obscured, but it is there. The individual steps in at this point, not as one about to take charge of a "masterful subjectivity," but as one who can access the alternate patterns of subjectivities and use the patterns to find or create affinities with others.

The lens of the macrosocial is muddy and cracked, and the organisms looking through the lens are misled in what they observe by faith in their own mythologies, categories, and hierarchies. The texts by Acker and Weeks seem fragmented and obscene only from within the narrow context of norms for literature and norms for female behavior, need, and desire. Outside of this context they are cogent, powerful, and clear documents not only of troubled and troubling female and other subjectivities, but also of patriarchal systems, as limited, limiting, and out of balance. *Zippermouth* provides many descriptions of how the patriarchal order functions on the most mundane level. In the following passage, it is embodied in the persona of young Wall Street executives:

---

[294] Laurie Weeks, "Laurie Weeks: Making Magic Out of the Real," interview by Karen Schechner, Lambda Literary, http://www.lambdaliterary.org/features/11/20/laurie-weeks-making-magic-out-of-the-real/.

Emerging from the subway into the miasma of workers, men striding superbly in their splendid suits, streaming currents of thick-headedness and cologne, ripe to bursting with generalized contempt, lost in thought no doubt of cigars growing cold on their tongues, the snaky veil of aggression and self-defense filming their eyeballs behind which circulated thoughts like *Should I buy a speedboat or what?,* the usual shock of cognitive dissonance hit me when I realized that many of them were at least seven years younger than me. I thought I was walking beside versions of my dad, strong-smelling, utterly unself-conscious, and middle-aged. But their smooth white skin and cherry cheeks gave them away. It's like these kids woke up in their little spaceship pajamas and stepped into the paradigm of successful manhood standing like an open sarcophagus next to the bed, an animatronic container for their lives.[295]

Later on, the protagonist visits a friend who is a Wall Street programmer and who is also a drug addict, a foil for the successful bankers and traders:

I recalled visiting Tony right after he'd done a speedball to find him standing in one place in his living room, sweating and shifting from foot to foot. Out of the blue he sank to his knees then stretched out full length to peer beneath the front door on his stomach, still wearing his suit from his programming job on Wall Street. There was nothing to see because the door extended all the way to the floor; there wasn't a crack or anything. "I think there might be cops out there," he said. I opened the door. "Tony, there are no cops." . . . After a moment he said, "I know this sounds crazy, but I think there's a rat sitting on the doorknob."[296]

The addicted Wall Streeter, Tony, is no better or worse, his situation no less real or false, than that of anyone else trying to fit together the puzzle pieces. When the narrative swings to

---

[295] Weeks, *Zipper Mouth,* 78.
[296] Ibid., 116.

Tony it situates the location of terror there. It is the nameless female protagonist who opens the door. For Tony, the rat sitting on the doorknob is the entire system he has succumbed to – the environment of his career condensed in the form of a menacing rat, one of the most common animals in New York. But there is no rat if you do not see one.

In the last paragraph of the book, the heroine walks the streets in a struggle with geometry:

> I couldn't see it, I was practically blind, all my senses were focused on whichever leg was in the process of touching down, my entire consciousness located in the supporting thigh. Then, once I had judged the possibility of a buckling knee to be minimal, there was the issue of pushing off and swinging the back leg forward. Plus I had to avoid knocking someone down. There was also the problem of the sidewalk itself. I was pretty sure it might suddenly swing down in front and up behind me to ninety degrees, a seesaw, no longer the ground but a vertical wall or chute. My stomach flipped as I walked and my internal gyroscope plunged from side to side. Is this machine going to slam me into the pavement and when it does will it take a long time?[297]

The sidewalk angles abruptly downward and the fractal reappears. In this slow motion kinhin, a belief in progress is rejected, not only because the narrator cannot progress from addiction into recovery, but also because there can be no progressive movement through space and time, or inside history as it is constructed in the intimate details of the everyday – except by putting one foot in front of the other. Progress, history, and the network of non-generic human interactivity occur within multiple simultaneous monologues and dialogues, moving with a great degree of uncertainty towards their next coherent iteration.

---

[297] Weeks, 164.

Part 4: Trans-border Agents

Digital *Flâneurs* Occupy Wall Street

A few weeks into the Occupy Wall Street demonstrations during the fall of 2011, media theorist Douglas Rushkoff wrote an online article for the Cable News Network (CNN) called "Think Occupy Wall St. is a phase? You don't get it,"[298] in which he discusses the apparent "incoherence" of the Occupy phenomenon to mainstream news media and political analysts. Early media reports, according to Rushkoff, "seem determined to cast [Occupy Wall Street] as the random, silly blather of an ungrateful and lazy generation of weirdos."[299] His assessment is that "They couldn't be more wrong and, as time will tell, may eventually be forced to accept the inevitability of their own obsolescence." CNN reporters themselves, after trekking to Zuccotti Park in New York's Financial District, were hard pressed to pinpoint the central theme of the protests after interviews with some of the occupiers. Not only did there seem to be no campaign platform, there was no unified strategy and no specific organizational hierarchy. This was not the grassroots version of any political machine and it did not rely on spokespersons or an agreed upon list of demands. Rushkoff claims that the media perceived an incoherent movement because they themselves were incoherent. He calls Occupy "America's first true Internet-era movement," and states that Occupy, "which -- unlike civil rights protests, labor marches, or even the Obama campaign – does not take its cue from a charismatic leader, express itself in bumper-sticker-length goals and understand itself as having a particular endpoint." This, he contends, is the contemporary space of protest action.

---

[298] Douglas Rushkoff, "Think Occupy Wall St. is a phase? You don't get it," CNN Opinion, October 5, 2011,
http://www.cnn.com/2011/10/05/opinion/rushkoff-occupy-wall-street/ (accessed October 6, 2011).
[299] Quotes of Rushkoff in this paragraph are taken from the same online article.

The Seattle, London, and Genoa protests of the beginning of the new millennium pre-figure Occupy by ten years. In notes on the translators' introduction to Guattari's *The Three Ecologies*, Ian Pindar and Paul Sutton note that Guattari's recommendation is that ecosophists work together and work without a leader. They footnote this observation with a description of the 1999 demonstration in London's financial district:

> It was a carefully planned day of anarchy that took the authorities completely by surprise and was co-ordinated through the Internet by hundreds of disparate protest groups. As was observed at the time, 'the very beauty of the operation was the apparent lack of organizers, leaders or any public face' (*Observer*, 20 June 1999: 'Virtual chaos baffles polices: recruited through an obscure website, organized in cells, the ecowarriors without a chief have redefined anarchy'). . . . As the website declared at the time: 'Resistance will be as transnational as capital.'[300]

The 1999 Seattle demonstrations during the World Trade Organization Conference (WTO) had a slightly more centralized organizational structure than those of Occupy, but the protestors relied on telecommunications technology to set up their actions including the obstruction of key intersections *en route* to the conference; because of the organized obstruction of roadways, official traffic to and from the WTO convention became virtually impossible. Demonstrators created a networked pattern in the real world, not of connectivity, but of obstruction, and it worked. The conference was closed down after three days of protest because it was difficult for the delegates to reach meeting sites.[301] The demonstrators' roadblocks also separated the conference delegates from their official facilitators, the police. This bit of psychogeography represented the most obvious, and

---

[300] Ian Pindar and Paul Sutton, from notes on the Translator's Introduction to Guattari, *The Three Ecologies*, 80.
[301] Paul de Armond, "Netwar in the Emerald City: WTO Protest Strategy and Tactics," Rand Corporation,
http://www.rand.org/content/dam/rand/pubs/...reports/.../MR1382.ch7.pdf, 2000 (accessed July 8, 2012).

perhaps the most unexpected, oppositional strategy. The Internet and mobile telecommunications were important tools of the early new millennium protests, and understanding the shared strategies of the 1999, 2001, and 2011 protests are pivotal to understanding the street politics of this entire new era: the movement is decentralized, leaderless – or having several or many people who act as organizers and teachers, rather than leaders or ideologues – they form around a number of issues formerly considered to be distinct, or requiring the attention of specialists, or requiring completely separate solutions. Nor do the new movements set up specific goals that would be end points for their movement. Emphasis for resistance has shifted from ideology to affinity, from reaching a goal to continuance.

The pattern for Occupy had been in the offing with trial runs in London, Seattle and Genoa. Decentralization is a troop strategy as well as an ethic. But in terms of how space is conceived and used, the Occupy strategy of setting up encampments perhaps diverges the most from earlier new millennium methods of open resistance. Seattle concerned itself with how to manage the WTO conferees, and in the process avoid being managed by the police. London concerned itself with organized chaos in terms of participant cells and leaderless affinity groups. Occupy, however, erased regional boundaries *within* the United States. The take-over of public and private land by sit-ins, and the setting up of campsites, calls the land itself that America is situated on into question, not simply as private or public land, but as a continuous borderless space. The myriad encampments, none of which needed central approval to be set up, created a different map of the United States, deterritorializing the country, and then reunifying it as a site of direct democracy, writing over the symbolic site of patriotism and nationalism. As Occupy encampments were set up across America and in other parts of the world, the scale of the space of resistance changed. The ordinary attachment to home was disrupted for participants and observers alike, as loyalties to other occupiers multiplied across a large, and now undifferentiated, landscape case by case. Regional issues were heightened to the point of the defense of individuals and families who were losing their homes in the foreclosure epidemic, for example. The foreclosure issue, for families in localized Oakland, California, or Queens, New York, was revealed to be an issue of global capitalism rather than personal finance.

The incoherence of the media was based on not knowing whom to call into account for the Wall Street actions, but more than that, it was based on the dislocation of American cities and states into sites of localized activity networked nationally and internationally. The links existed in real space and were mapped in cyberspace, where communication networks charted the physical ones. Digital *flâneurs* conducted a non-linear global ramble, reshaping real space and digital space as they went along. Social networking applications, for example, created the primary digital nodal point for millions of people, some of whom used social networking to locate and join a demonstration as it was happening; others used it to follow actions in other parts of the world, tracking the changing nature of new millennial protests, which were metamorphosing from calls against globalization to campaigns against totalitarianism. Lurkers were always welcome and they became the hordes of occasional, temporary, and part-time participants, whose commitment to a leaderless movement was based on what was happening in the moment. Within the new millennial protests, the voices of ordinary citizens have as much credibility, or even more, than the analyses of the experts because the ordinary citizens are in charge of the information and are exchanging information and data directly.

The network structure is an adhocracy that facilitates links between people and can shift focus readily based on shifting political realities. Rushkoff reads the new millennial language of protest in this way:

> Anyone who says he has no idea what these folks are protesting is not being truthful. Whether we agree with them or not, we all know what they are upset about, and we all know that there are investment bankers working on Wall Street getting richer while things for most of the rest of us are getting tougher. What upsets banking's defenders and politicians alike is the refusal of this movement to state its

terms or set its goals in the traditional language of campaigns.

That's because, unlike a political campaign designed to get some person in office and then close up shop (as in the election of Obama), this is not a movement with a traditional narrative arc. As the product of the decentralized networked-era culture, it is less about victory than sustainability. It is not about one-pointedness, but inclusion and groping toward consensus. It is not like a book; it is like the Internet.[302]

Once again, there is no central theme to Occupy Wall Street, but as the participants make clear by their inclusiveness and persistence, a central theme would not give it coherence. Nor does the Internet give it coherence. For Occupy, the Internet works brilliantly to do what it does best – send and receive information to people who are connected remotely. Occupy's longer term relevance is obvious if it is not viewed as a the one-off result of the 2008 collapse of Wall Street, but is placed, instead, into the larger sphere of anti-globalization and pro-democracy campaigns that have been occurring around the world since the beginning of the new millennium. There is no endpoint, and in order to keep endpoints at bay, the movement must keep moving and continue to resist ideologies and conclusions. The narrative arc has indeed changed and there are thousands of narrators. That the Rushkoff article itself has 75,953 Facebook recommendations[303] is a telling indication that

---

[302] Douglas Rushkoff, "Think Occupy Wall St. is a phase? You don't get it," CNN Opinion, October 5, 2011,
http://www.cnn.com/2011/10/05/opinion/rushkoff-occupy-wall-street/.
[303] This figure represents Facebook data as of October 6, 2011. When I accessed the article, I recognized the name of the last "recommender" listed next to the Facebook icon along with her Facebook photograph – someone I have known for decades. Seeing her picture gave me a sense of community, however uneasy it may have been and however suspicious I am of the process that places my friend's name and tiny photography on the CNN Opinion website. But this indirect access to my friend's moment of connection is not meant to connect her to me in an actual encounter. It is meant to reveal her place as well as my own in

his observations may be worth considering. There is trouble in paradise, however.

In contrast to the Occupy actions in the fall of 2011, the 2012 Occupy May Day demonstration in New York seemed like a street party, or perhaps a simulation of a street party. Although there were separate extra-legal actions around the city, the main demonstration was a legal march down Broadway. There was an amplified sound stage for music and speakers at Union Square and one at the southern tip of Broadway, delimiting the official space of the march. At Union Square, someone sang Woody Guthrie's "This Land is Your Land," encouraging everyone to sing along, but for many of the younger people, this song stirs up few associations. The organizers of the May Day Demonstrations secured a New York City Permit to March, as well, a legal document that must be obtained in advance and approved by the Police Commissioner. Everything was legitimate, by the book. The police did their job to keep the march moving and to allow other traffic to flow smoothly. There were few clashes and few arrests. Legitimization seemed to have swallowed up the movement.[304] Adbusters Magazine, who sent out a call for the initial September 17, 2011 action, and who continues to publicize Occupy news, sent out a post-May Day email claiming that the May Day march had failed:

> Last May 15 [2011], a hundred thousand *indignados* in Spain seized the squares across their nation, held people's assemblies and catalyzed a global tactical shift that birthed Occupy Wall Street four months later. Our movement outflanked governments everywhere with a thousand encampments in large part because no one was prepared for Occupy's magic combination of Spain's transparent consensus-based *acampadas* with the Tahrir-model of

---

the network of the article, the Occupy movement, and the sphere of colleagues to which I have agreed to belong within the Facebook social network.

[304] This report of New York's Occupy May Day celebration is based on my personal observations and comparisons with the Occupy actions I attended throughout the fall of 2011.

indefinite occupation of symbolic space. Now exactly a year later, a big question mark hangs over our movement because it is clear that the same tactics may never work again.

Spring re-occupations have largely failed here in North America. The May Day General Strike was stifled by aggressive, preemptive policing that neutralized Occupy's signature moves.[305]

The problem was not that the tactics had reached the limits of their effectiveness, as Adbusters claims. The General Strike – the May Day Demonstration – was not stifled by police action, but rather seemed stifled by its own legitimization in the form of a legal parade permit, a document that assures police protection, whether it covers a parade by Occupy Wall Street or the Ancient Order of Hibernians. The Occupy protest momentum was waylaid when the arena was legitimized and taken into the mainstream. A familiar social order was reestablished and all parties played their role satisfactorily.

Back in November 2011, Douglas Rushkoff addressed the occupiers of Zuccotti Park in a lecture that carries a warning about the need to move on and move out into a larger arena than the one they had been using in the tiny square in downtown Manhattan. His lecture begins with a simple analogy between computing systems and government systems. The government is the machine, the computer, and the economy is the program; central currency is the operating system, and "the corporation" is the software. Rushkoff delineated how the software's function, which is to prevent people from creating and exchanging value outside the corporate system, works in everyday reality: "We cannot work unless we have a job. We outsource our work. We outsource our savings. We outsource our borrowing. We outsource our investing. All instead of sourcing one another." He states that we are mistaking the current "operating system"

---

[305] Excerpted from an email sent to me from Adbusters Magazine on May 11, 2012.

for reality, for the way things have to be, so that part of the problem is about representation and perception. "We are not asking for wealth to be redistributed, we are asking for the redistribution to stop. The long extraction is over. The peer-to-peer society is back."[306] He suggested that the occupation of Zuccotti Park was over, and it was time to go into other communities, into "a bigger battlefield."[307]

During the most active period of the Occupy movement, the term "occupy" experienced a shift in use. It is generally used in reference to a place (the Occupied Palestinian Territories, for example) or a space (an occupied seat on public transit, or at the theater), or even abstract space (a thought that occupies one's mind, a pre-occupation). In the fall of 2011, "occupy" became a word that captured the imagination of many, a verb that seemed appropriate with almost any object, or as an adjective, one that described space, place, sign, and idea in spatial terms that suggested a complete taking, or hi-jacking, of an object, and re-contextualizing it in the willful reconstruction of political space. The term went from being used as a slogan to being used almost poetically, and certainly conceptually, until the taking over of Zuccotti Park was no longer just an action – it had taken on semiotic significance. In Rushkoff's Zuccotti Park lecture, he advocates resisting mass-market consumerism, as well as buying and growing local food crops, and using alternative currencies. These suggestions seem simple and doable on a personal or small group scale, but on a global scale, the project would be massive, taking decades to achieve. It would entail nothing less than an organized global economic revolution and a complete disruption of every system connected to agricultural production, systems of currency, technology, policing, migration and trade. Occupy Wall Street cannot accomplish a revolution within the scope of their project, but they can remain a global network, creating effective actions on a small group scale that connects, as we have seen, the intimate space of the local to an

---

[306] Douglas Rushkoff, "Occupy Reality – An Occupy Wall St. Teach-In," Rushkoff Blog, November 11, 2011 (accessed July 4, 2012).
[307] Ibid.

undifferentiated space of resistance. At this point, the active and multiple networks of digital *flâneurs* represent not so much the core of global activism per se, as a restructuring of activist strategies on a global scale, creating nodal points where people can become engaged, collectively, in a wide range of interconnected endeavors. However, there is even more trouble in paradise.

On October 3, 2011, in an open letter to Occupy Wall Street that was posted on his web log, "Unsettling America: Decolonization in Theory & Practice,"[308] Native American activist John Paul Montano (Nishnaabe) discusses the term "occupy." Montano first thanks the Occupy activists for "attempting to improve the situation in what is now called the United States." His analysis of Occupy's position in reference to the United States reminds the Occupy movement that the land is already occupied in the colonialist sense of the term. While he is not part of the ruling class, he makes it clear that he is also not one of the 99%.[309] He writes:

> I had hoped that you would address the centuries-long history that we indigenous peoples of this continent have endured being subject to the countless '-isms' of do-gooders claiming to be building a "more just society," a "better world," a "land of freedom" *on top of our indigenous societies, on our indigenous lands, while destroying and/or ignoring our ways of life.*

> I had hoped that you would acknowledge that, since you are settlers on indigenous land, you need and want our indigenous consent to your building *anything* on our land – never mind an entire society. See where I'm going with this? I hope you're still smiling. We're still friends, so don't

---

[308] John Paul Montano, "An Open Letter to the Occupy Wall Street Activists," Unsettling America: Decolonization in Theory & Practice, October 3, 2011, http://unsettlingamerica.wordpress.com/2011/10/03/decolonize-wall-street/ (accessed March 1, 2012).
[309] "The 99%" is a term the Occupy movement uses to identify anyone who is not a part of the ruling class, who are identified as "the 1%."

sweat it. I believe your hearts are in the right place. I know that this whole genocide and colonization thing causes all of us lots of confusion sometimes. It just seems to me that you're *unknowingly* doing the same thing to us that all the colonizers before you have done: you want to do stuff on our land without asking our permission.[310]

From Montano's perspective, the exclusion of Native Americans from consideration when planning the Wall Street occupation is due to Occupy's failure to consider the history of the earth beneath Wall Street and the people who lived there before the Europeans landed. Without full consideration of what *that* occupation has meant for the native inhabitants, the conflict is merely between two factions of occupiers – the government, on the one hand, and unhappy citizens of that same government, on the other, who are still negotiating within the contract that was established after the American Revolution of the 1700s. Montano's open letter makes several demands, one of which is for Occupy Wall Street to, "Make some kind of mention that you are indeed aware that you are settlers and that you are not intending to repeat the mistakes of all of the settler do-gooders that have come before you. In other words, that you are willing to obtain the consent of indigenous people before you do *anything* on indigenous land."[311] A week after Montano's open letter appeared, Occupy Boston posted the following "declaration" to their web site, with a link to Montano's web log:

> *Boston, MA, October 10, 2011* – Occupy Boston ratified a statement of solidarity with indigenous peoples at the Saturday October 8 General Assembly. Recognizing that "we are guests upon stolen indigenous land," the memo declares the Occupation movement must honor the history and wisdom of Native Americans and resolves that

---

[310] Montano, "An Open Letter to the Occupy Wall Street Activists," http://unsettlingamerica.wordpress.com/2011/10/03/decolonize-wall-street/.
[311] Ibid.

Columbus Day henceforth be referred to as Indigenous Peoples' Day.[312]

This seems a weak measure, at best, decided by people whose struggle to understand what full acknowledgement of their status as "guests" in their own country would mean produces only a symbolic gesture towards recognizing that Columbus Day celebrations are problematic.

On September 17, 2011, when the first Occupy Wall Street demonstration took place, the Grassroots Global Justice Alliance (GGJA), an international alliance of grassroots activist organizations, was in the middle of a three-day Congress in Raleigh, North Carolina. GGJA has been building an international alliance of grassroots activist organizations for the past five years. Their mission statement lists issues and goals that concern them: "Over the next 20 years, GGJA will work to achieve critical shifts in global issues including climate justice, trade, migration and militarization, because the time is now to make another world possible – a world where everyone matters and everyone can have enough."[313] Clayton Thomas-Muller, an activist at the GGJA Congress representing the Indigenous Environmental Network, and a member of the Mathias Colomb Cree Nation in Northern Manitoba, Canada, recalls the events of September 17, 2011. While at the GGJA Conference, he received a sudden influx of text and Twitter messages about the first Occupy demonstration in New York, as did many other attendees. They began discussing, somewhat confusedly, what was going on in New York, and the first question many of them had was why had their organizations not been notified in advance. Why had they been left out? In his address to a GGJA meeting in Toronto in January, 2012, Thomas-Muller talked about those moments of confusion that quickly turned into

---

[312] "Occupy Boston Declares Solidarity with Indigenous Peoples," Occupy Boston, October 10, 2011, http://www.occupyboston.org/2011/10/10/occupy-boston-declares-solidarity-with-indigenous-peoples/ (accessed March 1, 2012).
[313] Grassroots Global Justice Alliance, "GGJ Mission," http://ggjalliance.org/mission/ (accessed March 1, 2012).

moments of realization, of not only having been left out of the
Occupy planning discussions, but of not even having been
informed ahead of time that the first Wall Street action was
about to take place:

> Well, who's on Wall Street right now? And then we started
> looking at the live feeds, because the live feeds started
> coming in and it was all young, white, middle class youth,
> from all kinds of different walks of life, predominantly.[314]
> There was, like, a couple black folks in there, maybe a
> couple Latino folks, but I didn't see *any* Indians. But the
> point is . . . here I am at the premiere Congress of racialized
> communities gathering to talk about how we were going to
> utilize the limited resource power – but the infinite people
> power, the spiritual power, the resiliency that we have – in
> the year 2012, and how we were gonna do that. And none of
> us knew a damn thing about this action on Wall Street. That
> troubled me.

> I knew that the world was in a very serious situation of
> change. That the Arab Spring was spreading, that something
> was happening, and that technology played a part in that...
> and people are pissed off about the economic collapse, you
> know. And so for me, I started worrying. . . . [I had] fears
> that this Occupy movement, if not handled correctly, had
> the potential to set up a scenario where a lot of our existing
> social movements that have been gaining a lot of power
> lately through good, resilient leadership from local frontline
> communities supported by hard-core solidarity movements
> that are rooted in anti-colonial, anti-racist, anti-oppression
> brainworks – you know there's some big shit that's gone
> down in the last couple years . . . and I'm afraid that if we
> don't find a way to deal with this huge influx of activists, of

---

[314] Carl Franzen, "Occupy Wall Street Demographic Survey Results Will
Surprise You, Talking Points Memo (TPM)," Talking Points Memo,
http://idealab.talkingpointsmemo.com/2011/10/occupy-wall-street-demographic-
survey-results-will-surprise-you.php/ (accessed Nov. 1, 2011). Demographically,
over sixty-four percent of the Occupy Wall Street Movement is under 35 years of
age, and over ninety-two percent is college educated.

recently radicalized people, who for the most part have never been exposed to social movements, who for the most part have no idea about the history of the Civil Rights movement, or Black Panthers, or Red Power, or American Indian Movement, or even more contemporary stuff that's been happening, you know, if we don't have a solid group, of like a whole army of anti-racist trainers, you know, to like deal with these people, all of our people are gonna experience a whole shitload of lateral violence because these people don't know how to check their white privilege at the door.[315]

Thomas-Muller's analysis of the danger of a sudden uprising against government policies by people who have little or no previous experience in activism explains why Occupy would need permission. They are being called on to abandon race-based and economic privilege, to acknowledge that the right they have to protest came from an older source with a longer-term connection to the place, and working within a much longer timeline. In doing so, Occupy must also acknowledge a much broader view of its own history and ally it with a history of the continent that was ongoing before European expansion.

History is one consideration, but before history, there is a more primary consideration, which is, again, about space. In *Space and Place: The Perspective on Experience,* Tuan discusses the issue of the landmark as something in the public environment created in the image of the culture. The same landmark may mean something different to indigenous people than it means to colonizers or settlers, and it may have different meanings through time as well. His examples include Ayers Rock in Australia, which "dominated the mythical and perceptual field of the aborigines, but it remains a place for modern Australians

---

[315] Clayton Thomas-Muller, "Occupy Talks: Indigenous Perspectives on the Occupy Movement," Unsettling America, http://unsettlingamerica.wordpress.com/2012/01/29/occupy-talks-indigenous-perspectives-on-the-occupy-movement-tom-b-k-goldtooth/ (accessed March 1, 2012).

who are drawn to visit the monolith by its awesome bulk."[316]
Another of Tuan's examples is the monument at Stonehenge,
whose original use has not yet been determined, but it is a
landmark for contemporary travelers as well, who visit the site
because it represents an inspiring architectural feat and is a
source of wonder about what connection there could be in the
present to this ancient heritage. Both sites, the natural landmark
of Ayers Rock and the human construction at Stonehenge, have
general as well as specific significance. Tuan writes, "Most
monuments cannot survive the decay of their cultural matrix.
The more specific and representational the object the less it is
likely to survive."[317] Stonehenge has obviously lost its matrix,
but Ayers Rock has not. The "functional realm"[318] of the place
for the aboriginal people is different from that of the tourists and
government of Australia, but it has not been lost. The place is
significant in two separate realms, simultaneously.

The Native American claim to Wall Street is a decolonizing
move, a move to reclaim the functional realm of Wall Street as a
place of significance for Native people in the present time.
Decolonizing Wall Street changes the functional realm of the
entire Occupy phenomenon as well, to a realm of colonization.
The Occupy activists, like other American colonizers, not only
have a different historical sense than that of the indigenous
people, they have a different relationship to origins. They belong
to a group whose migration is not yet complete. They move not
only because they have colonized the continent – the second
colonization following the four thousand year trek by the first
people who walked across the Bering Strait from Asia fourteen
thousand years ago. Lineage is a marker of pride and reinforces
communal bonds for Native Americans, but it was once a
determination of legal status, potentially dangerous for people
not of European descent. Human pedigree is a strange idea in
itself considering the long history of human migration. Modern
societies are due for reconsideration in terms used by the pre-

---

[316] Tuan, *Space and Place: The Perspective of Experience*, 163.
[317] Ibid., 164.
[318] Ibid.

moderns anyway, based on recent revelations that Africans, for example, are the least likely to have inherited any amount of DNA from our kissing cousins, the Neanderthals, whom we *Homo Sapiens* colonized some time between twelve and twenty thousand years before the migrations into North America began. A new circle is drawn, providing an additional species that we must include in our families, modern as well as pre-modern/amodern, colonizer and native. The idea of origins fragments and disperses like pieces of a broken mirror, as the new guest takes a seat at the table.

The differences between Occupy Wall Street's organizing strategies and those of alliances that place a high value on leadership and face-to-face community building over months and years, indicate that global scale and perspective must be operational at the local level. This enables groups with differing or even opposing strategies to find useful connections, and groups that are organized differently can function together, some from within a strong tradition of homeland and others as migrants, guests, *flâneurs*, and the descendants of colonizers.

Archi-political Design and the Moveable Equator

"The *Aztecas del norte* . . . compose the largest single tribe or nation of Anishinabeg (Indians) found in the United States today. Some call themselves Chicanos and see themselves as people whose true homeland is Aztlán."[319] Between 1845 and 1850, during and just after the Mexican-American War, the United States annexed the Mexican lands of Texas, New Mexico, Arizona and Alta California in a truly audacious land grab. When lands were ceded to the Americans, Mexicans who had lived in these territories for generations became foreigners

---

[319] Jack D. Forbes, *Aztecas del Norte: The Chicanos of Aztlán* (Greenwich: Fawcett Publications, 1973), 13, 183, in Gloria Anzaldua, *Borderlands/La Frontera: The New Mestiza* (San Francisco: Aunt Lute, 1999), 23.

in their own country.[320] The border has continued to fluctuate with the continual crossing of citizens of both countries in both directions, but the border could never be properly forced closed. Unauthorized human, commercial (including drug-related), and cultural migrations continue to stymie the efforts of the governments of both nations to clearly delineate what part of the borderlands is culturally and politically American, and what part is Mexican. All of the American Southwest is Aztlán, however, the territory of *el mestizo*, and all of it was once Mexico.

From the perspective of the north, migrations from Mexico are migrations into another country. From the perspective of the Mexican migrants, trips north across the border are a return to the homeland. Poet and cultural writer Gloria Anzaldúa writes, "We have a tradition of migration, a tradition of long walks. Today we are witnessing *la migración de los pueblos mexicanos,* the return odyssey to the historical/mythological Aztlán. This time, the traffic is from the south to the north."[321] The long walks are across disputed ancestral territories, but the landscape is gendered as well, and is a different space for women. In describing the borderlands between the United States and Mexico, Anzaldúa states that "life in the borderlands" is a space-time of "intimate terrorism"[322] for Mexican, Mexican-American and indigenous women:

> *La mohada, la mujer indocumentada,* is doubly threatened in this country [Aztlán]. Not only does she have to contend with sexual violence, but like all women, she is prey to a sense of physical helplessness. As a refugee, she leaves the familiar and safe homeground to venture into unknown and possibly dangerous terrain.

---

[320] In a semiotic land grab the United States has absconded with the name "America," although it rightly belongs to all nations from the Canadian and Alaskan north to the southern tip of South America, including the island nations of the Caribbean.

[321] Anzaldúa, 33.

[322] Ibid., 44.

This is her home
   this thin edge of
     barbwire.

The world is not a safe place to live in. We shiver in separate cells in enclosed cities, shoulders hunched, barely keeping the panic below the surface of the skin, daily drinking shock along with our morning coffee . . . Woman does not feel safe when her own culture, and white culture, are critical of her; when the males of all races hunt her as prey.[323]

Alienated from her mother culture, "alien" in the dominant culture, the woman of color does not feel safe within the inner life of her Self. Petrified, she can't respond, her face caught between *los intersticios,* the spaces between the different worlds she inhabits.[324]

The alienation Anzaldúa describes is two-fold: she is alienated from her own *mestizo* culture because the white culture she lives in values living separately as a sign of success, independence, and possibility, and for her, living alone means being unsafe. The Mexican sense of community places a high value on inter-generational living in tight-knit neighborhoods – Anzaldúa does not want a room of her own. Secondly, she cannot live fully inside her own culture without being subject to physical abuse, subservience, and having no expectation of promise or fulfillment. *Las mestizas* inhabit a different world within their own culture, situated between home and selfhood.

Anzaldúa's confession – for what else is it when women express desire, whether about sexuality or selfhood? – is a cultural critique, but as in the writings of Kathy Acker and Laurie Weeks, women's confessional writing is a methodology seldom taken seriously, and given little respect in terms of its contributions to cultural theory, history, and literature. The

---

[323] Ibid., 34.
[324] Ibid., 42.

female subjective voice does not often carry the weight of empirical knowledge, as though women cannot be trusted to draw reasonable conclusions about their own relationships to the world. The personal stories of women are those for women's society, a practice made political when it was brought into feminist circles decades ago and links were established between the complaints of ordinary women and the power structures under which they must try to realize themselves. In those unsanctioned and unsupervised groups, personal and political realities merged and a syncretic analysis developed. These may seem like primitive or unsophisticated methods for forming theory, but they are direct and effective, and yield results that can be plotted over a wide range of specific experiences by millions of women. What may be considered primitive and simplistic is a reaction to women's survival tactics that devalues women's narratives. The cultural devaluation of these narratives represents a failure to comprehend the significance of women's otherness, a failure, in fact, to absorb otherness, become it, and re-inscribe it as part of the human experience. But it is also a failure to write an inclusive phenomenology, one that recognizes a complete and integrated humanity. The map that is being drawn here, then, is of the interstitial space between culture and survival, which, for Anzaldúa, is the space of *la mestiza*. Anzaldúa is a writer who confesses to everything except to the belief that "the inner life of her Self" is the measure of real oppression. The terror without – governments, laws, the Church, physical and psychological violence – is an amalgamation of influences on the terror within: "The ability to respond is what is meant by responsibility, yet our cultures take away our ability to act – shackles us in the name of protection. Blocked, immobilized, we can't move forward, can't move backwards. That writhing serpent movement,[325] the very movement of life, swifter than lightning, frozen."[326]

---

[325] The figure of the serpent is a guide throughout Anzaldúa's text. The serpent is one of several representations of fertility goddesses as mother and as warrior in Mesoamerican mythologies.

[326] Anzaldúa, *Borderlands/La Frontera: The New Mestiza*, 45.

Anzaldúa lives inside as well as outside the traditions of her people and regards gender inequality as an intruder, one that inflicts harm onto the entire collective spirit. For her, the oppressive intruder, *machismo,* is not indigenous to her culture:

> "You're nothing but a woman" means you are defective. Its opposite is to be *un macho.* The modern meaning of the word "machismo," as well as the concept is actually an Anglo invention. For men like my father, being "macho" meant being strong enough to protect and support my mother and us, yet being able to show love. Today's macho has doubts about his ability to feed and protect his family. His "machismo" is an adaptation to oppression and poverty and low self-esteem. It is the result of hierarchical male dominance. The Anglo, feeling inadequate and inferior and powerless, displaces or transfers these feelings to the Chicano by shaming him.[327]

Blame shifts upward in this interpretation of *machismo.* The Anglo not only feels inadequate but his system of equating difference with division is a tidy re-classification of places that already had significance prior to his arrival. The Anglo logic is fulfilled in separating, renaming, and controlling the borderlands. In order for this be accomplished, the *mestizo* population has to be engaged in a continuous internal conflict along gender lines. The *macho* character must compete with the male posturing of its Anglo counterpart in the social realm, attaching cultural significance to behavior that is divisive within its own culture. To Anzaldúa, this Americanized *macho* man is a foreigner.

The confessional narrative, which in Anzaldúa's writing is part rant, part analysis, and part poetry, is a place where women can discard the abject self. It is not a place where women must remain – it is not a permanent home for women. As Irigaray reminds us, women often do things, including writing history, differently from men. The issue, if we go back to Irigaray's

---

[327] Ibid., 105.

gender theory, is one of a female subjectivity that cannot be "bridged" in a patriarchal economy. Irigaray, too, has observed that even within her own culture, woman is not native. Irigaray finds sexual difference to be the basis for identity:

> To refound society and culture upon sexual difference is also to radically put back in question the notion of the proper, propriety, of appropriation that governs our mental and social habits. It is to learn, at the most intimate, at the most passionate and carnal level of the relation to the other, to renounce all possession, all appropriation, in order to respect, in the relation, two subjects, without ever reducing one to the other.

> Man and woman are *culturally* different. And it is good that it is so: this corresponds to a different construction of their subjectivity. The subjectivity of man and that of woman are structured starting from a *relational identity* specific to each one, a relational identity that is held between nature and culture, and that assures a bridge starting from which it is possible to pass from one to the other while respecting them both.[328]

Irigaray's ideal human subjectivity represents a spiritually heightened heterosexuality within which each cultural element, male and female, is "based on irreducible givens"[329] of anatomy and the social world that may be constructed around it. Woman gives birth to both male and female. Male engenders only the masculine. Her partitioning of the human into male and female, as complementary polar opposites outside of patriarchy would be a starting point for the coupling, then, that forms the basis of an identity dependent on affinities. These affinities are based in chemistry, biology, and a bifurcated humanity, only male or female, only in relation to each other. Irigaray's perspective represents gender polarization as a principle of necessary difference, in contrast to the terror that Acker, Weeks and

---

[328] Irigaray, *Between East and West*, 128 – 129.
[329] Ibid., 129.

Anzaldúa express as the milieu of the feminine. Irigaray's relational situation seems to limit human subjectivity as well, not perhaps in terms of the body, but in terms of an ability to inhabit the space of the other, to become the other, and to not only bridge differences with virtuous respect, but to mix them up, to acknowledge cultural factors and to mis-use them, in a sense, as Acker's writing does.

Irigaray's feminism at least provides a picture of what exists now in terms of the place of the feminine in the system of male privilege and power, wherein all sexuality is in the service of male sexuality, and all sexuality is, therefore male sexuality. Patriarchal cultural systems are based on the appropriation and colonization of others' subjectivities. The relational aspect to Irigaray's assertion is that a lateral model of difference, rather than a hierarchical one, imagines a situation in which interdependent individual and collective subjectivities exist and flourish together, as a bridge of respect passes between them. According to Irigaray, the exchange is primarily a cultural one. As a model for cultural exchange, the bridge of respect is a good one. Heterosexuality as a model for a society's foundations, however, is still fraught with problems of relying on sexual and cultural norms to stabilize society, and imposes gendered models of social significance that disregard a full spectrum of sexualities. Perhaps most troubling is the unspoken next step, the isolated enclave of the heterosexual family. Anzaldúa, who is a lesbian, complicates the issue of cultural marginalization by her unwillingness to assimilate into white culture, and her unwillingness to participate in the misogyny of her own culture. She keeps alive *mestizo* perceptual influences, yet challenges the authenticity of the culture of an ancestral homeland, Aztlán, that is a prison to half the population. Anzaldúa's predicament is how to be at home, how to be human, within the complex of interstitial spaces, cultures and identities that characterizes the borderlands.

In *Space and Place,* Tuan discusses homeland in terms of attachment, scale and "cosmic" geometry:

> Homeland is an important type of place at the medium
> scale. It is a region (city or countryside) large enough to
> support a people's livelihood. Attachment to homeland can
> be intense. . . . Human groups everywhere tend to regard
> their own homeland as the center of the world. A people
> who believe they are at the center claim, implicitly, the
> ineluctable worth of their location. . . . home is the focal
> point of a cosmic structure.[330]

Humanity is adaptable, however, and has a very long history of
roaming. Tuan observes that, "Cosmic views can be adjusted to
suit new circumstances. With the destruction of one 'center of
the world,' another can be built next to it, or in another location
altogether."[331] The enterprises of global capitalism require a
labor force of migrant workers who leave hearth and home to do
the work that the local citizens may reject. It requires the
migration of commerce, as well, of corporations themselves that
must relocate in order to profit from the exploitation of cheap
labor. These types of migrations are not generally seen in the
light of our million-year trek, but the migrations engendered by
globalized industry and finance are responsible for the
establishment of new communities that bring many aspects of
their primary culture with them. Assimilation occurs, partly, but
mostly the "bridge" model that Irigaray puts forth for gender
equality could better represent the bridge that joins migrant
communities to the new societies in which they gradually
become an embedded cultural force. In his book *Magical
Urbanism: Latinos Reinvent the U.S. Big City,* urban theorist
Mike Davis describes the Mexico-U.S. border as "a lusty bastard
offspring of its two parents." He calls the nineteen hundred mile
stretch of border, *La Línea,* an "historically specific institution,"
that operates like a "dam, creating a reservoir of labor-power on
the Mexican side of the border that can be tapped on demand . . .
by *polleros, iguanas,* and *coyotes* for the farms of south Texas,

---

[330] Tuan, *Space and Place: The Perspective of Experience,* 149.
[331] Ibid., 150.

the hotels of Las Vegas and the sweatshops of Los Angeles."[332] The American Border Patrol imagines itself as a defense against a threatening alien invasion, but as one side constructs a wall and massive systems of surveillance, the other sets up a flowing economy.

The North America Free Trade Agreement (NAFTA), which came into effect in the mid-1990s, spawned a borderland of U.S. and Asian-owned *maquiladoras* – factories that import raw materials and export finished products while using cheap Mexican labor – on the Mexican side. The *maquiladoras* sustain "only a mirage of national economic development, [which] nonetheless has dramatically reshaped the culture of *La Frontera* and the inter-relationships of the dozen or so twin cities that span the border from Matamoros/Brownsville on the Gulf to Tijuana/San Diego on the Pacific."[333] While work may seem steady, wages in the *maquiladoras* are low and environmental pollution, especially in terms of wastewater runoff into the drinking water supply, is high. Although twenty-five percent of jobs in Mexico are at the *maquiladoras*,[334] the Mexican workforce outnumber the jobs these factories can provide, and both documented and undocumented workers continue to travel north for work, bringing with them the most mundane and therefore vital aspects of their old communities – neighborhoods consisting of outdoor *mercados*, small playgrounds, multi-generational housing, and their own micro-economies of buying and trading goods and services within their migrant communities. These communities dot the San Diego area, creating a practical re-zoning that puts living, working and finding recreation all within the same area. And what flows from north to south? Waste, debris, and abandoned building materials flow south as people haul American waste for re-use across the border. Eventually they improvise uses for the discarded tires, building materials, and even entire abandoned houses, which

---

[332] Mike Davis, *Magical Urbanism: Latinos Reinvent the U. S. Big City*, (New York: Verso, 2000), 25.
[333] Ibid., 29.
[334] Anzaldúa, *Borderlands/La Frontera: The New Mestiza*, 32.

they transport from San Diego to build additions to their homes in Mexico. Tijuana is built with the excess of the American system.

San Diego-based architect and alternative developer Teddy Cruz considers Mexican immigrant neighborhoods in the U.S. to be more sustainable than what he refers to as the "oil-hungry development" of typical Southern Californian suburban housing complexes that rely on the privatization of transportation, and which lack a basic village infrastructure. Cruz suggests that urban planners examine the kinds of communities that immigrants from Mexico build in the U.S., studying what he calls the "informal" and "non-conforming spatial and entrepreneurial practices"[335] of the immigrants. The immigrants create specific uses for the cities and neighborhoods to which they migrate partly because of the living practices in neighborhoods from which they came. The Mexican neighborhood is a site of production on both sides of the border. From studying the immigrant models that spring up organically, Cruz recognizes how the local becomes enabled in bottom-up types of dynamics and believes these dynamics can "trickle up to produce top-down changes – the idea of transitional infrastructures" that create not only a specificity of the public, but also a "specificity of rights."[336] According to Cruz, a neighborhood is "performed" through its social, political, and economic realities, and performing a neighborhood well means designing against homogenization and a neutral idea of the public realm. It means developing areas incrementally in order to enable a variety of informal economies to build up, and acknowledging the specificity of the inhabitants and the location. Neighborhoods perform themselves, becoming sites of production within micro-economies and local cultures that have

---

[335] "Profile Overview: Estudio Teddy Cruz," California-Architects, http://www.california-architects.com/en/estudio/en/ (accessed March 4, 2012).
[336] Quotes from Teddy Cruz are taken from his lecture, "Creative Acts of Citizenship – Performing Neighborhoods," at the Designing Civic Encounters Symposium, Ramallah, July 2011, http://www.youtube.com/watch?v=95cAIs9VNZI&feature=related (accessed March 4, 2012).

the potential, through interrelation and diversity, to become sustainable environmentally and financially. This must happen from within a radicalized and nonhierarchical sense of the local. The idea of style in architectural design, which is frequently the main focus of urban planners of low-income housing for marginal communities, becomes a moot point. "Informal" describes praxis as well as economics, and is a method of democratizing development; aesthetics develop from specific plans for use and the availability of materials locally, and are not related to symbolic embellishment or simulations of traditional styles of architecture.

Cruz situates the flow of people across the Mexico-U.S. border within a larger consideration of worker migrations from south to north across the globe. He has created a diagram that repositions the geographical equator politically, moving it northward to the San Diego/Tijuana Border, and continuing the line of the newly positioned equator across America, Africa, the Middle East, and Asia to reflect the trends in a global economic division that result in large waves of immigration from the southern hemisphere to the northern, "between enclaves of mega-wealth and sectors of poverty."[337] The newly positioned equator reflects the movement of populations looking for work from south to north, and the global outsourcing of jobs from north to south, revealing what Cruz calls a "global corridor of [economic] conflict." Laborers migrate from South and Central America, as well as Mexico, to the United States; they migrate from Northern and Central Africa to Europe and the Middle East; they migrate from Asia to the Middle East, and from Eastern Europe as well, to Western Europe. Money earned by migrant workers crosses the border in the other direction, toward home. For Cruz, it becomes evident that "the conflict embedded globally or locally begins with the recognition of the conflict between geopolitical boundaries, natural resources, and marginal

---

[337] Teddy Cruz, Estudio Teddy Cruz, "Profile Overview, Projects," http://www.california-architects.com/en/estudio/en/.

communities."[338] The dependency of the global economy on migrant worker communities requires new strategies for performing the local. The global economy forces the establishment of transitional spaces as well as less transitional, but perhaps not permanent, new communities. A new sense of the local develops, informed by the basic cultural needs that immigrant communities bring with them, and by the need for cheap labor in the wealthier sectors.

Cruz's archi-political practice is based on design being practical, in dialogue with regional lifestyles rather than with contemporary formal investigations or symbolic references to a cultural architectural style. Unlike the neutral architecture of Supermodernity, which lacks reference to human identity, archi-political design is essentially regional and specific to the cultural practices of the community in its new location. The private-public functions of many of the supermodern designs designate how the space is to be used: airport layouts are designed not only for travelers, but also function as international border-crossings; any one hotel that is part of an international chain has operating procedures based on the needs of the hotel managers and serves only the most general or basic needs of the broadest number of guests, with little regard for the needs of the region in which the hotel is situated. Operational functions are built into the architecture; the systems of use are based on the needs of the operators rather than those of the users. Cruz's design standards, in contrast, include interactivity, mobility, and even portability. The concept of a transitional infrastructure almost defines the patterns of living that migrant workers establish – the patterns themselves are the infrastructure, and they are based on moving, on being in transit, on situations that can be set up and dismantled when needed. The idea of "temporary" is displaced in this case. The migrants are not temporarily in a situation; their mobility is longer-term, which is the nature of their situation. Cruz's architectural practice takes into account not only the users, but also the geography, climate, and history of land

---

[338] Cruz, "Creative Acts of Citizenship – Performing Neighborhoods," lecture, Designing Civic Encounters Symposium, Ramallah, July 2011.

development in a region, including the local availability and cost of materials, and the general costs of living that the individual or family can expect as the intended occupants to his border neighborhood developments. Unlike the non-places of airports and corporate chains, the practice of archi-political design for living is specific to the inhabitants – the people together with their cultural needs form the design basis.

Because this approach to architecture addresses real issues on the ground rather than engaging formalist concerns or corporate efficiency, it brings into question the fact of formalism itself, regardless of whether the presentation is of modern, post-modern, or supermodern concerns. When issues of perception and representation become solidified in architecture, the buildings cease to be in dialogue with the changing nature of the real world, having little to do with development of communities or the establishment of neighborhood and home. They immediately exist as a part of the past, referencing an era in formal terms. The "other" that these buildings perform is almost everyone. Sinking oneself into the experience of the other in the non-space of homogenous, neutral architecture creates an enduring contradiction that operates to imprison the inhabitant or user in a condensed space of an artificially created status quo. Conformity replaces community in such a situation.

Artist and trans-border activist Ricardo Dominguez engages the Mexico-U.S. border as well, dealing with the process of transition between countries by engaging in radical space hacking practices in the trans-border zone. Dominguez, a former member of Critical Art Ensemble, and his group, the Electronic Disturbance Theater (EDT), work with people on both sides of the border to provide border-crossers with mobile phones that have been hacked for use as global positioning devices that guide travelers to locations in the desert where NGOs have placed drinking water. The phones are available for free at locations in Tijuana frequented by people looking for help in crossing the border. EDT calls the device a *Transborder Immigrant Tool,* and its creation and use are acts of electronic civil disobedience that carry real life-saving significance as well as representational significance. The total action, consisting of the hacking of phones, their distribution, and the border-crossings they enable, is a performance that re-maps the international border, using mobile telecommunications to highlight areas of danger to human life that the heightened defense of the border carries within the logic of its operations.

Dominguez, founder of EDT and Associate Professor of Art at the University of California, San Diego, investigates linguistic border crossings as well. In an interview about the *Transborder Immigrant Tool* (TBT) he evokes Donna Haraway's cyborg in breaking down some of the relational aspects of the border conflict:

> Part of the TBT project is to call into question the northern cone's imaginary about who has priority and control of who can become a cyborg or "trans" human – and immigrants are always presented as less-than-human and certainly not part of a community which is establishing and inventing new forms of life. When in fact these flowing in-between immigrant communities are a deep part of the current condition that Haraway's research has been pointing towards – for us it is a queer turn in its emergence, both as unexpected and as desire. The investigation of queer technology and what this queering effect has been or might be is an important part of our conversations . . . This gesture dislocates the techno-political effect with aesthetic affects that become something other than code: a performative matrix that fractalizes and reverses the disorder of things with excessive transbodies acting from the inside-out of those enforced borderless borders. These affects assemble new empirico-tran(s)cendental forms of multi-presence(s) incommensurable with the capitalist socius of the so-called "immaterial" Empire. As the Zapatistas say, "we do not

move at the speed of technology, but at the speed of dreams" - the heart of the trans-border-borg.[339]

Dominguez's reference to both "trans" and "queer," as bodies and as consciousness, lifts these terms from the earlier dialogues of Identity Politics and places them within an open arena where humanity itself is revealed as the queer contestant against state and corporate control of place. The fractal emerges as well, a model here for humanizing the borderlands against the deadly policies of *La Migra* by performing resistance that grows exponentially from the "inside-out." The TBT hacks queer identity and global positioning, creating a symbiosis of systems (queer and global) that have always drifted towards each other, but whose real relational functioning has been prevented by governments and denied by science. Now science comes to the foreground, by virtue of the assistance of technology in orbit in outer space, providing a basic necessity of life: water for the desert travelers. The transcendent factor is obvious in terms of what Irigaray calls:

> An irreducible difference of the other really considered as other, in the fact that their otherness is thus never knowable nor appropriable by myself – although it appears limited to my perceptions and even my intuitions – then transcendence no longer amounts to merely making objective a projection of my own subjectivity. So long as the other remains alive and free with respect to another world, especially to my world, time and space are kept in a dialectical process between us in an always indefinite and open way.[340]

Haraway's transcendent other is an insistent presence as well. In "Ecce Homo, Ain't (Ar'n't) I A Woman, and Inappropriate/d Others: The Human in a Post-Humanist Landscape," she discusses figuration in terms of "disarticulated bodies" and the

---

[339] Lawrence Bird, "Global Positioning: An Interview with Ricardo Dominguez," Furtherfield, October 10, 2011, http://www.furtherfield.org/features/global-positioning-interview-ricardo-dominguez (accessed January 5, 2012)
[340] Luce Irigaray, *Sharing the World* (New York: Continuum, 2008), ix-x.

fictive figure of humanity as a "modernist invention."[341] Her feminism disregards man and woman, humanity, and a "generic universal" as the elements of an Enlightenment era design for a human subjectivity based in the male of the propertied classes, whose privilege includes the right to rule, the right to establish norms, and to claim a true scientific knowledge of their own manifest destiny. Haraway suggests an alternative to the hierarchies of gender, class, origins, and ways of accessing the world through daily living that acknowledges the feminist practice of self-criticism rooted in information from physical, sacred/mythical, experiential, emotional, and learning intelligences. Through this practice, human universality is broken apart and difference is acknowledged, examined, and put into practice to connect others to others. For Cruz, the border is a zone of creation. The twinning effect of reconstructing the praxis of the old community in the new place means that the new is authentic as well, not a representation and not a simulation of the culture left behind. For Dominguez, the border is a zone where a migratory tradition is enabled by queer technologies, and where the guiding star is a satellite. Both Cruz and Dominguez work within, and place a high value upon, the traditions of the border crossers and border dwellers, transcendent others whose actions in the present constitute the development of practices that open up their traditions to the future.

Decoders of border languages such as Anzaldúa, Cruz, and Dominguez are not working within a system that was created by NAFTA, or the Border Patrol, or other representatives of either the Mexican or the U.S. governments. They work against them and around them, and in the case of satellite connectivity, through them. They are "reconfiguring the border and immigration"[342] in an enactment of permeability, mutation, and

---

[341] Haraway, "Ecce Homo, Ain't (Ar'n't) I A Woman, and Inappropriate/d Others: The Human in a Post-Humanist Landscape," in *The Haraway Reader*, 47.

[342] Ricardo Dominguez, in Lawrence Bird, "Global Positioning: An Interview with Ricardo Dominguez," Furtherfield, October 10, 2011, http://www.furtherfield.org/features/global-positioning-interview-ricardo-dominguez.

transformation. In the case of the Mexico-U.S. border, cultural traditions include frequent border-crossings and produce a twinning of communities, as villages and towns migrate south to north, recreating the spaces they left behind in an ongoing reclamation of Aztlán by descendants of its earlier inhabitants. According to Tuan, the "original inspiration" for establishing a homeland was "to consort with the gods,"[343] protectors that enable life, family, and community to flourish. The gods created order out of an unspecified place, making it unique and giving it significance as the center of the world. All places, then, can be the center of the world, ruled by their gods, and locative through all kinds of continuously forming networks of ancestors, physiologies, machines, texts and technologies.

Homeland

An indigenous group's claim to homeland is different from a colonizer's, or from someone's whose ancestors were enslaved and brought to a new place, or from that of a refugee who may be fleeing a bad situation. Since the indigenous people of North America migrated from Asia thousands of years ago, the American continent might actually belong to them. But even in the present day, across heavily populated territories, human migration continues. Tuan describes the sense of home as a sense of "rootedness" experienced on a deep personal level as well as on a collective level, providing an insight into the human scale of place. The experience occurs among settled people as well as traditional nomads, whose sense of home and community may be of a wider territory traversed seasonally, but is nonetheless a sense of home. Tuan discusses rootedness as being based in rituals of ancestor worship; the sacred fire, the hearth, and the tomb are the spaces of the rituals of belonging and of home. It was the ancestor, in whose memory history is kept, who "became a protecting god. . . . He was good to and provident to his own family but hostile to those who had not descended from

---

[343] Tuan, *Space and Place: The Perspective of Experience*, 150.

him."[344] Another aspect of the god's benevolence is that the power of the ancestor to protect the group is limited to the home territory, outside of which the god has no influence. The hearth and its protection represent the first experience of home.

According to Tuan, Western ideals of rootedness are a tradition we borrow from our knowledge of the ancient Greeks and Romans, who "valued autochthony," and "took great pride in being natives, in the fact that they could trace their long and noble lineage in one locality."[345] He quotes from Isocrates:

> We did not become dwellers in this land by driving others out of it, nor by finding it uninhabited, nor by coming together here as motley hordes composed of many races; but we are of a lineage so noble and so pure that throughout our history we have continued in possession of the very land which gave us birth, since we are sprung from its very soil and are able to address our city by the very names which we apply to our nearest kin; for we alone of all the Hellenes have the right to call our city at once nurse and fatherland and mother.[346]

Isocrates' text from the fourth century BCE calls on Athenians and Spartans to settle their differences, to recognize a national identity based on homeland, and to prepare together for war with Persia. First, homeland; second, war. The sentiments behind the call from grassroots political organizers within the American aboriginal community for Occupy Wall Street to formally announce its presence to them and request permission from them to stage occupations on stolen land bears some resemblance to the sentiments that Isocrates called forth twenty-four hundred years ago. The claim of the Native Americans is that the entire North American continent is their homeland. Who can argue with this? The homeland of the non-native, therefore, must be

---

[344] Tuan, 152-153.
[345] Tuan, 154.
[346] Isocrates, "Panegyricus," *Great Books*, vol. 6, trans. George Norlin (Cambridge: Harvard University Press, 1952), 396, quoted in Tuan, 154.

elsewhere, but certainly their homeland is no longer Europe, Africa, Asia, India, the Middle East or anywhere in between. Where, then, is the elsewhere that they can claim as home, which provides the reassurance of familiarity, which holds memories of family and history, in which rituals are enacted and ancestors are buried, and which deserves the protection of their gods? The sense of history that the colonizers/migrants possess is vastly different from that of the indigenous people. They bring their protective gods with them and their history, in this way, is continuous.

In Ireland, nationalism defines and radicalizes attachments to territory and is a psychic defense against continuing British colonialism in the North and the terrible history of colonialism on the Island overall. As the Irish write a Celtic heritage into their narrative, far right nationalism and socialism become uneasy companions in claiming Celtic roots. Celtic Ireland is the myth used to create an authentic non-British racial identity, a story that separates Irish blood from English and presents a specific Irish racial presence and deep history to the world. On the political far right, there is a campaign to limit immigration and create laws against automatic rights to citizenship at birth, spawned by a fear of the influence of African immigrants and their offspring on the DNA of the Irish race. This is racism and nationalism, to be certain. But nationalism is strong in the Irish Left as well, which sees no irony in making claims to an authentic Irish-ness while welcoming new immigrants and lobbying for the creation of a multicultural, multi-ethnic society.[347] Rootedness may beget nationalism, and migration may be the result of either colonialism or political or other disasters, but a god figures into the debates too. Ireland, like America, has a history of genocidal oppression, and holds on to indigenous identity by giving it a place of honor in the

---

[347] Based on my observations and conversations with people while living in Ireland between 2002 and 2007. Irish nationalism runs deep in both conservative nationalism and left-leaning socialism alike, but it rarely surfaces in conversation. It appears, instead, as legislation or as motions under consideration at the ballot box.

mythologies of the past. In Ireland, the past is a sacred place; the reconstructed Celtic identity is the face it shows the world, while the authentic objects of ancestors, ritual, and homeland have been secured in vitrines in the Folklife Collections at the National Museum, where they tell a different story to those who know how to listen.[348]

Homeland became a suspect word when the Office of Homeland Security, soon to become the Department of Homeland Security, was named shortly after the 9/11 disaster. Homeland Security is a term that invokes another nationalist term, Fatherland. Patriarchy and manifest destiny are imbedded in these terms. Manifest destiny privileges ownership over use, prefiguring a claim on all land and animals that come within view. Homeland Security and Fatherland reference aspects of nationalism, ownership, and stewardship in a scenario where the human has a divine rather than earthly duty. In further writing about landmarks, Tuan describes the ordinary practice whereby humans take stewardship over land:

> Think of the way a new country is settled. At first there is wilderness, undifferentiated space. A clearing is made in the forest and a few houses are built. Immediately differentiation occurs; on the one side there is wilderness, on the other a small, vulnerable, man-made world. The farmers are keenly aware of their place, which they have created themselves and which they must defend against the incursions of wild nature.
>
> With the continual extension of clearings the forest eventually disappears. An entire landscape is humanized. The fields belonging to one village adjoin those of another. The limits of a settlement are no longer clearly visible. They are no longer dramatized by the discernible edges of the

[348] For alternative Irish histories I recommend *The Atlantean Irish: Ireland's Oriental and Maritime Heritage*, by Bob Quinn (Dublin: Lilliput Press, 2006), and *Ploughing the Clouds: The Search for Irish Soma*, by Peter Lamborn Wilson (San Francisco: City Lights, 2001).

wilderness. Henceforth the integrity of place must be ritually maintained.[349]

Eventually the place acquires meaning, not only as home or homeland, but also as concept. Localism – as a practice of being concerned with home and the things or places nearby where one can acquire goods and services – as well as nationalism —a practice of constructing a mental concept of traits and values that distinguish a place worth defending from other places, even those that are contiguous – designate an occupant's status as insider. Others, of course, are outsiders and a fractal formation begins again: the spiral of categorizing, dividing and partitioning turn the homeland into a site of contention and conflict. At this point, cultural homogenization, caused by globalization, at first makes other places seem familiar because the same objects and products are found there, but this is merely an appeasement that masks the overarching economic influence of global corporatism. What we are seeking is difference without nationalism, familiarity without homogenization, and homeland without xenophobia. Some identities have long roots, and these occupy space and create consciousness in the same places as those that have been uprooted in recent generations. The long view of history is extant and has withstood change for millennia. The short view is mapped over the long view. Diversity is not a concept nor is it a construct. It is a process, and in this process, homeland, identity, insider, and outsider communicate in a continuous renegotiation of the present.

---

[349] Tuan, *Space and Place: The Perspective of Experience*, 166.

Conclusion: Technically Sweet

Diversity, difference, growth, mutation, unsettlement, chaos, motion, contradiction, paradox and uncertainty are the milieu of authentic daily life. The subjectivity of the individual is essential, but it is also indefinite. Identity is mutable, however strong it may remain; the formation of identity and subjectivity are active agents in the formation of everyday life and in the phenomenon of the continuous creation of the social realm. The continuous interaction of human and nonhuman actors, objects, ideas, events, and processes that create the social realm can be characterized as a network of affinities of indefinite dimension, a network always in the process of becoming.

The framework within which contemporary Western society is officially organized is a hierarchical arrangement of authority and privilege, based on governmental and socio-economic power structures that are fixed or are slow to change. The hierarchical structure organizes aspects of the contemporary into systems of control of populations and resources. The most powerful system of control is the system of global corporatism, which is a non-nationalized, decentralized network of global corporations that require not only a compliant labor force, but also an acquiescent consumer force, to form the backbone of its power base. Global corporatism operates across various types of governments including dictatorships, oligarchies, theocracies, and democracies, forming alliances where necessary and occasionally operating outside the authority of governments. Consumerism and the globalized marketplace represent the current dominant milieu of daily life, and the principles and values of mass marketing have been mapped over all aspects of daily life.

Do the forces of mass marketing change the significance of what is called common? What does resistance to consumerism and the creation of an authentic experience of the everyday look like? Avital Ronell puts the question this way: "How do you fight the power without rallying the troops? How do you break off or break up something without destroying or demeaning and undermining the other? How do I hold the fire? How do I not hit my target?"[350] These questions address measures of resistance, but also the scale of the influences that impact an individual's sense of the everyday – the information and knowledge she acquires in the lived space of the present. The scale of resistance is a human scale and not a corporate scale, nor is it the scale by which the maintenance of control is stretched over the matrix of experience. The scale of resistance is a personal scale, but is enacted by many actors and agents, and resistance is therefore something that spreads from many points, to many other points, at once. Consequently, actions taken in the intimate moments of the everyday are the first means by which an individual gains agency against consumer culture in the production of society. The most important action to be taken, on a consistent basis, is to question the organization of the space in which the body is situated.

In his 1975 essay "Culture Industry Reconsidered," Adorno discusses mass media as having not so much a subject in the consumer, as having an object. "The masses are not the measure but the ideology of the culture industry, even though the culture industry itself could scarcely exist without adapting to the masses."[351] To miss the target is to resist; to ignore the target is to resist. But another question arises: if the test is not the structure, if hitting the target represents a painful acquiescence to conformity and life based on survival rather than authentic living, how does a collective action composed of individual moments of resistance deconstruct global corporate domination of popular culture, servitude to the state, and the ever-present technology-testing of war?[352] This seems like a tall order.

---

[350] Ronell, "Test Drive: The Test, and Testing," lecture, European Graduate School, 2011.
[351] Theodor W. Adorno, "Culture Industry Reconsidered," *The Culture Industry: Selected Essays on Mass Culture* (New York: Routledge, 2001), 108.
[352] Avital Ronell discusses war as the testing of technologies in her 2011 European Graduate School lecture, "Test Drive: The Test, and Testing," in which she states, regarding the technologies of the first Gulf War, "There is no

The term "technically sweet" comes to mind, attributed to J. Robert Oppenheimer regarding the creation of atomic weapons. According to Oppenheimer, "When you see something that is technically sweet, you go ahead and do it and you argue about what to do about it only after you have had your technical success. That is the way it was with the atomic bomb."[353] Science and technology drive the mission regardless of its content. Science is amoral, ostensibly, but an amorality of this sort is housed within the morality of hierarchical value systems and sheltered behind urgings toward patriotic and nationalistic mandates that seem to require the technology of one society to destroy large parts of another. As Ronell explains, George W. Bush stated, "I can't call it off anymore," in speaking about an imminent attack on Iraq after the destruction of the World Trade Center in 2001. Even though he knew that Iraq had no part in the destruction of the Twin Towers, the American president could not call off the strike, "Because the technology needed to be tested."[354] But perhaps the technically sweet drive works in other processes, and not only in regard to atom bombs or non-retaliatory retaliations.

This study examines the relationship of states of oppression to the formation of a non-polemical and non-ideologically-based movement towards radical social change. Our personal identities, group identities, and the categories that we claim to identify ourselves can only make sense within a field of difference, where identity is not fixed and where mutable subjectivities converge, connect, and continue on. The mutability of identity, the irreducibility of the I, is one part of the network of resistance, a network that is mutable and changing, always becoming something other. Our technology is in place,

---

technology that won't be tested, which is to say that the limits between the test and the real really, really are reduced. . . . We had a whole arsenal of technologies that had not had their field tests. In other words, that didn't get to be used. And there's no technology that won't be tested or deployed."
[353] Maria Finn and Yvette Brackman, eds., *The Making of Technically Sweet: One Script/Thirteen Points of View/Allusions – Endless* (Copenhagen: Plum Velvet, 2008), 12.
[354] Ronell, lecture, European Graduate School, 2011.

the actors and agents are ready; we need to not call it off
anymore.

Appendix

On Exactitude in Science
By Jorge Luis Borges and Adolfo Casares

... In that Empire, the Art of Cartography attained such Perfection that the map of a single Province occupied the entirety of a City, and the map of the Empire, the entirety of a Province. In time, those Unconscionable Maps no longer satisfied, and the Cartographers Guilds struck a Map of the Empire whose size was that of the Empire, and which coincided point for point with it. The following Generations, who were not so fond of the Study of Cartography as their Forebears had been, saw that that vast Map was Useless, and not without some Pitilessness was it, that they delivered it up to the Inclemencies of Sun and Winters. In the Deserts of the West, still today, there are Tattered Ruins of that Map, inhabited by Animals and Beggars; in all the Land there is no other Relic of the Disciplines of Geography.

Suarez Miranda,Viajes de varones prudentes, Libro IV, Cap. XLV, Lerida, 1658[355]

---

[355] Jorge Luis Borges and Adolfo Casares, "On Exactitude In Science," in *Jorge Luis Borges, Collected Fictions*, trans. Andrew Hurley (New York: Penguin Books, 1988), 325.

Bibliography

Acker, Kathy. *Hannibal Lecter, My Father.* New York: Semiotext(e), 1991.

_____. "Kathy Acker." In *Angry Women,* edited by Andrea Juno and V. Vale, 177 – 185. San Francisco: Re/Search Publications, 1991.

_____. *Blood and Guts in High School.* New York: Grove Press, 1989.

_____. *Literal Madness.* New York: Grove Press, 1987.

_____. *Portrait of an Eye: Three Novels.* New York: Pantheon, 1980.

Adorno, Theodor W. *The Culture Industry: Selected Essays on Mass Culture,* New York: Routledge, 2001.

Agamben, Giorgio. *The Coming Community.* Translated by Michael Hardt. Minneapolis and London: University of Minnesota Press, 2009.

_____. *Homo Sacer: Sovereign Power and Bare Life.* Stanford: Stanford University Press, 1998.

Anker, Michael. *The Ethics of Uncertainty: Aporetic Openings.* New York: Atropos Press, 2009.

Anzaldúa, Gloria. *Borderlands: La Frontera.* San Francisco: Aunt Lute Books, 1999.

Atlas, Charles, and Antony, *Turning.* DVD. Directed by Charles Atlas. Produced by Vibeke Vogel and Lucy Sexton. Denmark: Turning Film, Bullitt Film and Beo Film, 2011.

Augé, Marc. *Non-Places: Introduction to An Anthropology of Supermodernity.* Translated by John Howe. New York: Verso, 2006.

Bachelard, Gaston. *The Poetics of Space.* Translated by Maria Jolas. Boston: Beacon Press, 1994.

Baudrillard, Jean. *Simulations.* Translated by Paul Foss, Paul Patton and Philip Beitchman. Los Angeles: Semiotext(e), 1983.

Bellos, David. *Georges Perec: A Life in Words.* London: Harvill Press, 1999.

Bender, Gretchen and Timothy Druckrey, ed. *Culture on the*

Brink: Ideologies of Technology. Seattle: Bay Press, 1994.

Benjamin, Walter. "The Work of Art in the Age of Mechanical Reproduction." *One-way Street and Other Writings*, translated by J. A. Underwood, 228 – 259. New York: Penguin, 2009.

Bey, Hakim. *T.A.Z. The Temporary Autonomous Zone, Ontological Anarchy, Poetic Terrorism*. Brooklyn: Autonomedia, 2003.

Bird, Lawrence. "Global Positioning: An Interview with Ricardo Dominguez." Furtherfield, October 10, 2011, http://www.furtherfield.org/features/global- positioning-interview-ricardo-dominguez (accessed January 5, 2012).

Borges, Jorge Luis. *Jorge Luis Borges, Collected Fictions*. Translated by Andrew Hurley. New York: Penguin Books, 1988.

Buber, Martin. *I and Thou*. Translated by Walter Kaufmann. New York: Touchstone, 1970.

_____. "Distance and Relation." In *Psychiatry 20* (1957), 97 – 104.

Burden, Ernest. *Illustrated Dictionary of Architecture*. New York: McGraw-Hill, 2002.

Caillois, Roger. "Mimicry and Legendary Psychasthenia." Generation Online, http://www.generation-online.org/p/fpcaillois.htm (accessed March 10, 2012).

Certeau, Michel de. *The Practice of Everyday Life*. Translated by Steven Rendall. Berkeley: University of California Press, 1988.

Cixous, Hélène. "The Laugh of the Medusa." In *Continental Aesthetics: Romanticism to Postmodernism: An Anthology*, edited by Richard Kearney and David Rasmussen, 388 – 399. Malden, MA and Oxford: Blackwell, 2008.

Critical Art Ensemble. "Nomadic Power and Cultural Resistance." In *The New Media Reader,* edited by Noah Wardrip-Fruin and Nick Montfort, 783 – 790. Cambridge: The MIT Press, 2003.

Cronenberg, David. *Videodrome*. DVD. Directed by David Cronenberg. Toronto: Canadian Film Development Corporation, 1983.

Cruz, Teddy. "Creative Acts of Citizenship – Performing

Neighborhoods." Designing Civic Encounters Symposium, Ramallah, July 2011, http://www.youtube.com/watch?v=95cAIs9VNZI&feature= related (accessed March 4, 2012).

Davis, Mike. *Magical Urbanism: Latinos Reinvent the U.S. Big City.* New York: Verso, 2000.

Debord, Guy. *The Society of the Spectacle.* Detroit: Black & Red, 1983. Debord, Guy and Gil. J. Wolman. "A User's Guide to *Détournement.*" In *Situationist International Anthology,* edited and translated by Ken Knabb, 14 – 21. Berkeley: Bureau of Public Secrets, 2006.

Deleuze, Gilles and Félix Guattari. *A Thousand Plateaus: Capitalism and Schizophrenia,* translated by Brian Massumi. Minneapolis: University of Minneapolis Press, 1987.

Du Bois, W. E. B., *The Souls of Black Folk.* New York: Signet Classic, 1995.

Ferguson, Russell and others. *Out There: Marginalization and Contemporary Cultures.* New York: New Museum of Contemporary Art, 1990.

Finn, Maria and Yvette Brackman, ed. *The Making of Technically Sweet: One Script/Thirteen Points of View/Allusions – Endless.* Copenhagen: Plum Velvet, 2008.

Forbes, Jack D. *Aztecas del Norte: The Chicanos of Aztlán.* Greenwich: Fawcett Publications, 1973.

Galloway, Alexander R. *Protocol: How Control Exists After Decentralization.* Cambridge: The MIT Press, 2004.

Giedion, S. *The Beginnings of Art.* Washington: The National Gallery of Art, 1957.

Guattari, Félix. *The Three Ecologies,* translated by Ian Pindar and Paul Sutton. New Brunswick, NJ: Athlone Press, 2000.

Hall, Stuart. "Race, the Floating Signifier." Google Video, http://video.google.com/videoplay?docid=84713835802829 07865 (accessed May 9, 2012).

Hammer, Barbara. *Hammer! Making Movies out of Sex and Life.* New York: Feminist Press, 2010.

_____. *Dyketactics and Other Films from the 1970s.* DVD. Directed by Barbara Hammer. Barbara Hammer, 2007.

Haraway, Donna. *The Haraway Reader.* New York and London: Routledge, 2004.

_____. *Modest_Witness@Second_Millennium.FemaleMan©_ Meets_OncoMouse™: Feminism and Technoscience.* New York: Routledge, 1997.

_____. *Simians, Cyborgs, and Women: The Reinvention of Nature,* New York: Routledge, 1991.

Heidegger, Martin. *Being and Time,* translated by John MacQuarrie and Edward Robinson. New York: Harper Perennial, 2008.

hooks, bell. *Feminist Theory: From Margin to Center.* New York: South End Press, 1984.

_____. "marginality as a site of resistance." In *Out There: Marginalization and Contemporary Cultures,* edited by Russell Ferguson and others, 341 - 343. New York: New Museum of Contemporary Art, 1990.

Horkheimer, Max and Theodor Adorno. *Dialectic of Enlightenment.* New York: Continuum, 1969.

Ibelings, Hans. *Supermodernism: Architecture in the Age of Globalization.* Rotterdam: NAi Publishers, 2002.

Ingram, Gordon Brent and others. *Queers in Space: Communities, Public Spaces, Sites of Resistance.* Seattle: Bay Press, 1997.

Isocrates. "Panegyricus." *Great Books*, vol. 6, translated by George Norlin. Cambridge: Harvard University Press, 1952.

Juno, Andrea and V. Vale, ed. *Angry Women.* San Francisco: Re/Search Publications, 1991.

Kaplan, Alice and Kristin Ross, ed. "Everyday Life." *Yale French Studies,* No 73. New Haven: Yale University Press, 1987.

Kearney, Richard and David Rasmussen, ed. *Continental Aesthetics: Romanticism to Postmodernism: An Anthology.* Malden, MA and London: Blackwell, 2008.

Khayati, Mustapha. "On the Poverty of Student Life." In *Situationist International Anthology,* translated and edited by Ken Knabb, 408 – 429. Berkeley: Bureau of Public Secrets, 2006.

Kingwell, Mark. "Meganarratives Of Supermodernism: The

Spectre Of The Public Sphere." Phaenex: Journal of Existential and Phenomenological Theory and Culture, http://www.phaenex.uwindsor.ca/ojs/leddy/index.php/phaenex/ (accessed February 20, 2012).

Klein, Naomi. *Fences and Windows: Dispatches From the Front Lines of the Globalization Debate.* New York: Picador, 2002.

_____. *No Space, No Choice, No Jobs: No Logo.* New York: Picador, 2002.

Knabb, Ken, trans. and ed. *Situationist International Anthology.* Berkeley: Bureau of Public Secrets, 2006.

Koolhaas, Rem and others. *Mutations.* Barcelona: ACTAR, 2000.

Latour, Bruno. *Reassembling the Social: An Introduction to Actor-Network-Theory.* Oxford and New York: Oxford University Press, 2007.

_____. *We Have Never Been Modern,* translated by Catherine Porter. Cambridge: Harvard University Press, 1993.

_____. "The Trouble With Actor-Network Theory." CSI-Paris/Science Studies-San Diego, 1990, http://www.cours.fse.ulaval.ca/edc65804/latourclarifications.pdf (accessed March 9, 2012).

Law, John. "Notes on the Theory of the Actor Network: Ordering, Strategy and Heterogeneity." Centre for Science Studies, http://www.lancs.ac.uk/fass/sociology/papers/law-notes-on-ant.pdf (accessed January 16, 2012).

Lefebvre, Henri. *The Production of Space,* translated by Donald Nicholson-Smith. Malden, MA: Blackwell, 1997.

Lippard, Lucy R. *On the Beaten Track: Tourism, Art and Place.* New York: The New Press, 1992.

Lovink, Geert. *Zero Comments: Blogging and Critical Internet Culture.* New York and London: Routledge, 2008.

Mackay, Polina and Kathryn Nicol, ed. *Kathy Acker and Transnationalism.* Newcastle upon Tyne: Cambridge Scholars Publishing, 2009.

Mandelbrot, Benoit. "A Theory of Roughness." Edge, http://www.edge.org/3rd_culture/mandelbrot04/Mandelbrot04_index.html (accessed February 25, 2012).

Manovich, Lev. *The Language of New Media,* Cambridge: The MIT Press, 2001.

_____. "New Media from Borges to HTML." In *The New Media Reader,* edited by Noah Wardrip-Fruin and Nick Montfort, 13 – 25. Cambridge MA and London: The MIT Press, 2003.

Montano, John Paul. "An Open Letter to the Occupy Wall Street Activists." Unsettling America: Decolonization in Theory & Practice, October 3, 2011, http://unsettlingamerica.wordpress.com/2011/10/03/decolonize-wall-street/ (accessed March 1, 2012).

McDonough, Tom, ed. *The Situationists and the City.* New York: Verso, 2009.

Negroponte, Nicholas. *Being Digital.* New York: Vintage Books, 1995.

Nietzsche, Friedrich. *The Gay Science: With a Prelude in Rhymes and an Appendix of Songs.* Translated by Walter Kaufmann. New York: Vintage Books, 1974.

Occupy Wall Street. "A Modest Call to Action on this September 17." Occupy Wall Street, http://occupywallst.org/article/September_Revolution/ (accessed February 10, 2012).

Perec, Georges. *An Attempt at Exhausting a Place in Paris,* translated by Marc Lowenthal. New York: Wakefield Press, 2010.

_____. *Life A User's Manual.* Translated by David Bellos. Boston: David R. Godine, 2004.

_____. *Species of Spaces and Other Pieces,* translated and edited by John Sturrock, London: Penguin Books, 1999.

Quinn, Bob. *The Atlantean Irish: Ireland's Oriental and Maritime Heritage.* Dublin: Lilliput Press, 2006.

Rancière, Jacques. *The Emancipated Spectator,* translated by Gregory Elliott. London and New York: Verso, 2009.

_____. *Hatred of Democracy,* translated by Steve Corcoran. London and New York: Verso, 2006.

Riley, Shannon Rose. "Kathy Goes to Haiti: Sex, Race, and Occupation in Kathy Acker's Voodoo Travel Narrative." In *Kathy Acker and Transnationalism,* edited by Polina Mackay and Kathryn Nicol, 32 – 33. Newcastle upon Tyne:

Cambridge Scholars Publishing, 2009.

Robertson, Lindsay G. "Native Americans and the Law: Native Americans Under Current United States Law." University of Oklahoma Law Center, http://thorpe.ou.edu/guide/robertson.html (accessed May 4, 2012).

Ronell, Avital. "Test Drive: The Test, and Testing." European Graduate School, 2011. http://www.youtube.com/watch?v=nvR4cKYzuxc (accessed April 16, 2012).

———. *The Test Drive.* Champaign: University of Illinois Press, 2005.

———. *Stupidity.* Urbana: University of Illinois Press, 2003.

———. "Avital Ronell." In *Angry Women,* edited by Andrea Juno and V. Vale, 127 – 153. San Francisco: Re/Search Publications, 1991.

Ronell, Avital, Eduardo Cadava, and Jean-Michel Rabaté. "On Testing, Torture, and Experimentation: The Test Drive." Slought Foundation, March 15, 2006, http://slought.org/content/11317/ (accessed August 8, 2012).

Rouch, Jean. *Petit à Petit,* DVD. Panthéon Distribution: Paris, 1994.

Rushkoff, Douglas. "Think Occupy Wall St. is a phase? You don't get it." CNN Opinion, October 5, 2011, http://www.cnn.com/2011/10/05/opinion/rushkoff-occupy-wall-street/ (accessed October 6, 2011).

Schirmacher, Wolfgang. Homo Generator: Media and Postmodern Technology." In *Culture on the Brink: Ideologies of Technology,* edited by Gretchen Bender and Timothy Druckrey, 65 – 82. Seattle: Bay Press, 1994.

Scholder, Amy, Avital Ronell, and Carla Harryman, ed. *Lust for Life: On the Writings of Kathy Acker.* New York: Verso, 2006.

Soja, Edward W. *Postmodern Geographies: The Reassertion of Space in Critical Social Theory.* London and New York: Verso, 1989.

Solnit, Rebecca. *A Field Guide to Getting Lost.* New York: Viking, 2005.

Spargo, Tamsin. *Foucault and Queer Theory.* London and New

York: Totem Books, 1999.

Sterling, Bruce. "Closing Keynote: Vernacular Video and Saffo's Law." Aku Aku, http://www.akuaku.org/2011/01/vernacular-video-and-saffos-law.html (accessed January 28, 2012).

_____. *Tomorrow Now: Envisioning the Next Fifty Years.* New York: Random House, 2002.

_____. *Islands in the Net.* Springfield, MA: Ace Publications, Inc, 1989.

Sylvester, David. *The Brutality of Fact: Interviews with Francis Bacon.* London: Thames and Hudson, 1987.

Taussig, Michael. *Mimesis and Alterity: A Particular History of the Senses.* New York: Routledge, 1993.

Thomas-Muller, Clayton. "Occupy Talks: Indigenous Perspectives on the Occupy Movement." Unsettling America, http://unsettlingamerica.wordpress.com/2012/01/29/occupy-talks-indigenous- perspectives-on-the-occupy-movement-tom-b-k-goldtooth/ (accessed March 1, 2012).

Tuan, Yi-Fu. *Space and Place: The Perspective of Experience.* Minneapolis: The University of Minnesota Press, 1977.

Turkle, Sherry. "The Flight From Conversation." The New York Times Sunday Review, http://www.nytimes.com/2012/04/22/opinion/sunday/the-flight-from-conversation.html?pagewanted=all (accessed June 11, 2012).

Vaneigem, Raoul. *The Revolution of Everyday Life,* translated by Donald Nicholson-Smith. London: Rebel Press, 2006.

_____. Interview by Hans Ulrich Obrist. "In Conversation with Raoul Vaneigem." E-Flux, May 2009, http://www.eflux.com/journal/in-conversation-with-raoul-vaneigem/ (accessed March 12, 2012).

Virno, Paulo. *A Grammar of the Multitude For an Analysis of Contemporary Forms of Life,* translated by Isabella Bertoletti, James Cascaito and Andrea Casson. New York: Semiotext(e), 2004.

Wardrip-Fruin, Noah and Nick Montfort, ed. *The New Media Reader.* Cambridge: The MIT Press, 2003.

Weeks, Laurie. *Zipper Mouth.* New York: The Feminist Press,

2011.

_____. "Laurie Weeks: Making Magic Out of the Real." Interview by Karen Schechner. Lambda Literary, http://www.lambdaliterary.org/features/11/20/laurie-weeks-making-magic-out-of-the-real/ (accessed January 21, 2012).

Wilson, Peter Lamborn. "My Summer Vacation in Afghanistan." In *The Fifth Estate* (Summer 2002): 15 – 19.

_____. *Ploughing the Clouds: The Search for Irish Soma.* San Francisco: City Lights, 2001.

Wittig, Monique. *The Straight Mind.* Boston: Beacon Press, 1992.

Wollen, Peter. "Death (and Life) of the Author." London Review of Books 20.3 (1998): 8 – 10, http://www.lrb.co.uk/v20/n03/peter-wollen/death-and-life-of-the-author (accessed January 12, 2012).

Think Media: EGS Media Philosophy Series

Wolfgang Schirmacher, *editor*

A Postcognitive Negation: The Sadomasochistic Dialectic of American Psychology,
Matthew Giobbi

A World Without Reason, Jeff McGary

All for Nothing, Rachel K. Ward

Asking, for Telling, by Doing, as if Betraying, Stephen David Ross

Betraying Derrida for Life Perhaps..., Stephen David Ross

Memory and Catastrophe, Joan Grossman

Can Computers Create Art?, James Morris

Community without Identity: The Ontology and Politics of Heidegger, Tony See

Deleuze and the Sign, Christopher M. Drohan

Deleuze: History and Science, Manuel DeLanda

DRUGS Rhetoric of Fantasy, Addiction to Truth, Dennis Schep

Facticity, Poverty and Clones: On Kazuo Ishiguro's 'Never Let Me Go', Brian Willems

Fear and Laughter: A Politics of Not Selves 'For' Self, Jake Reeder

Gratitude for Technology, Baruch Gottlieb

Hospitality in the Age of Media Representation, Christian Hänggi

I see. Do you? Thinking seeing, Anne-Laure Oberson

Itself, Robert Craig Baum

Jack Spicer: The Poet as Crystal Radio Set, Matthew Keenan

Laughter and Mourning: point of rupture, Pamela Noensie

Letters to a Young Therapist: Relational Practices for the Coming Community,
Vincenzo Di Nicola

Literature as Pure Mediality: Kafka and the Scene of Writing, Paul DeNicola

Lyric Dwelling, Gina Rae Foster

Media Courage: Impossible Pedagogy in an Artificial Community, Fred Isseks

Metastaesthetics, Nicholas Alexander Hayes

Mirrors triptych technology: Remediation and Translation Figures, Diana Silberman Keller

Necessity of Terrorism political evolution and assimilation, Sharif Abdunnur

No Future Now, Denah Johnston

Nomad X, Drew Minh

On Becoming-Music: Between Boredom and Ecstasy, Peter Price

Painting as Metaphor, Sarah Nind

*Performing the Archive: The Transformation of the Archive in Contemporary Art from
Repository of Documents to Art Medium*, Simone Osthoff

Philosophy of Media Sounds, Michael Schmidt

Polyrhythmic Ethics, Julia Tell

Propaganda of the Dead: Terrorism and Revolution, Mark Reilly

Repetition, Ambivalence and Inarticulateness: Mourning and Memory in Western Heroism,
Serena Hashimoto

Resonance: Philosophy for Sonic Art, Peter Price

Other books available from Atropos Press

CPSIA information can be obtained at www.ICGtesting.com
Printed in the USA
BVOW03s0123040414

349694BV00006B/131/P